STUDIES IN ECONOMICS AND P
*edited by*
THE DIRECTOR OF THE LONDON SCHOOL OF E
SCIENCE

No. 66 in the series of Monographs by wi
London School of Economics and Political Science

# PRINCIPLES OF PUBLIC FINANCE

# PRINCIPLES
# OF PUBLIC FINANCE

by

## HUGH DALTON
P.C., M.A., D.Sc.(Econ.), M.P.
*Sometime Reader in Economics in the University of London*

*Sometime Chancellor of the Exchequer,*
*President of the Board of Trade, etc.*

**ALLIED PUBLISHERS PVT. LIMITED**
New Delhi Mumbai Kolkata Chennai Nagpur
Ahmedabad Bangalore Hyderabad Lucknow

# ALLIED PUBLISHERS PRIVATE LIMITED

1/13-14 Asaf Ali Road, **New Delhi**–110002
**Ph.**: 011-23239001 • E-mail: delhi.books@alliedpublishers.com

**47/9** Prag Narain Road, Near Kalyan Bhawan, **Lucknow**–226001
**Ph.**: 0522-2209942 • E-mail: lko.books@alliedpublishers.com

17 Chittaranjan Avenue, **Kolkata**–700072
**Ph.**: 033-22129618 • E-mail: cal.books@alliedpublishers.com

15 J.N. Heredia Marg, Ballard Estate, **Mumbai**–400001
**Ph.**: 022-42126969 • E-mail: mumbai.books@alliedpublishers.com

**60** Shiv Sunder Apartments (Ground Floor), Central Bazar Road,
Bajaj Nagar, **Nagpur**–440010
**Ph.**: 0712-2234210 • E-mail: ngp.books@alliedpublishers.com

F-1 Sun House (First Floor), C.G. Road, Navrangpura,
Ellisbridge P.O., **Ahmedabad**–380006
**Ph.**: 079-26465916 • E-mail: ahmbd.books@alliedpublishers.com

751 Anna Salai, **Chennai**–600002
**Ph.**: 044-28523938 • E-mail: chennai.books@alliedpublishers.com

5th Main Road, Gandhinagar, **Bangalore**–560009
**Ph.**: 080-22262081 • E-mail: bngl.books@alliedpublishers.com

3-2-844/6 & 7 Kachiguda Station Road, **Hyderabad**–500027
**Ph.**: 040-24619079 • E-mail: hyd.books@alliedpublishers.com

**Website:** www.alliedpublishers.com

First published in Great Britain, December, 1922
Fourth revised edition, October, 1954
First Indian Reprint, 1978
Reprinted 1978, 1980, 1983, 1985, 1989,
1991, 1993, 1995, 1998, 2004, 2012
ISBN 81-7023-133-7

ISBN 13: 978-81-7023-133-2

Reprinted in India by Allied Publishers Pvt. Limited, New Delhi 110002,
under special arrangement with Routledge & Kegan Paul Ltd.
Broadway House, 68-74 Center Lane, London, E.C. 4.

# PREFACE TO THE FOURTH EDITION

THERE has been no new edition of this book for eighteen years, but it has continued to be in demand, both in this country and overseas. For close on eleven years out of these eighteen I have been a Minister of the Crown and, in that capacity, have held six different offices, first in war and then in peace. And I have had the uncommon experience of writing a textbook in my middle thirties and becoming a Minister of Finance in my late fifties, with the duty to practise what I had preached.

Since 1936 our understanding of many of the problems of Public Finance has greatly increased, partly through new thought, by the late Maynard Keynes and other economists, partly through new events, which have disproved or discredited some old opinions regarding, for example, the balancing of the budget, and the effects of continuing high taxation on production and employment.

In the course of preparing this new edition, I have, therefore, found myself writing what is very nearly a new book, though within the old framework and even under the old chapter headings. I have added two new chapters, one on modern ideas of budgetary policy, the other giving a brief account of my period of office as Chancellor of the Exchequer, of the special problems of that time, of what I tried to do, and of the considerable changes which were carried through. To make room for this and other new matter, I have saved space on the old. And, as I wrote in the Preface to the Second Edition in 1928, 'I have tried not to sacrifice compactness, nor an eclectic brevity.'

In August and September, 1953, I was in Brazil and lectured on Public Finance to University and other audiences in Rio de Janeiro, Sao Paulo and Belo Horizonte. I experimented there with some new ideas and methods of presentation, and am grateful to those who discussed these points with me.

I am also most grateful to Mr. I. M. D. Little and Mr. Brian Abel-Smith for helping me with criticisms and suggestions.

HUGH  DALTON

*House of Commons*
  *April, 1954.*

# PREFACE TO THE FIRST EDITION

THIS book contains the substance of lectures on the Theory of Public Finance delivered at the London School of Economics. It is designed, in Bacon's words, 'to excite the judgment briefly, rather than to inform it tediously'. I have aimed at setting out, without undue elaboration, the chief general principles which are applicable to the public finance of a modern community. For the study of first principles is a necessary preliminary to an effective discussion of practical problems, and should be helpful in providing a framework of general ideas, into which particular ideas and particular facts can be fitted, so as to appear, not as unique and isolated things, but in their true relation to a larger whole.

Though I may seem occasionally to have yielded a little to temptation, it is not my object in this book to advocate any detailed practical policy, but only to indicate some of the general considerations on which any sound policy must be based. Facts, in the field of public finance, are moving so rapidly at the present time that realistic studies are soon out of date and the form, in which practical problems present themselves, is constantly changing. But there are certain general principles of which this is not true. . . . In the course of my argument, therefore, I have occasionally turned aside to criticise certain current opinions on questions of taxation, public expenditure and public debts, which I believe to rest upon errors of judgment and confusions of mind.

It has been customary with the majority of economists to adopt a somewhat negative attitude towards public expenditure. I have attempted to treat this part of the subject more positively and to exhibit the parallelism which exists between the theory of public expenditure and that of taxation.

*London School of Economics*

# CONTENTS

## PART ONE. INTRODUCTORY

# PART TWO.  PUBLIC INCOME

## PART THREE. PUBLIC EXPENDITURE

## PART FOUR.   PUBLIC DEBTS

## PART FIVE.  SOME PROBLEMS OF POLICY

# PART ONE

# INTRODUCTORY

★

## CHAPTER I

## THE NATURE OF PUBLIC FINANCE AND THE MAIN DIVISIONS OF THE SUBJECT

§ 1. Public finance is one of those subjects which lie on the border line between economics and politics. It is concerned with the income and expenditure of public authorities, and with the adjustment of the one to the other; adjustment not necessarily to equality, but to whatever arithmetical relationship, in given conditions, is best.[1]

'Public authorities' include all sorts of territorial governments, from parish councils up to national, federal and even international governments. They differ widely, of course, as regards the magnitude of the areas and populations which they govern, the range of functions which they exercise, their methods of obtaining income, the objects of their expenditure, and their financial relations with other public authorities, superior or subordinate to themselves. In a broad survey of the subject most of these differences are only of secondary importance, but a clear distinction should be drawn between public authorities which have the power to issue currency and those which have not. Most 'central' governments, whether national or federal, have this power.

§ 2. In modern civilised communities the income and expenditure of public authorities consist, almost exclusively, of money

[1] The conditions in which a budget surplus or deficit of a given size is desirable are discussed in Ch. XXVII.

receipts and money payments. The word 'finance' signifies
'money matters' and their management, and public finance in
its modern sense presupposes the existence of a money economy.

The expenditure of public authorities, indeed, consists practically without exception of money payments. But we may
notice two sorts of public receipts which are not money receipts,
namely (1) certain unpaid personal services, and (2) the payment of certain taxes otherwise than in money. Some unpaid
services are rendered voluntarily to public authorities, others
under legal compulsion. Examples of the former in Britain
are the services of magistrates and members of local authorities.
Examples of the latter are the services of jurors, and the
obligation resting upon all citizens under the Common Law to
assist in sweeping snow from the streets, in extinguishing fires
and in helping the police to catch murderers and thieves. A
more important form of compulsory service, in many modern
communities, is compulsory military service. But this is paid
for, though at a much lower rate than it would be necessary to
offer in order to secure an equal amount of voluntary paid
service.

The payment of taxes in money has gradually superseded
their payment in kind, for the same reason that a money
economy has gradually superseded a barter economy, that is to
say, on grounds of general convenience. But in Britain there are
a few exceptions. Thus since 1909 the death duties of land-
owners may, with the consent of the Inland Revenue authorities, be paid in land,[1] though, when this proposal was first made
in the House of Commons in 1906, it was ridiculed on the
ground that, if it was accepted, distillers would next be asking
to pay their death duties in whisky. Again, since 1919 death
duties may be paid by handing over Victory Bonds.

[1] This provision was practically inoperative until 1946. In my budget of
that year I established a National Land Fund of £50 millions out of the
proceeds of the sale of war stores, and I encouraged the idea that, in suitable cases, land and houses should be accepted in payment of death duties.
I provided that these properties might be handed over either to public
bodies, such as the Forestry Commission or the Agricultural Land Commission, or to non-prof:  aking private bodies, such as the National
Trust or the Youth Hostels Association. In such cases the Inland Revenue

And since 1920 in the United States royalties, payable under leases of publicly owned oil-bearing lands, may be paid to the Federal Government in oil.[1]

§ 3. The main division in public finance is between public income and public expenditure, which form two symmetrical branches of the subject. Public debts are often treated as a separate branch and this is convenient, since they give rise to a number of special problems.

Financial administration likewise raises many problems and is sometimes treated as a separate branch of the subject. It is not dealt with in this book, since the general principles which can be laid down with regard to it are few, and their effective discussion presupposes in the reader a detailed acquaintance with existing financial systems. Nor have I touched, except lightly and in passing, on public accounting methods.

Part II of this book is devoted to public income, Part III to public expenditure, Part IV to public debts and Part V to some problems of public policy, including the balancing of the budget, the balancing of the economy as a whole with the aid of a budget which may be deliberately unbalanced, and an account of the problems which confronted me, when I was in charge of British Public Finance in 1945-7.

The two remaining chapters of Part I are concerned respectively with the fundamental principle which should govern all problems of public finance, and with the relation of public to private finance.

§ 4. Every writer, who aims at organising a general discussion of public finance, must be conscious of a conflict between two personalities, those of the practical and of the analytical man. And, in seeking to resolve this conflict, he is in danger of getting the worst of both worlds, missing both the perfection of

receives from the National Land Fund what it would have received if the tax had been paid in cash. Under these arrangements a number of beautiful and historic houses and gardens, and some fine and unspoilt open country, have passed into public or semi-public hands. But less than I had hoped, since valuation for death duty is generally lower than in the open market, so that the National Land Fund is still growing through reinvestment of unspent interest. In 1954 it reached £57 millions.

[1] Lutz, *Public Finance*, p. 132.

theory, boldly guided by pure reason, and the wisdom of states-manship, cautiously guided by administrative officialdom. Public finance lies very close to practical politics. It is, in this sense, the most live branch of economics. Its precepts and its formulæ may change, at the wave of a politician's wand, into the clauses of an Act of Parliament. Here, more easily than anywhere else in economics, theory and practice may either play into each other's hands, or remain at cross purposes. Studies in public finance have, for this reason, a special fasci-nation, but for the same reason an excess of abstraction is apt, in this sphere, to seem especially unreal and an excess of conventional rule-of-thumb especially half-witted.

A good example of the conflict between theory and practical statesmanship is the assumption that the marginal utility of income diminishes, as income increases. Some theorists shy at this assumption, because, they say, it can't be proved. But most statesmen, keeping in closer touch with common opinion, are willing to accept it and work out its consequences.

# CHAPTER II

## THE PRINCIPLE OF MAXIMUM SOCIAL ADVANTAGE

§ 1. In public finance we are still haunted by the superficial views and shallow precepts of an earlier age. 'The very best of all plans of finance', said J. B. Say, a hundred and fifty years ago, 'is to spend little and the best of all taxes is that which is least in amount.' He would still find many to agree with him. Much current discussion starts from the assertion that 'every tax is an evil'. Credulous minds are thus biased in advance against all forms of public expenditure. We might, just as plausibly, start from the assertion that 'all public expenditure is a good'.

It is not true that every tax is an evil. One may admit, without being a total abstainer from alcohol, that a tax, which by raising its price diminishes its consumption, may be a positive good. For it was not a good state of things, when in the eighteenth century in England 'a man could get drunk for a penny and dead drunk for twopence'. Further, as we shall see later, taxes sometimes stimulate their victims to greater or more sustained exertion, and this may be an economic good.

Similarly, of course, it is not true that all public expenditure is a good. Expenditure on unnecessary wars is an obvious evil. And so, some might argue, are large and long continuing payments of interest on war debt. Nor is it ever difficult to find, in any scheme of public expenditure, some elements which are wasteful, or even do more harm than good, though we may just as easily find others which could with great advantage be increased.

But it is not possible to pass a complete judgment upon any operation in public finance without balancing against one another both sides of the operation, the effects of the raising, and the effects of the spending, of public revenue. It is idle to

speak, as many do, of the 'burden of taxation', regardless of the
benefit of the corresponding public expenditure. No sensible
person speaks of the 'burden' of drawing cheques, regardless of
the purposes for which they are drawn.

Historically the idea that all taxes are an evil stems from the
facile individualist doctrine that, outside the narrow sphere of
its traditional minimum of activities, the State can do no right.
But this doctrine is now seen to be too simple-minded. Historically also the idea is connected with a supposed distinction
between 'productive' and 'unproductive' expenditure. It was
imagined by early economists, including Adam Smith and
Ricardo, that most of the private expenditure, which taxation
checked, was 'productive', while all public expenditure, which
taxes paid for, was 'unproductive'. But this supposed distinction has long been discredited. The only economic test of the
'productiveness' of any expenditure is its productiveness of
economic welfare, and public expenditure on education and
health, for example, is often more productive in this sense than
private expenditure on luxuries, or even on new capital goods.[1]

None the less, it is an ingrained habit with many 'respectable
authorities', in the City of London and elsewhere, somewhat
uncritically to deplore that growth of public expenditure which,
quite apart from war and preparations for war, has been
steadily proceeding in all civilised communities for many years
past. It is a truth not confined to public finance that 'our great
need is economy'. But there is a sharp distinction to be drawn
between false and true economy, between spending as little as
we can, regardless of the results attained, and spending whatever is necessary in order to get the best results attainable—in
short, between spending little and spending wisely.[2]

§ 2. One fundamental principle must lie at the root of public

[1] See Ch. XVIII, and especially § 7.
[2] 'Mere parsimony is not economy. Expense and great expense may be
an essential part in true economy. Economy is a distributive virtue and
consists not in saving but in selection. Parsimony requires no providence,
no sagacity, no powers of combination, no comparison, no judgment.
Mere instinct may produce this false economy in perfection. The other
economy has larger views. It demands a discriminating judgment and a
firm sagacious mind' (Burke, *Works*, V, p. 229).

finance. This we may call the Principle of Maximum Social Advantage. All the operations of public finance resolve themselves into a series of transfers of purchasing power, or of variations in total purchasing power, and of consequential changes in the use of economic resources. These transfers are made, by taxation or otherwise, from certain individuals to public authorities, and back again from these authorities, by way of public expenditure, to other individuals, some of whom, such as policemen or contractors, render services in return, while others, such as old age pensioners, do not.[1] This distinction between transfers in payment for services rendered, and transfers to which no services are related, is important. But it need not detain us here.

Variations in total purchasing power are made either through the budget, or through the banks, or both. Broadly, there is a net increase in purchasing power when the budget shows a deficit, or when the banks extend credit; a net decrease when the budget shows a surplus, or when the banks restrict credit.[2]

As a result of all these operations of public finance, changes take place in the amount and in the nature of the wealth which is produced, and in the distribution of that wealth among individuals and classes. Are these changes in their aggregate effects socially advantageous? If so, the operations are justified; if not, not. The best system of public finance is that which secures the maximum social advantage from the operations which it conducts. This principle is obvious, simple and far-reaching, though its practical application is often very difficult. But the difficulty is inherent in the subject, and cannot legitimately be avoided by substituting a wrong principle for a right one, in order to arrive more easily at practical conclusions.

§ 3. In seeking to apply this principle we need to have before us certain tests of social advantage. The first which suggests

[1] Sometimes the beneficiaries of public expenditure receive, not purchasing power in the form of money, but specific goods or services, such as uniforms, education or medical treatment.

[2] Variations in total purchasing power can only, of course, to any significant extent, be brought about by public authorities which can influence the supply of money within their areas. The British government at Westminster can do this, but not British local authorities.

itself is the need to preserve the community, assuming it to be worth preserving in its existing form, against internal disorders and external attacks. How this should best be done falls outside the scope of this discussion. But it is a question of wise public policy at home and abroad, and not merely of expenditure on police and armed forces. If any community in its existing form is not worth preserving, it is the duty of statesmen to change its form. And, in any case, it is their duty to increase the welfare, both economic and non-economic, of its members.

This brings us to the more strictly economic tests of social advantage, with which this book is primarily concerned. The two chief conditions of an increase in the economic welfare of a community are, first, improvements in production and, second, improvements in the distribution of what is produced.

Improvements in production resolve themselves into (1) increases of productive power, so that a larger product per worker shall be obtained with a smaller effort, (2) improvements in the organisation of production, so as to reduce to a minimum the waste of economic resources through unemployment and other causes, and (3) improvements in the composition, or 'pattern', of production, so as best to serve the needs of the community.[1]

Improvements in distribution resolve themselves into (1) a reduction in the great inequality, which is found in most civilised communities, in the incomes of different individuals and families, and (2) a reduction in the great fluctuations, between different periods of time, in the incomes of particular individuals and families, especially among the poorer sections of the community. Less inequality is desirable, in order that income may be distributed, at any given time, more in accordance with individual and family needs at that time, and with capacity to make good use of income.[2] To meet changes,

---

[1] A large increase, for example, in British production of food, coal, steel and engineering goods, relatively to other goods and services, to help to balance our overseas trading accounts by saving imports and increasing exports. See C. A. R. Crosland, *Britain's Economic Problem* (Cape, 1953), for a very able study of this question.

[2] This theme, already mentioned in Ch. I, § 4, recurs in Ch. IX, § 2, and in Ch. XI, § 1. It grows out of the concept of diminishing marginal utility

through time, in individual and family needs, is a separate problem of redistribution. Some inequalities in earned incomes, representing differences in responsibility or skill or effort, are, if they increase production, justifiable. The most unjustifiable inequalities are large differences in unearned incomes.

Less fluctuation means more stability, through time, in the economic life of the community, and particularly in the incomes and employment of individuals. More stability is another aspect of the better organisation of production. But it should be stability at a high level of employment, not merely less fluctuation around a lower level.

Full employment is now generally accepted as one of the first economic aims of a well-organised society. It is defended, not only because it helps to increase production, and to promote a greater equality of incomes, but also for its own sake. Unemployment, especially if widespread or prolonged, is now viewed as an offence against the proper treatment of human beings, and full employment in Britain, from 1945 onwards, as our greatest peace-time revolution.

It should be added that the statesman is a trustee for the future, no less than for the present. Individuals die, but the community, of which they form part, lives on. The statesman, therefore, should prefer a larger social advantage in the future to a smaller one today.

§ 4. With these applications of the Principle of Maximum Social Advantage we shall be concerned in more detail later. But at this point a few negative conclusions may usefully be drawn, as correctives to certain popular arguments.

It is impossible 'to make an estimate', as is sometimes suggested, 'of what this country, taking its income into consideration, could really afford in the way of public expenditure'. For what can be 'afforded' depends partly on how the money is raised, and partly on how it is spent. We cannot afford the expense of an unnecessary war, or even of an unnecessary public department, however the money is raised. On the other hand,

of income, with possible variations for individual need and individual capacity. This concept makes sense to most ordinary people, though some economists question its logical basis.

we may be able to afford a large expenditure in various desirable directions, if the money is raised by one scheme of taxation, but not if it is raised by another.

Again, it is not generally true that 'private individuals spend money better than government does'. Gladstone, indeed, used to speak of 'leaving money to fructify in the pockets of the people', as though it were a ripening cheese, and to defend this policy as preferable to the maintenance of taxation, no matter for what purpose. But he and most of his generation were blind to the advantages of public expenditure on such objects as old age pensions, and other developments of the modern Welfare State. We should scrutinise closely the expenditure of private individuals, no less than of public authorities, and judge its social value. In the summer of one of the early inter-war years I noticed one day the headlines of two newspapers, side by side. One pilloried 'The Spendthrifts' and contained an article attacking the government for paying large salaries to officials at the Ministry of Transport; the other advertised 'Ascot Last Day', and informed me, with an air of regret for the good old days, that some ladies were wearing only four new dresses during the six days of that race meeting, instead of the six which were customary before the first world war. This contrast still carries its moral. 'Retrenchment' is a blessed word, but it should be applied to private no less than to public extravagance. It is not wisdom to cut down public expenditure simply in order that private individuals may have more to spend as they please.

On the other hand, it is not generally true, as some modern writers suggest, that 'government spends money better than private individuals do'. A government with more money to spend may spend it on projects which are not worth what they cost. A rich frequenter of Ascot, with more taxes to pay, may pay them, not out of what he spends on his wife's dresses or his own drinks, but out of what he might otherwise have saved, thus helping to make possible some useful enterprise, such as the building of working-class houses.

Leaving these false trails, to this simple but comprehensive doctrine of Maximum Social Advantage we continually return. Take account of all the probable effects, which can reasonably be foreseen, of any financial proposal which is under discussion; strike a balance of probable gain and loss to the community; compare this balance with that of alternative proposals, and act upon the results of this comparison. Those who are oppressed by a sense of the difficulty of this calculus, should console themselves with the saying of the ancient Greeks that 'it is not the easy things, but the difficult things, which are beautiful'. And there is no short cut.

# CHAPTER III

## PUBLIC FINANCE AND PRIVATE FINANCE

§ 1. It is instructive to compare public with private finance, and this is the task of the present chapter. Broadly speaking, it is true to say that, while an individual's income determines the amount of his possible expenditure, a public authority's expenditure determines the amount of its necessary income. In other words, while an individual adjusts expenditure to income, a public authority adjusts income to expenditure. But to this broad statement there are qualifications.

To some extent an individual adjusts income to expenditure. If he marries, and still more if he becomes responsible for a number of dependants, his estimate of necessary expenditure will rise and he may decide to increase his income by working harder and sacrificing leisure. On the other hand, when his children have become self-supporting, his estimate of necessary expenditure may fall, and he may decide to work less hard and take more leisure. To some extent, again, a public authority adjusts expenditure to income. In bad times, when its income falls off, it may practise retrenchment, and in good times, when its income increases, it may embark on policies hitherto considered too expensive.

The adjustment of an individual's income and expenditure need not be exact in any given year. 'There is no special sanctity in the period in which the earth revolves round the sun.' A year is a convenient accounting period for some purposes, but not for others. If an individual's expenditure exceeds his income, the excess may be met out of savings made in previous years, or from the sale of assets. Or he may run into debt, either by straightforward borrowing, or by leaving bills unpaid, in which case, in effect, he borrows from his creditors. And if his income exceeds his expenditure, the surplus income is available for expenditure in the future.

Similarly, the adjustment of a public authority's income and expenditure need not be exact in any given year. When its income exceeds its expenditure, it has a surplus, which is available for future uses. Again, when its expenditure exceeds its income, a public authority, like an individual, may draw on its savings, if any, or sell some of its assets, or run into debt. But here some points of difference arise. A public authority may raise either an internal or an external loan, that is to say, may borrow either from those who are subject to its authority, or from those who are not. Or, if it has the legal power, it may make ends meet by issuing more currency. But an individual cannot raise an internal loan. The nearest approach he can make to such a transaction is, if he keeps two banking accounts, by borrowing from one for the benefit of the other. Nor can an individual increase the currency by decreeing that his I.O.U.s shall be legal tender.

It has also been noted above, and will be argued in more detail later,[1] that a public authority may do much to achieve full employment and to stabilise the economic life of its community by deliberately aiming at a surplus or a deficit, not only in one year, but over a longer period. A budget surplus one year does not mean that it is necessarily in the public interest to have a deficit the next. But all this is public policy, with no counterpart in individual finance.

§ 2. In some economic text-books it is said that an individual so distributes his expenditure on various commodities and services, that the marginal utilities of all these expenditures are equal, and the total utility of the whole expenditure a maximum. It is one of the chief advantages of a money economy that it enables this to be done, and for this reason we may anticipate the survival of money even in the most socialistic communities which the future may bring forth.[2] In reality most individuals do not thus equalise their marginal utilities with any great

---

[1] See Ch. XXVII.
[2] In the Soviet Union the use of money was soon resumed after a brief and unsatisfactory experiment in 'moneyless economy'.

exactitude, but in the schemes of expenditure of all except the
least intelligent, who have no scheme at all, there is an approach
towards such equalisation.

A public authority, not being a person except in a legal sense,
cannot estimate the marginal utilities of its various expenditures
as an individual can. But the general principle, on which statesmen should attempt to act, is the same. The marginal utility *to
the community* of all forms of public expenditure should be
equal[1] and the distribution of a given total of expenditure
between different objects is thus theoretically determined.

A statesman, in estimating the marginal utility of any form
of public expenditure, tries to find an objective standard of
public welfare, or social advantage. An individual, on the other
hand, follows a subjective standard of utility, or private
advantage, linked with an objective standard of price.

§ 3. What should determine the total of public expenditure?
Here, again, at first sight the theoretical answer is clear. Public
expenditure in every direction should be carried just so far, that
the advantage to the community of a further small increase in
any direction is just counterbalanced by the disadvantage of
a corresponding small increase in taxation or in receipts from
any other source of public income. This gives the ideal total both
of public expenditure and of public income. The ideal distribution of this total public income between different taxes and
other sources of income is similarly given by the requirement
that the marginal social disadvantages, or disutilities, of raising
income from all these sources should be equal.[2]

It is not to be imagined that public authorities, any more
than individuals, ever achieve perfect solutions of these complex problems of balancing marginal utilities and disutilities.
But some statesmen miss perfection by a longer chalk than
others. In practice these problems of public finance are settled

[1] Or as nearly equal as possible, allowing for the indivisibilities of
economic resources.

[2] But there is no reason why equalising all these marginal utilities and
disutilities should automatically equalise public income and expenditure,
or give a budget surplus or deficit of any desired size. To achieve such a
result the equalised marginal utilities might have to diverge widely from
the equalised marginal disutilities.

by a tug-of-war between rival spending departments, and between spending departments and the Treasury, modified by pressure from other influential quarters—elected persons, organised interests, newspaper editors and so forth. And, in practice, neither public authorities nor individuals are ever required to rearrange the whole of their schemes of expenditure from top to bottom. Certain expenditures are actually going on, and the problem is usually restricted to the desirability of making changes, which affect only a small proportion of the whole. Moreover, much expenditure, particularly by public authorities, is commonly based on legal contracts, or on quasi-contractual assurances which cannot, without serious disturbance, be varied at short notice.

§ 4. None the less, for making deliberate changes in its income and expenditure, and particularly for making increases, a public authority is generally in a much better position than an individual. The chief reason for this is obvious; it has the whole taxable wealth of the community on which to draw, in addition to the possibility of raising external loans. But there is another reason. In some theoretical discussions it is suggested that individuals go on working, until the marginal utility of more product, or more pay, just falls short of the marginal disutility of more work. But this is only true of those who work independently of others, boys picking blackberries, to take Marshall's classical example, or artists, or free-lance journalists. But most people have to fit in their hours of work with those of others, and often with collective agreements and sometimes with Acts of Parliament. Some would like to work more and others less than they do, but have to conform with general arrangements. Public authorities are usually free from this disability and can make their own financial arrangements without much regard to what others are doing. Expenditure on armaments is an exception to this rule.

§ 5. In the pure theory of individual finance, the principle of the equalisation of marginal utilities includes, as a special case, the equalisation of the marginal utilities of present and future expenditure, and hence determines the provision which individuals make for the future. Most people, however, discount the future to some extent. For its satisfactions, and equally its dissatisfactions, quite apart from any factor of uncertainty, look shrivelled to the normal eye beside equal satisfactions, or dissatisfactions, in the present. Moreover, one's life is uncertain and one's descendants, after a certain point, uninteresting. Most individuals, therefore, make less provision for the future than they would do if their power of visualising it were stronger or if they expected their earthly life to last for ever, or even for a hundred years. But, since the community outlasts the individual, and since, as was pointed out in the last chapter, the statesman should regard himself as trustee for the future, he is not entitled to discount it at so high a rate as most individuals in their private capacity normally do. Indeed, it is doubtful[1] whether he should discount it at all. It follows that, in so far as future conditions can be reasonably foreseen, statesmen should sometimes aim at making a more generous provision for the future than would be made by private individuals left to themselves. Important examples of this principle will be given later, when we come to deal with public expenditure. But the task of statesmen will often be rendered difficult by the political pressure of those who repeat the ancient question, 'What has posterity done for me, that I should do so much for posterity?'

[1] So doubtful that it would require a long digression to examine this most interesting problem of moral duty.

# PART TWO

# PUBLIC INCOME

★

## CHAPTER IV

## SOURCES OF PUBLIC INCOME

§ 1. The income of a public authority may be defined either in a broad or a narrow sense. In the broad sense it includes all 'incomings' or 'receipts', in the narrow sense only those receipts which are included in the ordinary conception of 'revenue'. As between these two senses, the context is generally a sufficiently good interpreter, but, where necessary, ambiguity may be avoided by using the terms 'public receipts' and 'public revenue' to denote public income in its broad and in its narrow sense respectively. The chief elements included in the conception of public receipts, but excluded from that of public revenue, are receipts from public borrowings and from the sale of public assets, such as war stores.

§ 2. The first and most important practical distinction is between taxation and other sources of public income. A tax is a compulsory charge imposed by a public authority and, as Taussig puts it, 'the essence of a tax, as distinguished from other charges by Government, is the absence of a direct *quid pro quo* between the taxpayer and the public authority'.[1] We have, on the other hand, as an important source of public income, the prices charged by a public authority for specific services and commodities supplied by it, including the prices charged for the use of public property. Generally speaking, these prices are paid voluntarily by private persons, who enter into contracts, express

[1] *Principles of Economics*, II, p. 483.

or implied, with public authorities, whereas taxes are paid compulsorily.

Developing the broad distinction between taxes and prices, we have on the one side (1) taxes ordinarily so called; (2) tributes and indemnities, whether arising out of war or otherwise; (3) compulsory loans;[1] and (4) pecuniary penalties for offences, imposed by Courts of Justice. On the other side we have (5) receipts from public property passively held, e.g. public lands leased to tenants, or the British Government's Anglo-Iranian or Suez Canal shares; (6) receipts from enterprises carried on by a public authority which does not use its monopoly power to raise its prices above 'the competitive level'; (7) fees or payments made for services, not in the nature of business services, performed by a public official, such as the registration of births; and (8) receipts from voluntary public loans.

Four other sources of public income may be distinguished which do not fall completely under either of our two main headings, namely, (9) receipts from enterprises carried on by a public authority which *does* use monopoly power to raise its prices above 'the competitive level'; (10) receipts from 'special assessments'; (11) receipts from the use of the printing press, for the purpose of meeting public expenditure by the issue of new paper money; and (12) voluntary gifts. Many enterprises are carried on by public authorities with the primary object of raising revenue by the use of monopoly power. Thus some governments have established State monopolies of matches and tobacco. That part of the price of such commodities, which exceeds their cost of production (including normal profits), is indistinguishable, in principle, from a tax on such commodities.[2] A special assessment is an American invention, defined by Seligman as 'a compulsory contribution, levied in proportion to the special benefits derived, to defray the cost of a specific

[1] A recent example is British post-war credits, which bear no interest and are repaid only when the holder reaches the age of sixty-five (male) or sixty (female), or inherits from a deceased holder who would now have reached these ages.

[2] In practice, it is not a simple matter to divide, with any degree of precision, the price of a commodity or service monopolised by a public authority into its component parts, competitive price plus tax. For, in the

improvement to property undertaken in the public interest'.[1] It is a device for securing for the public treasury part of the unearned increment in the value of fixed property, which arises, for example, in the neighbourhood of a newly opened thoroughfare. A special assessment resembles a tax in that it is a compulsory payment, but differs from it in that the payer has received a definite and direct *quid pro quo*. In the latter respect it resembles a price, but differs from it in that the payment is not voluntary and does not arise out of a contract with the public authority. In the same class is the development charge, imposed by the British Town and Country Planning Act of 1947, but repealed in 1953. This charge was equal to the added value given to land by permission granted by the Planning Authority (normally a Borough, County Borough or County Council) to develop it.

The issue of new paper money by a public authority is not quite the same thing as the imposition of a tax, though its effect, through reducing the value of money, is similar to that of a general tax upon all commodities and services.[2] Voluntary gifts form, unfortunately, only an infinitesimal part of the income of public authorities. They are exemplified in this country by 'conscience money', which, however, is usually only a delayed part-payment of taxes which have already been evaded. Also by occasional gifts for the reduction of the national debt.[3] More substantial is the steady flow of gifts to hospitals.

§ 3. The boundary lines between the various kinds of public income just enumerated are not, in most cases, clear cut, but one kind shades gradually into another. Thus taxes shade gradually into prices, since the services rendered by public

---

absence of competition, the competitive price can only be roughly estimated. And the cost of production of either a private competitor or a private monopolist might differ widely from that of the public authority.

[1] *Essays in Taxation*, p. 283.

[2] See Ch. XV for a further discussion of this point. The issue is often made indirectly, in response to increased bank credits.

[3] See Ch. XXIII, § 7, note.

[4] Receipts from gifts, legacies and trusts in favour of hospitals in England and Wales were over £2 millions both in 1950–1 and 1951–2 (Annual Accounts under Section 55 of National Health Service Act, 1946).

authorities to taxpayers often stand in a somewhat indefinite relation to the payments made by the latter. Local rates for the supply of water, where no meters are used, illustrate this.

Again, Taussig's description of a tax, quoted above, would cover penalties for offences.

The distinction between taxes and penalties is one of motive; a public authority imposes taxes mainly to obtain revenue and enacts penalties mainly to deter from certain acts. If motorists were fined £1 for every infraction of the speed limit, and the money were collected periodically, such fines might be regarded as a tax on high speed, comparable to a tax on petrol. But if, at each successive offence by the same motorist, the fine were increased, and the offender finally put in prison or deprived of his licence to drive, so that no more fines were obtainable from him, those already collected would clearly be in the nature of penalties and not taxes. Similarly with customs duties, in the language of which, as Swift remarked, two plus two is often less than three. If, as the rate of a particular duty is increased, the revenue yielded increases, the duty is predominantly a tax. But when the rate is increased above the point at which the yield in revenue is a maximum, it is clear that some element of penalty is present, and we finally reach a duty of prohibitive amount, whose yield is very small or even non-existent. This is closely akin to a simple prohibition of production or importation, with a penalty for infraction.

§ 4. It has already been pointed out that the monopoly profits, if any, of a public enterprise are very like a tax. There is no substantial distinction, from this point of view, between the French Government's monopoly profits from the sale of tobacco and the British Government's revenue from tobacco duties imposed on private traders. Public enterprises, which make monopoly profits, shade into those which do not. The test is not whether a public authority has an absolute monopoly of the supply of any commodity or service, for very few monopolies are absolute, when substitutes, actual and potential, are taken into account. A Government monopoly of railway transport, for instance, is open to competition from private (or public) transport by water, road and air. But monopoly need not be absolute, in order to permit of the use of monopoly power to raise prices above cost of production. This power is available, as a general rule, wherever a considerable proportion of the total supply of any commodity or service is under a single control. The test is whether such monopoly power is, or is not, actually used. A public authority conducting an enterprise may have a large degree of monopoly power, but may decide that it is in the public interest that the product of the enterprise shall be sold at, or even below, cost price. A practical difficulty often arises in determining the cost of production of the products of a public enterprise. What allowances for interest, depreciation, etc., should be made? Anyone who doubts the reality of these difficulties should try to work out the cost of production of British postal services.

There is no sharp distinction between fees on the one hand and taxes and public monopoly profits on the other. For the cost of performing a service is often less than the fee charged for performing it. Nor is there any sharp distinction between fees and receipts from public enterprises generally. For there is no sharp distinction between those services which are 'in the nature of business services' and those which are not. Thus some writers have proposed to class all postal receipts as fees. Again, there is no sharp distinction between receipts from public enterprises and receipts from public property passively held, for some supervision and management are required even in the most humdrum administration of public lands and, if schemes of afforestation, irrigation, etc., are undertaken, these constitute an enterprise no less than the delivery of letters and telegrams.

Since 1945 in Britain a number of public boards have been created to conduct the coal, electricity, gas and other industries. These boards are not, of course, 'public authorities' in the ordinary sense, but they are public monopolies, subject to some degree of Ministerial and Parliamentary control. The statutes creating them require these boards, 'taking one year with another', to balance their accounts, and this requirement heavily influences their price policy. The requirement is no more than a practical politician's rough rule of thumb, and it may be persuasively argued that other rules, resulting in some cases in a large profit, in others in a large loss, would give much greater social advantage.[1]

The general conclusion of this discussion is that the sources of public income may indeed be classified, but that many of the distinctions involved are not clear cut and that, here as elsewhere, the search for a classification is more instructive than the classification when found.

[1] See Ch. XIV, § 8.

# CHAPTER V

## TAXATION AND SOME
## DISTINCTIONS BETWEEN TAXES

§ 1. We have seen that a tax is a compulsory contribution imposed by a public authority, irrespective of the exact amount of service rendered to the taxpayer in return, and not imposed as a penalty for any legal offence. Auberon Herbert, who was a philosophic anarchist, thought that taxation was never morally justifiable, but this is an eccentric opinion which may be ignored. Yet taxation, though justifiable, might not be necessary, or might be necessary only to a small extent, if other sources of public income were more prolific, if, for instance, public authorities owned larger quantities of income-yielding property or if it was more the fashion among wealthy people to make large voluntary gifts to the State. If the London County Council had been, since its foundation, the sole landlord within its area, London rates would be much lower than they are.[1]

As things are now ordered, however, a large amount of taxation is necessary in nearly all modern communities and, as public expenditure increases, taxation increases also.

§ 2. The classification of taxes need not detain us long, but a few distinctions may be noticed in passing. The commonest is between direct and indirect taxes. The idea often underlying this distinction is that a direct tax is really paid by the person on whom it is legally imposed, while an indirect tax is imposed on one person, but paid partly or wholly by another, owing to a consequential change in the terms of some contract or bargain

[1] A Canadian who attended my lectures told me that the Municipality of Guelph, Ontario, imposed no local taxation, but lived entirely on the rent of municipally owned land leased to the Canadian Pacific Railway. And oil royalties amount to one-third of the public income in Iraq, to three-quarters in Bahrein, and to more than four-fifths in Kuweit (*Economist*, February 26, 1954).

between them. Thus an indirect tax is conceived as one which can be shifted or passed on; a direct tax as one which cannot. This distinction is less fundamental and useful than is sometimes supposed.[1] The reasons for this will appear more clearly when we come to consider the incidence and effects of taxation. Nor is the distinction always clear in particular cases. An income tax is generally regarded as a direct tax; but the United States Supreme Court in 1868 held it to be indirect, when they wished to declare it constitutionally valid. This, however, was only the economics of clever lawyers in a tight place. An inheritance tax is generally regarded as a direct tax and so are other taxes on property. On the other hand, taxes on commodities and transactions are generally regarded as indirect. But doubts begin to arise when we reflect that most commodities only differ from most other forms of material property in being less durable, and that an inheritance tax is merely a tax on a particular class of transactions.

It is often vaguely supposed to be a sign of financial virtue to 'keep a balance' between direct and indirect taxation, an idea encouraged by Gladstone's well-known simile, in which he likened these two sources of revenue to 'two attractive sisters', as between whom he was 'perfectly impartial', believing that, as Chancellor of the Exchequer, it was 'not only allowable, but even an act of duty, to pay my addresses to them both'.

This notion of 'keeping a balance' is bound up with ideas about the proper distribution of the burden of taxation between persons, which will be discussed later, and with the belief that direct taxes are paid by the rich and indirect by the poor. There are no theoretical, but some practical, grounds for this last belief. Most existing direct taxes in modern communities do, in

[1] The distinction has been made by some writers to turn on whether or not it is intended by the statesmen, who impose it, that a tax shall be shifted. But the intentions of statesmen and the facts of incidence may be at variance. I asked a member of the British Government in 1911, whether either the Cabinet or the Treasury had made any estimate of the incidence of the weekly levies imposed on employers and employees under the National Insurance Act of that year. But the Minister could not see that there was anything to estimate. 'The men pay 4d.,' he said, 'and the employers pay 3d. and the State pays 2d., and so the men get 9d. for 4d.'

fact, involve larger contributions from the rich than from the poor, in proportion to their incomes, and the opposite is the case with many existing indirect taxes. But the position would be reversed, if direct taxation were limited to a poll tax of equal amount on every citizen, and indirect taxation to duties on luxuries which only the rich could afford to buy.

Disregarding incidence, it accords pretty well with common usage to say that indirect taxes are those levied on the sale or purchase of any goods or services other than personal services, and that all other taxes are direct.

This definition avoids some awkwardness to which the criterion of incidence gives rise.[1]

§ 3. Consider next the distinction between taxes on income and taxes on capital. It can make no difference whether a given revenue is raised by a flat-rate tax assessed on the annual value, or by a similar tax assessed on the capital value, of property, so long as the ratio of annual value to capital value is the same in all cases affected by the tax. If, for instance, this ratio is one to twenty, a tax of one and eightpence in the pound on an income, or annual value, of £500 will bring in the same revenue as a tax of a penny in the pound on a capital value of £10,000. If, however, the ratio varies, a tax on capital value will be heavier than a tax on annual value, yielding the same revenue, in those cases where the ratio of capital to annual value is abnormally high, and less heavy where it is abnormally low. For example, owners of undeveloped or 'under-developed' land will be hit harder than the owners of fully developed land. This is why those, who wish to compel land-owners to 'put their land to the fullest use',[2] advocate a tax based on the capital, rather than the annual, value of the land. Similarly holders of gilt-edged securities would be hit harder than holders of equities.

The above distinction between taxes *assessed on* income and capital respectively is often confused with the quite separate

[1] See Ch. VII, § 2.

[2] 'Fullest use' here means that which, taking account of the tax, is most profitable to the private owner. This is often not identical with the use which brings the maximum social advantage. To secure the latter intelligent geographical planning is required.

'.stinction between taxes *paid out of income* and c pu.. respectively. But a tax assessed on capital may be paid out of income,
and conversely. A man liable to death duties may pay them out
of income; a man may sell securities or borrow from his bank
in order to pay income tax. A tax assessed on capital may, however, be too heavy to be paid out of income. And thus, in
practice, there is a link, in the case of heavy taxes on capital,
between basis of assessment and source of payment. This is
important, as we shall see later, in relation to a stabilising
budgetary policy.[1]

§ 4. Another distinction sometimes drawn is between taxes
assessed on property and taxes assessed on commodities. This
distinction seems at first sight to turn on relative durability.
From this point of view, land is evidently property, sugar
evidently a commodity. Houses and machines are intermediate,
being less durable than land, but more durable than sugar. But,
in practice, this distinction often turns on whether the tax is
imposed periodically or once for all. In the former case the
object of the tax may be regarded as property, in the latter as a
commodity. Nor in the former case need the period be regular.
An inheritance tax, though levied at irregular intervals, may
reasonably be called a tax on property, even though the inheritance includes a stock of sugar. British local rates, being a
periodic tax on the annual value of land and buildings, treat
houses as property, but a tax levied once for all on the value of
newly built houses would treat these as commodities.

Taxes on commodities may be either specific or *ad valorem*.
A specific tax is based upon some physical measurement, such
as a unit of weight or volume, e.g. a tax of a shilling a pound on
tea or fifty shillings a gallon on beer. An *ad valorem* tax is based
upon a unit of value, e.g. a tax of a third of their value on
imported mouth-organs.

§ 5. A distinction of a different kind is between taxes intended
to be only temporary and taxes intended to be comparatively
permanent. A special tax, whether assessed on an individual's
income, his capital, or his 'excess' profits, designed to pay off in
a short time a large amount of public debt, or to help to pay

[1] See Ch. XXVII, §§ 3–4.

for a war in progress, or for a special rearmament programme, would be an example of the former. The British income tax, at any rate since Gladstone's death,[1] is an example of the latter, though many taxpayers hope that the present rates of tax will not be permanent. The chief value of this distinction lies in its bearing on the probable conduct of taxpayers, which will vary with their expectations regarding future taxation.[2]

§ 6. A distinction is sometimes suggested between taxes on persons and taxes on things. This form of words may be used in two different senses. First in relation to assessment. Thus taxes on persons might include, on the one hand, a poll tax, either equal for all or assessed on different persons in some quite arbitrary manner, and on the other, all taxes based on purely personal characteristics of the taxpayer, such as his height, weight or religion, or the colour of his eyes or hair, while taxes on things would include all taxes based on criteria external to the taxpayer, such as his income, the rent which he pays for his house, or the amount of tobacco which he smokes. But in this sense the distinction is without much practical value, since nearly all actual taxes are on things and not on persons. But national insurance contributions, when levied as poll taxes, are personal taxes in this sense. So was the tax on the wearing of beards, imposed by Peter the Great to encourage cleanliness,—though this was easier to escape.

A second sense, in which the distinction has sometimes been used, implies that some taxes are *paid* by persons and others by things.[3] But this is a very gross error. It is natural, when thinking of the basis of assessment, to speak of taxes on land, on imports, on industry and trade. But neither inanimate objects,

[1] Gladstone always regarded it as temporary and in 1874, on the eve of a general election, promised to repeal it. But he lost the election.

[2] See Ch. X, §§ 3–8.

[3] See, for example, Giffen's observations on pp. 83–4, of *Memoranda on the Classification and Incidence of Imperial and Local Taxes* (C. 9258, 1899): 'Rates on real property are for the most part burdens on the property itself, and therefore not taxation in the proper sense of the term; in other words not contributions to the expense of the State by the individuals who bear the rates in the same way that the Income Tax is a contribution by those who bear it. . . . Duties upon the succession to property at death are

such as plots of land and bundles of imported goods, nor abstractions, such as 'industry' and 'trade', are endowed with pockets or banking accounts, out of which they, as distinct from persons, can pay taxes. It is a platitude that all taxes are paid by persons, not by things.

§ 7. There are some taxes, the place of which in tax classifications may at first sight seem doubtful. Stamp duties, taxes on business profits, and on trade turnover are examples. But a little reflection will make it clear that a stamp duty is not a special kind of tax, but only a special method of collecting taxes. People are required in certain circumstances to buy stamps of a certain value and to stick them on certain documents, or to buy the documents ready stamped. Many taxes on transactions are thus collected, and any tax could be so collected. The question is simply one of administrative convenience. Again, a tax on business profits is only a tax on a particular kind of income, while a tax on turnover is only a tax on the value of the commodities turned over.

not taxes upon the dying, because they are not levied till they have ceased to own the property, and not taxes upon the inheritors because they only inherit by the will and permission of the State itself.' This official publication can still be skimmed by the modern student with profit, and perhaps also with some amusement. It contains the answers to an examination paper set by the Treasury to a number of civil servants, professors and other eminent persons. These examinees were fortunate in being allowed ample time for their answers and unlimited access to books and papers!

# CHAPTER VI

## SOME CHARACTERISTICS OF A GOOD TAX SYSTEM

§ 1. Any system of public finance must be looked at as a whole, before any final judgment can be passed upon its merits or demerits. So, too, any tax system must be looked at as a whole. For different taxes may, in some of their effects, correct and balance one another.

If in a given year a given revenue is to be raised by taxation, alternative tax systems will result in alternative distributions of the total burden of taxation, which will itself be greater under some systems than others, and in other alternative effects on the economic welfare of the community. These matters will be discussed in the next seven chapters. But in this chapter a few preliminary points will first be noticed.

§ 2. The comparative advantages of single tax and multiple tax systems have been much argued. Various types of single tax have been proposed. The Physiocrats proposed a single tax on the economic rent of land, because they thought that this was where all taxes ultimately fell, and that it would, therefore, save trouble and misunderstanding to put them there straight away. But this idea involved a false theory of incidence. Henry George made a similar proposal, partly because he thought that a tax on rent did not check industry, whereas all other taxes did, in which opinion there is a grain of truth, and partly for reasons of a supposedly ethical character, which carry less weight. But there are two grave objections to a single tax of this kind. The first is that it would not, in most modern communities, bring in enough revenue. The second is that it would lead to a very bad distribution of the burden of taxation. For a millionaire, who owned no land, would pay no taxes, while a poor man, who had invested all his savings in the purchase of his house, might pay in taxation, in respect of the land on which it stood, a considerable proportion of his income. A single tax on land has no relation to individual 'ability to pay'.

There is a much stronger case for a single tax assessed on income. This could be made to yield all the tax revenue normally required and, by means of graduation, differentiation and other devices, could be made to distribute the burden of taxation between individuals in whatever way was thought best. There are, however, in addition to arguments against *any* single tax, three objections to exclusive reliance upon an income tax. The first is that such a tax imposed on small incomes is relatively difficult and expensive to collect. The second is that it secures no special contribution from inheritors of wealth, a pre-eminently taxable class. The third is that it tends to check saving more than most other taxes do. The first objection might be overcome to some extent by administrative improvements, and indeed would not arise at all, if it were decided to distribute the burden of taxation in such a way as to exempt small incomes altogether. The second could be overcome by treating wealth acquired by inheritance or gift as taxable income at the time of its acquisition. There is something to be said for doing this and it was done in the United States income tax of 1861. The third could be overcome by exempting savings from taxable income, and imposing a single tax, not upon personal income, but upon personal expenditure.

Such a tax has great attractions. It would also fall upon dissavings, i.e. on personal expenditure financed by selling securities or other assets and 'living on capital'; also on capital gains, if these were spent, though not if they were saved. In principle, there is a strong case for making such an expenditure tax, not indeed a single tax, but one of the more important revenue raisers, graduated and differentiated, as with an income tax, so as to give the desired distribution of the tax burden. But, in practice, there are great administrative difficulties, much greater than with income tax, and it is not yet clear that these could be effectively surmounted.[1]

§ 3. Arguments against particular forms of single tax are

[1] A most persuasive advocate of such an expenditure tax is Mr. Nicholas Kaldor, with whom I have several times discussed the question.

reinforced by certain general arguments against any form of single tax. Anomalies as between persons, which are liable to arise under a single tax, are liable to be corrected under a multiplicity of taxes. And evasions, which may be comparatively easy under a single tax, are more readily detected under the check and counter-check which a multiple tax system may provide. Thus valuations for death duties and the previous income tax returns of the deceased may be checked against one another.[1] Again, the land value duties of the British budget of 1909, though they never brought in any appreciable revenue, necessitated a land valuation which, though never completed, is said to have more than paid for itself by the additions which it indirectly brought to the death duty revenue.

In general, the weight of argument is against a single tax. In the case of local authorities, exercising comparatively few functions over a comparatively small area, there is something to be said, on ground of convenience, for a single tax on 'immobilia' or immovable property. Local rates in Britain are a tax of this sort, based on the annual value of land plus buildings, though some classes of land and buildings are subject to exemption or abatements by way of 'derating', and there are great complications both of law and fact, increased by the wide range of rent control, in the valuation of various classes of property. It is often argued, with some force, that rates would be better based on the capital, or even the annual, value of land only, as is done in many parts of the world. For British local rates are in great measure, a tax on houses, which are not a good object of taxation. But these local rates are not, in reality, a single tax, for British local authorities derive a large part of their revenue from grants-in-aid out of the proceeds of national taxation, and from the ownership of public property and the conduct of public enterprises in their own areas. And local rates are only in part a genuine tax. In part they represent prices paid by ratepayers for specific services rendered to them by local authorities.

[1] In Sweden, where the supply of spirits is limited to a fixed ration per head, a ration card is only issued if the applicant can produce a certificate to show that he has paid his income tax.

An interesting case is the State of Nevada, which raises nearly all its revenue by the taxation of legal gambling. 'It has no state income tax, no retail sales tax and no state inheritance tax.'[1]

§ 4. But though a multiple tax system is generally preferable to a single tax system, too great a multiplicity is not desirable. Advocates of 'broadening the basis of taxation' are to be distrusted. Of this fellowship was Arthur Young who said, 'if I were to define a good system of taxation, it should be that of bearing lightly on an infinite number of points, heavily on none'.[2] But there is not necessarily any less total pressure under such a system, for, as mathematicians know, the sum of an infinitely large number of infinitely small weights may be greater than a single moderate weight. Moreover, a large number of taxes, however small, usually involves a large cost and a large amount of vexation in collection.

The path of wisdom in this matter, for a modern community with a well developed economic life and a reasonably efficient administrative system, is fairly clear. It is best to rely on a few substantial taxes for the bulk of the tax revenue. In so far as it is desired to tax the rich, income and inheritance taxes are the best means; in so far as it is desired to tax the poor, taxes on a few commodities of wide consumption, preferably commodities not necessary to health and efficiency. Some commodities, such as alcohol and tobacco, may indeed be taxed on their merits, or, as some would say, on their demerits, apart from any question of the distribution of the burden of taxation between different sections of the community. Other taxes on luxuries

---

[1] 'Tourism is officially listed as the leading industry but unquestionably it owes a great deal to public gambling which has become the fifth largest industry, and to the divorce business, which is conservatively listed tenth among the sources of income. Both help to maintain hotels, restaurants, motor courts, night clubs, etc. . . . Las Vegas, with a population of 24,000, took $122 millions from tourists last year. Roughly 50 cents out of every dollar of this sum went for whisky and gambling. . . . The voters have tended to become apathetic in a state too long bossed by a bipartisan coalition of millionaire refugees from taxation' (*Economist*, January 2nd, 1954, p. 28).

[2] Quoted by Bastable, *Public Finance*, p. 344.

have their legitimate place and some taxes with special objects may be added, but it is desirable to keep their number within bounds.

Almost everywhere, and even in Great Britain, whose tax system is simpler and more efficient than that of any other important modern community, so-called 'historical causes' have led to a needless multiplicity of taxes and to needless complexity in methods of assessment. But, especially where multiplicity is reduced, particular taxes may need to be complex—the British income tax for example—if the tax system as a whole is to be satisfactory.

§ 5. A further point of occasional controversy may be noticed here. Is it a characteristic of a good tax system that taxes should be 'felt' as much, or as little, as possible? The plain man will be inclined to think that the best tax is that which is least felt, that is to say which causes the least inconvenience and conscious sacrifice to those who pay it. But some austere thinkers take the view that mankind can only learn through suffering, and that political responsibility can only be brought home to us through conscious payment of the price of greatness—or of folly, as the case may be. Thus after the first world war a Scottish Professor of Economics thought that we might be tempted to go to war again, if we rashly destroyed, by means of a capital levy, the Great War Debt, which would otherwise be one of the most impressive of our national war memorials. It used also to be maintained that, if income tax were resolutely imposed upon all, however poor, all would eagerly co-operate in checking wasteful expenditure, while the poor would also gain in moral stature. Men take sides in this controversy according to opinions not exclusively economic. Personally, I take sides with the plain man. And experience after the second world war has now shown that, in a modern democratic state, the reaction to a nearly universal income tax, newly imposed, is not that imagined by the austere. The public mind is less preoccupied with checking public expenditure than with redistributing the burden of taxation, so as to relieve the poorer sections of the community of their recently acquired income tax. On the other hand, an increase in a well-established tax, such as local rates,

P.P.F.—D

tends to create a somewhat undiscriminating demand for 'economy'.

§ 6. The practical application of a decision, in either sense, of the main controversy is not wholly clear. Thus it is commonly supposed that an income tax is more keenly felt than taxes which, being levied on commodities, are wrapped up in their prices, as some of the medicines of our childhood were wrapped up in jam. But on the other hand, it is sometimes said, an income tax hits only marginal expenditure and marginal savings all round, whereas a tax on a particular commodity hits expenditure, including non-marginal expenditure, on that commodity only, and is thus apt to cause a greater loss of satisfaction. Moreover, when income tax is 'deducted at the source', that is to say intercepted before his money income actually reaches the taxpayer, it is apt to be less keenly felt, than if he first receives his income in full and then at a later date, when he has already spent most of it, receives a demand note from the tax collector.[1] An inheritance tax, again, is often less keenly felt than might be supposed, since its payment is generally made through the agency of executors, before the inheritors receive the balance of the property, and since the payment coincides both with a positive accretion of personal wealth to the inheritors and with other events, which often force considerations of tax payments into the background of their minds.

§ 7. An ingenious formula, of Cambridge origin, is that the rich should pay more taxation than they think, while the poor should think they pay more than they do. This double illusion, it is argued, will keep the rich contented and the poor virtuous, and will tend to maximise work and saving by all classes. But it would be hard to create, and still harder to maintain, such an unstable equilibrium of errors.

A distinction may, indeed, be drawn between the subjective and the objective burden of taxation.[2] Corresponding to the

[1] For a further discussion of what taxes cause most loss of satisfaction, see Ch. X, §§ 3–4, and of my own opinion, and my action based upon it while I was Chancellor of the Exchequer, see Ch. XXVIII.

[2] And similarly between the subjective and the objective benefit of public expenditure

same objective burden, as seen by the statesman, there may be a different subjective burden on two different taxpayers, due to differences of taste and temperament, even if their economic situation, as regards income and other factors, is the same. Corresponding to a given objective burden, taxes which are 'much felt' impose a heavier, and taxes which are 'little felt' a lighter, subjective burden. But, in general, this distinction is only of secondary importance. The primary consideration is the objective burden, as measured by a given loss of resources to a taxpayer in a given economic situation. To this there corresponds what may be called a normal subjective burden. Deviations on either side from this normal are mainly due either to personal peculiarities of taxpayers, which cancel out in the average, or to transitory conditions, such as the novelty of a particular tax, which pass with time. The objective burden will vary only with variations in the loss of resources imposed by taxation, or in the economic situation of the taxpayer, as measured by his income, number of dependants, etc.

We may also, if we choose, distinguish between the weight and the burden of taxation; the weight absolute, in terms of commodities surrendered, the burden relative to the taxpayer's power to carry the weight.

# CHAPTER VII

## INCIDENCE OF TAXATION

§ 1. The problem of the incidence of a tax is commonly conceived as the problem of who pays it. More precisely we may say that the incidence is upon those who bear the direct money burden of the tax. Every tax causes a number of economic effects, and it has been questioned whether we either can or should try to separate the special problem of incidence from the more general problem of effects. But clearly the attempt must be made, if anything is to be said on the distribution of the direct money burden of taxation, a subject to which many theorists and most plain men attach importance.

A distinction must be drawn between the direct and the indirect burden of a tax, and also between the money burden and the real burden. The total direct money burden is equal to the total yield of the tax to the public treasury. To every shilling of revenue raised there corresponds a shilling of direct money burden, or incidence, falling upon someone.[1] To part with a shilling in payment of a tax means a greater sacrifice of economic welfare for a poor man than for a rich man. But that is a question, not of the incidence, but of the direct real burden of the tax. Again, when the price of sugar is raised by taxation, a family may have to eat less sugar, and so make a sacrifice of economic welfare. But that is a question, not of the incidence, but of the indirect real burden, of the tax. Again, when the tax on sugar is collected from the dealer in respect of his stocks and some time elapses between the collection of the tax and the sale of the stocks, the dealer is out of pocket by the amount of the interest, which he could otherwise have obtained during that period on the money paid to the tax collector. But that is a

[1] Except in the limiting case of escheat, that form of inheritance tax, under which the property of an intestate, who possesses no discoverable relatives however remote, reverts at his death to the State.

question, not of the incidence, but of the indirect money burden, of the tax.

§ 2. Thus the incidence of a tax on sugar collected from the seller is wholly on the buyer, if, as a direct result of the tax, the price rises by at least the full amount of the tax; wholly on the seller, if the price does not rise at all; partly on the buyer and partly on the seller, if the price rises by an amount less than the full amount of the tax.

We may illustrate at this point the unsatisfactory character of the distinction, based on incidence, between direct and indirect taxes.[1] Before we can decide whether a particular tax is direct or indirect, in this sense, we must know its incidence, and this may depend, not only on the nature of the tax, but on other circumstances. It is commonly assumed that a tax on a commodity is an indirect tax, since it is 'passed on', in whole or in part. But if, whether collected from buyers or sellers, it leaves the price unchanged, then it must be classed as a direct tax. For it is not then passed on. And, as will be seen later, such circumstances are not impossible. Again, the incidence of a tax on a monopolist varies with the character of the tax and, therefore, to take two examples which will be discussed later in this chapter, a tax proportionate to output must be classed as indirect, while a tax independent of output will be direct.

It is commonly assumed, on the other hand, that an inheritance tax is a direct tax, though there has been some dispute as to whether its incidence is on the successor or the predecessor. Clearly it is on the successor, for the predecessor must be dead before the tax can be levied and dead men, like other inanimate objects, can pay no taxes. The fact that the predecessor may have insured against the tax beforehand is irrelevant to the question of incidence, though not, of course, to the wider question of effects. The burden of such an insurance policy must be classed, not as a direct, but as an indirect, money burden on the predecessor, due to anticipation of the tax.

Again, it is commonly assumed that an income tax is a direct tax. The extent to which income tax payers can shift the incidence of the tax is, no doubt, so small, especially in the short run,

[1] See Ch. V, § 2.

as to be practically negligible. But exceptional conditions may make even an income tax, or parts of it, indirect, as judged by incidence.[1]

§ 3. Regarding taxes on particular commodities or services, two general propositions may be laid down. The first is that, other things being equal, the more elastic the demand for the object of taxation, the more will the incidence of the tax be upon the seller. And the second is that, other things being equal, the more elastic the supply of the object of taxation, the more will the incidence of the tax be upon the buyer. These propositions follow immediately from the definition of elasticity. They are considered further in the note to this and the next chapter.

Take first the case when competition prevails both among buyers and sellers. It makes no essential difference whether the tax is legally imposed on buyers or sellers, though this may affect the length of time which will elapse before the process of shifting the direct money burden, or part of it, from one side to the other is completed. Every tax tends, for a time, to 'stick where it falls'.

Cases of absolutely inelastic demand are seldom, if ever, found in practice. But the demand for luxuries is more elastic than the demand for necessaries and, therefore, other things being equal, a tax on necessaries will raise their price by a larger amount than an equal tax on luxuries. Again, the demand for new durable objects, of which a large stock is already in use, is generally more elastic than the demand for commodities which are perishable or quickly consumed.

Cases of absolutely inelastic supply are less remote from reality. Thus the supply of land in well populated districts may be regarded as absolutely inelastic. It follows that a tax on land, as distinct from improvements, will not raise the price of land, and its incidence will be wholly on the owner.

Where, however, the supply of a commodity is at all elastic, it is generally very elastic in the long run, and considerably more elastic than the demand. When, therefore, conditions of production have had time to adjust themselves to changes due to taxation, the greater part of the incidence will generally be

[1] This case is further examined in the Note following Ch. VIII.

upon buyers, and not upon sellers. But, during the period of adjustment, the elasticity of supply may be small and then a large part of the incidence may be upon the sellers. Thus, in the case of commodities produced by means of an expensive plant and much fixed capital, the elasticity of supply may remain small for a considerable time after a tax has been imposed upon them.

Our two general propositions may now be combined into one. The direct money burden of a tax imposed on any object is divided between the buyers and the sellers in the proportion of the elasticity of supply of the object taxed to the elasticity of demand for it. Thus in the particular case when the elasticity of supply is equal to the elasticity of demand, the burden is equally divided, and the price of the object taxed rises by half the amount of the tax.

This is a first approximation, based on the assumption that a tax on a commodity leaves unchanged the conditions of demand for, and supply of, all other commodities. This assumption is seldom completely justified, but often sufficiently so for rough practical purposes. Clearly, however, part of the incidence of a tax imposed upon the sellers or buyers of a commodity may fall, not upon these sellers or buyers, but upon the sellers of some other commodity, which is necessary to the production of the former, or upon the buyers of some other commodity, to the production of which the taxed commodity is necessary. Thus part of the incidence of a tax on jam may fall upon the sellers of tins or glass jars, who may be compelled by the tax to reduce their price to the jam makers.

§ 4. The preceding theory has been stated, so as to apply to the incidence of taxes on the internal trade of a community, but substantially the same theory applies to the incidence of taxes on international trade, in the form of customs duties on imports or exports. In the case of internal trade we have considered the exchange of goods for money, the elasticity of demand of the buyers, who give money for goods, and the elasticity of supply of the sellers, who give goods for money. In the case of international trade we may consider the exchange of goods for goods, and the elasticities of demand of the two groups of buyers for the goods respectively furnished by the other group in exchange for their own. Thus in the exchange of Canadian wheat for British woollen goods, assuming that no other goods are exchanged between the two countries, the elasticity of supply of Canadian wheat in Great Britain is the same thing as the elasticity of demand for British woollen goods in Canada.

Taxes on imports and exports may, then, be regarded as obstacles to exchange and, in accordance with the preceding theory, the direct money burden of any such obstacle is divided between the two parties to the exchange in inverse proportion to the elasticities of their respective demands. In other words, it is divided in direct proportion to the urgencies[1] of their respective needs, which are satisfied by the exchange. For, the more urgent the need of either party, the less elastic his demand. Other things being equal, the less elastic the British demand for Canadian wheat, the greater the proportion of the incidence, of a tax either on British woollen goods or Canadian wheat in transit between the two countries, which will fall upon the British party to the exchange. Similarly, the less elastic the Canadian demand for British woollen goods, the greater the proportion which will fall upon the Canadian party to the exchange.

§ 5. The inhabitants of a region, in which is produced a large proportion of the world supply of some commodity essential to outsiders in the rest of the world, could make these outsiders pay a large part of export duties on this commodity, or of import duties on what the outsiders offered in exchange for it. We in Britain were in such a favourable position, when this country was practically the only source of supply of wool to Flanders during the Middle Ages, of machine-made manufactured goods to the continent of Europe in the early nineteenth century, and of steam coal to the world's navies in the later nineteenth century. On the other hand, the inhabitants of a region, in which is produced no commodity very essential to outsiders, or only a small proportion of the world supply of essential commodities, cannot throw any appreciable part of any customs duties, which they may impose, upon outsiders, while, if outside products are essential to them, outsiders can

---

[1] Ignoring differences in the wealth of the two parties.

impose customs duties, a large part of the incidence of which will fall upon the inhabitants of this less fortunate region.

In the present conditions of international trade, the incidence of customs duties imposed in countries, whose exports are chiefly manufactured goods and whose imports are chiefly food and raw material, can hardly be, to any appreciable extent, upon outsiders. For the outside demand for their manufactures is, in most cases, much less keen, that is to say much more elastic, than their demand for the outsiders' food and raw material. The inhabitants of Britain, in particular, are not now in a position to make outsiders pay British customs duties, except in rare and unusual cases. It has been suggested that the British import duty on Greek currants is largely paid by the Greeks, but even this exception to the general rule is doubtful.

Further, commodities, which have a wide world market, have a very elastic supply to any small part of that market. Thus a tax imposed on the imports of such a commodity into a single 'national' market, provided that sales in that market are small relatively to world sales, will generally raise the price *in that market* by about the amount of the tax. Again, the demand of the inhabitants of a country for a commodity from *any particular outside market* is much more elastic than their demand for that commodity from the outside world as a whole. Thus the inhabitants of a number of important countries acting in combination would have a better chance, than the inhabitants of any one acting alone, of throwing the incidence of their customs duties upon those outside the combination.

And if, indeed, all manufacturing countries, each acting independently, protect their agriculture by import duties, they will be able to throw the incidence of these duties on to any primary producing countries, whose supply of food and materials and demand for manufacture are both inelastic.

§ 6. It remains to consider how far the theory of incidence should be modified in the case of taxes on monopolists. Where a tax is imposed upon a commodity, whose seller is a monopolist—or even an oligopolist—the effect on the price and hence the incidence, varies according to the character of the tax. Assuming that the monopolist will fix his price so as to secure for himself the maximum monopoly profits, the incidence of a tax, whose total amount is proportionate to the volume of his output, or, more generally, whose total amount increases as his output increases, will be similar to that of the taxes discussed in preceding sections of this chapter. Except in the event of either the supply being absolutely inelastic or the demand absolutely elastic, the tax will raise the price of the commodity to some extent and, other things being equal, this rise in price will be greater, the less elastic the demand and the more elastic the supply.[1]

If, however, the tax is one whose total amount is independent of the size of the monopolist's output, it will not raise the price and its incidence will be wholly on the monopolist. An example of such a tax would be a fixed contribution, independent of output.

There is also a third possibility, that of a tax whose total amount diminishes as the monopolist's output increases. Such a tax, if its imposition were practicable, would in some cases[2] cause the monopolist to increase his output and lower his price. An example would be a tax, whose total amount was proportionate to the price of the commodity per unit, or a lump sum with a rebate proportionate to output. In favourable cases the incidence of such a tax would be entirely on the monopolist who, in addition, would be compelled to transfer part of his monopoly profits to the buyers of his product in the form of lower prices. One practical obstacle in the way of carrying out this policy arises from the difficulty of checking the quality of the monopolist's product. For it will obviously pay him, if subjected to such a tax, to sell an inferior product at a lower price.

Where the product of the monopolist is an import from abroad, it will sometimes be possible to make him bear the incidence of an import licence, such a licence being a fixed payment for any given period, with or without a rebate proportionate to his importation during this period.

[1] But elasticity of supply has different meanings under monopoly and under competition. See note to Chs. VII and VIII, §§ 6 and 7.

[2] In those cases, namely, in which, as his output increases, his tax payments diminish faster than his monopoly profits, apart from the tax.

# CHAPTER VIII

## INCIDENCE OF TAXATION (*continued*)

§ 1. The argument of the last chapter needs to be supplemented by various considerations, some of which blunt the sharp edge of the general theory of incidence as applied to practical problems.

§ 2. The argument that the incidence of a tax on the value of land, as distinct from improvements, falls entirely on the landowner, assumes that the latter is already securing the highest rent that he can from his land. If not, one of the effects of the imposition of a new tax, or the increase of an existing tax, may be to make him 'look sharply to his rents and take in the slack'. In this case part of the incidence will be upon the occupier. The practical valuation of land, as distinct from improvements, is often difficult, though many experts consider it to be quite feasible, and taxes in many parts of the world are based upon such valuations. We need not separate the value of land from that of all improvements, but only from that of temporary, as distinct from permanent, improvements. But the line of division between temporary and permanent is apt to be hazy.

§ 3. The incidence of a tax on buildings presents many complications. Not only the owner and the occupier, but also the builder, may bear part of the incidence. Further, the occupier of a building, if engaged in trade, may be able to shift part of the incidence, which would otherwise fall on him, on to the purchasers of his products. And where these products are not consumable commodities, but machinery, etc., to be used in the production of further commodities, the purchasers of the machinery may, in turn, be able to shift part of any incidence falling on them on to the purchasers of their own products.

The power of shopkeepers to shift their local rates on to their customers is greater when the purchases of the latter are restricted to shops in their own neighbourhood than when they are not. For in the former case the demand of customers for goods sold at shops in their own neighbourhood is less elastic than in the latter. Thus the development of postal and telephone communications, the increasing circulation of price lists and the increasing use of motor transport, both for the delivery of goods at a distance and for carrying purchasers further afield, make it less easy for shopkeepers in any particular district to shift their rates on to their customers. But the poorer customers are at a disadvantage as compared with the richer, in so far as they are less able to make distant purchases.

§ 4. As regards the effects of a tax on a commodity upon its price certain further points are worth notice.

It has already been mentioned that, where a tax is collected from the seller in a lump sum in respect of a large quantity of the commodity, he will be out of pocket by the amount of interest, which he would otherwise have obtained, on the sum paid to the tax collector during the period between the payment of the tax and the sale of the goods. He will, therefore, attempt to shift on to the buyers of the commodity, not only the sum paid in taxation, but also the sum lost in interest. How far he will be able to do this, i.e. how far he will be able to raise the price of the commodity, depends, as before, upon the elasticity of the demand for, and of the supply of, the commodity. But, if the former elasticity is small and the latter large, it is possible that the price of the commodity will rise by more than the amount of the tax.

Similarly with the 'piling-up process', by which retail margins are increased, because wholesale prices and those of other intermediaries have been raised by the imposition of the tax.

Another case in which a tax on a commodity may raise its price by more than the amount of the tax is that of a commodity produced under conditions of 'increasing returns', that is to say under such conditions that the cost of production per unit diminishes, as the amount produced increases. In this case not only does an increased price mean a decreased demand, but a decreased supply means increased cost of production and hence an increased price, apart from the increase directly due to the tax.

It is doubtful whether the three cases discussed in this section properly belong to the theory of incidence, as distinguished from the more general theory of the effects, of taxation. For when the price of a commodity rises, owing to any of the causes just mentioned, more than it would have risen apart from these causes, the extra rise in price should, perhaps, be described as an indirect, rather than a direct, money burden on the buyer. In conformity with the definition of incidence given in Chapter VII, § 1, the test would appear to be, whether such an extra rise in the price of the taxed commodity leads to an increased revenue, *per unit of commodity*, to the public authority imposing the tax.[1] That is to say, the test is whether the tax is *ad valorem* or specific. In the former case the extra rise in price is partly a question of incidence and partly of other effects; in the latter case it is entirely a question of other effects. The need for introducing such a distinction here shows the difficulty of effectively separating incidence from other effects.

§ 5. The argument of the preceding chapter regarding the incidence of taxes on a monopolist must be applied with discretion to practical problems. In reality perfect competition is rare, and perfect monopoly still rarer. Some element of monopoly enters into the determination of nearly all prices, and fear of competition, actual or potential, affects nearly all apparent monopolists. Price may be influenced by the exercise of monopoly power, as soon as a single seller, or group of sellers acting in combination, controls a considerable proportion of the commodity to be sold. But where monopoly power exists, though we may assume that it is seldom neglected, yet it is not always fully exercised.

It follows that a tax on a monopolist, such that its incidence, according to the argument of the preceding chapter, would be entirely on him, may sometimes be shifted on to his customers by means of a more rigorous exercise than before of monopoly power. A monopolist, in fact, like a landowner, may react to

---

[1] This is not, of course, the same thing as an increased tax revenue in respect of the commodity. For the total tax revenue may be diminished by a falling off of demand owing to the extra rise in price, though the tax revenue per unit of commodity may increase.

taxation by 'taking in the slack'. Further, a group of sellers (or buyers), who have previously competed against one another, may react to taxation by acting in combination and thus enabling themselves to exercise monopoly power.

§ 6. Many schemes of social insurance are partly or wholly financed by weekly contributions from employers and workers. The incidence of these contributions may be traced as follows. The employers' contributions, being proportionate to the number of workers employed, are a tax on employment. The workers' contributions are a tax on wages. The incidence of both sets of contributions depends on the relative elasticity of the demand for, and supply of, labour. In general, the demand for labour is much more elastic than the supply. In general, therefore, much the greater part of the incidence is on the workers, and much the smaller part on the employers. The workers, therefore, pay by far the greater part both of the employers' contributions and of their own, and the employers pay by far the smaller part. The proportions will vary according to the circumstances of particular industries and localities and in exceptional cases, where the demand for labour is less elastic than the supply, the relative situation of employers and workers will be reversed. An example of such an exceptional case is, perhaps, that of domestic servants.[1]

Such, broadly, is the incidence when employment is not full. But, with full employment and strong Trade Unions, both sets of contributions are probably passed on to consumers through price increases.[2]

§ 7. Before leaving the subject of incidence, we may notice a few mistaken ideas, which are sometimes put forward.

It is sometimes said that 'an old tax is no tax', by which it is intended to imply that a tax which has been in existence a long time imposes no present burden on anyone.[3] Thus Mill said of

[1] Professor Pigou (*Theory of Unemployment*, p. 41) argues that the employers' contributions come out of wages, since the marginal net product of labour equals wages plus employer's contribution. Therefore, an increase in the contribution means an equivalent decrease in wages.

[2] See, Kaldor, 'The Beveridge Report : the Financial Burden' (*Economic Journal*, April, 1943, pp. 25–6).

[3] It is true, but comparatively unimportant, that for a while people feel

the 'old land tax' that 'there is not the smallest pretence for looking on this tax as a payment exacted from the existing race of landlords'. But this is quite fallacious. The incidence of any tax, however old, is its direct money burden, and falls on those who would derive a direct money benefit, if it were now repealed. If the 'old land tax' had been repealed in Mill's time, those members of 'the existing race of landlords' who then paid it would have secured a direct money benefit in the form of an increase in income and in the selling value of their land. Its incidence, therefore, would previously have been upon them.[1]

Another form of the same fallacy is the so-called 'doctrine of capitalisation' of taxes. It is argued that taxes on land and other more or less permanent sources of income, such as government securities, depress the selling value of the object taxed when they are first imposed, but that no burden is transmitted to subsequent purchasers of this object, since they buy knowing that the tax is payable, and reduce accordingly the price which they are willing to pay. But they are willing to pay less, precisely because they realise that they will have to pay the tax. And clearly, if the tax were to be repealed, the holders for the time being of the taxed object would gain through an increase of its selling value, or of their income, or both. And, therefore, the incidence of the tax is on them.

Finally, it is sometimes argued that the incidence of a tax on a commodity can be determined by a comparison of the price of the commodity at two different dates, before and after the imposition of the tax, in the same country, or at the same date in two different countries, in one of which there is a tax and in the other no tax, or a tax at a different rate. Thus some economic historians have tried to prove that the repeal of the Corn Laws in Britain had no effect upon the price of bread, except perhaps slightly to raise it. The attempted proof consists of the statement, which is true, that the price of bread rose slightly in the years immediately following the repeal. But all prices were

the incidence of a new tax more keenly than that of an equally heavy old tax, to which they have become accustomed. Compare Ch. VI, § 7.

[1] In fact, it was repealed in 1949, but only for the smallest taxpayers, the rest being required to extinguish their liability by a single lump sum payment.

rising at this time, chiefly owing to increasing gold production in California and Australia, and the price of bread rose less than other prices in this country and less than the price of bread in other countries during the same period.

In order to determine the incidence of a tax from price statistics, what should be compared with the price of the commodity at one time or place with the tax on, is not the price at a *different* time or place with the tax off, but the price at *the same* time or place with the tax off. And obviously there will be no statistical record of the latter price. For it is not any price which ever actually existed, but a price which would have existed, if certain conditions had been different. Nearly all statistical arguments on incidence are worthless, because a tax is only one of many factors which determine the price of a taxed commodity, and the effect on its price of changes in the tax may be, and often are, small compared with the effect of changes in the other factors.

## NOTE TO CHAPTERS VII AND VIII

§ 1. Some parts of the theory of incidence may be conveniently expressed by geometrical or algebraical methods. What follows is not intended to be an exhaustive discussion, but only to illustrate the use of mathematical methods in this field.

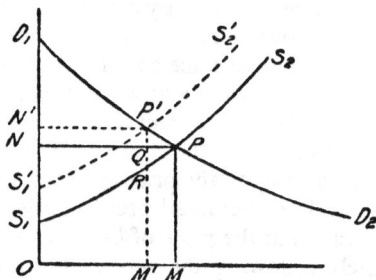

Let $D_1D_2$ be the demand curve, $S_1S_2$ the supply curve for a particular commodity (or service), PM the price per unit, and PN the amount sold per unit of time.

Now impose a tax on the commodity and collect it from the sellers. Let $S_1'S_2'$ be the new supply curve, P'M' the new price, P'N' the new amount sold, and P'R the tax per unit.

Thus the price rises by P'Q and the sales fall by PQ.

The incidence of the tax, P'R, is divided between buyers and sellers. The buyers bear P'Q, the sellers QR.

Now the elasticity of demand, $e_d = \dfrac{MM'}{OM} \Big/ \dfrac{P'Q}{PM}$

and the elasticity of supply, $e_s = \dfrac{MM'}{OM} \Big/ \dfrac{QR}{PM}$

$\therefore \dfrac{P'Q}{QR} = \dfrac{e_s}{e_d}$

That is to say, the incidence is divided between buyers and sellers in the ratio of the elasticity of supply to the elasticity of demand.

If the same tax were collected from buyers, instead of sellers, the only difference would be that, instead of a rise in the supply curve, there would be a fall in the demand curve.

If $t$ is the tax per unit, it is obvious that, since

$$t = P'R = P'Q + QR$$

$$P'Q = \frac{te_s}{e_d + e_s} \text{ and } QR = \frac{te_d}{e_d + e_s}$$

The following limiting cases obviously suggest themselves: (a) with perfectly elastic demand, $D_1D_2$ becomes a horizontal straight line, and P' coincides with Q, so that P'Q vanishes and the price is unchanged by the tax, though sales diminish; (b) with perfectly inelastic demand, $D_1D_2$ becomes a vertical straight line, P coincides with both Q and R, and $P'Q = t$, so that the price rises by the full amount of the tax, and sales are unchanged; (c) with perfectly elastic supply, $S_1S_2$ and $S_1'S_2'$ become horizontal straight lines, Q coincides with R and $P'Q = t$, so that the price rises by the full amount of the tax and sales diminish; (d) with perfectly inelastic supply, $S_1S_2$

becomes a vertical straight line and $S_1'S_2'$ coincides with it, while P, P , Q and R all coincide with one another, so that P'Q vanishes, the price is unchanged by the tax and sales are likewise unchanged.

§ 2. It is not necessary to assume, so far as the preceding geometrical proof is concerned, that the tax is small relatively to the price or to the amount sold. The proof holds good equally for small taxes and for large. In the former case the elasticities of demand and supply are 'point elasticities', in the latter they are 'arc elasticities'. But no ambiguity results from this in the present context.[1]

Nor is it necessary to assume that the rate of tax per unit is independent of the price, or of the sales, though this assumption represents the simplest case, that of a 'specific tax'. The geometrical proof remains unaffected, if we assume that the tax per unit is proportionate to the price per unit (the case of an 'ad valorem tax'), or if we assume, more generally, that the tax per unit is *any* function of the price, or of the sales. For P R will still represent the tax per unit, when equilibrium is reached with price P'M' and sales P'N'. But the position and shape of the new supply curve will, of course, vary in relation to the old according to the nature of the tax.

§ 3. An independent algebraical proof is as follows.

Before the tax is imposed, let $y$ be the price and $x$ the sales, and let $y = D(x)$ represent the demand curve and $y = S(x)$ the supply curve. Then equilibrium is given by $y = D(x) = S(x)$.

If a (specific) tax of $t$ per unit is imposed on the sellers, we have a new supply curve $y = t + S(x)$, but the old demand curve $y = D(x)$.

Therefore the new equilibrium is given by

$$y + \delta y = D(x - \delta x) = t + S(x - \delta x)$$

where $\delta y$, the increase in price, and $\delta x$, the decrease in sales, are both measured positively.

Assuming that $\delta x$ is small, so that its squares and higher

[1] For a discussion of the distinction between these two conceptions of elasticity, and of the ambiguities which are apt to arise from failure to make this distinction clear, see my *Inequality of Incomes*, pp. 186–90 and pp. 192–7.

powers may be neglected, we have

$$y + \delta y = D(x) - \delta x D'(x) = t + S(x) - \delta x S'(x)$$
$$\therefore \ \delta y = - \delta x D'(x) = t - \delta x S'(x)$$
$$\therefore \ \delta x = \frac{t}{S'(x) - D'(x)} \text{ and } \delta y = - \frac{t D'(x)}{S'(x) - D'(x)}$$

Now $\quad e_d = - \dfrac{y}{x D'(x)}$ and $e_s = \dfrac{y}{x S'(x)}$

$$\therefore \ - D'(x) = \frac{y}{x} \frac{1}{e_d} \text{ and } S'(x) = \frac{y}{x} \frac{1}{e_s}$$

$$\therefore \ \delta y = \frac{t \dfrac{1}{e_d}}{\dfrac{1}{e_d} + \dfrac{1}{e_s}} = \frac{t e_s}{e_d + e_s}$$

This algebraical treatment can be generalised, though the geometrical treatment cannot, to cover the case of specific taxes at different rates on a number of different sources of supply. If taxes $t_1, t_2 \ldots t_n$ are imposed on $n$ sources of supply, with supplies $x_1, x_2 \ldots x_n$ and elasticities of supply, $e_1, e_2 \ldots e_n$, and if $e_d$ is the elasticity of demand, it is easily shown that the increase in price

$$\delta y = \frac{t_1 e_1 x_1 + t_2 e_2 x_2 + \ldots + t_n e_n x_r}{e_d(x_1 + x_2 + \ldots + x_n) + (e_1 x_1 + e_2 x_2 + \ldots + e_n x_n)}$$

A similar formula would represent the effect on price of the differential taxation of a number of sources of demand.

But the algebraical treatment cannot be so easily generalised, as the geometrical, to cover the case of large taxes and arc elasticities, as distinguished from small taxes and point elasticities.

§ 4. The possibility that the price may rise by more than the amount of the tax, owing to loss of interest by the seller, may be thus exhibited.

If a tax $t$ per unit be imposed on the seller, and if, in addition, he suffers a loss of interest $i$ per unit during the interval between the collection of the tax and the sale of the commodity, he will try to pass on $i$, in addition to $t$.

Let $t + i = t'$

Then the price will rise by $\dfrac{t'e_s}{e_d + e_s}$

This quantity will be greater than $t$, if

$$\frac{(t + i)e_s}{e_d + e_s} > t$$

that is to say, if

$$\frac{i}{} > \frac{e_d}{e_s}$$

This result is, therefore, the more likely, (a) the less elastic the demand, (b) the more elastic the supply, and (c) the larger the loss of interest relatively to the tax, or, in other words, the higher the rate of interest and the longer the interval.

§ 5. In the case of increasing returns, we have the supply curve sloping downwards and $e_s$, the elasticity of supply, negative.

The geometrical construction of § 1 must, therefore, be modified accordingly. It is then evident that the increase in price, P'Q, is greater than the tax, P'R.

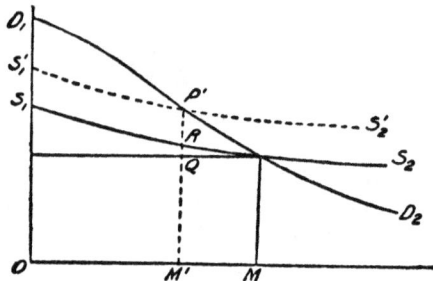

But we still have

$$e_d = \frac{MM'}{OM} \bigg/ \frac{P'Q}{PM} \text{ and } e_s = -\frac{MM'}{OM} \bigg/ \frac{QR}{PM}$$

$$\therefore \frac{P'Q}{QR} = -\frac{e_s}{e_d}$$

Thus the rise in price will be greater, other things being equal, (a) the greater the elasticity of demand, and (b) the smaller the negative elasticity of supply, or, in other words, the more rapid the rate of increase of returns.

§ 6. The incidence of various types of tax on a monopolised commodity may be treated either geometrically or algebraically.

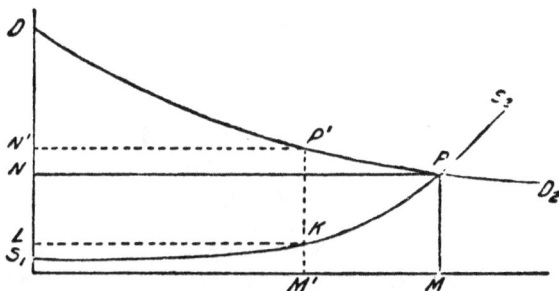

As before let $D_1D_2$ be the demand curve, and $S_1S_2$ the supply curve[1] for the commodity, with diminishing returns. Then PM may be called the competitive price and PN the competitive sales. But, since the commodity is monopolised, the price will be P'M', the sales P'N', and the restriction of sales (or output) by reason of monopoly MM'. The position of P' will be determined by the condition that the monopoly profits, represented by the rectangle P'KLN', shall be a maximum.

The extent to which it will pay the monopolist to raise price and restrict sales depends on the shapes of the relevant portions of $D_1D_2$ and $S_1S_2$, that is to say on the elasticities of demand and supply. The profits of restriction will evidently be greater, the smaller the elasticity both of demand and of supply. Apart from the possibility of endangering his monopoly, there is no limit to profitable restriction of output, so long as the elasticity of demand at each point of the demand curve, going upwards, is less than unity. For then, with each additional restriction, he

[1] Strictly speaking, under monopoly this is not a supply curve but a marginal cost curve. Supply, under monopoly, is a function not only of price, but of elasticity of demand.

will produce a smaller output at less cost and sell it for more money. But, in reality, the demand for any commodity, even if it shows a low degree of elasticity over a considerable range of price variation, becomes much more elastic at comparatively high prices. A point must sooner or later be reached, when the will of consumers to keep their demand for a particular commodity inelastic is broken by their inability to do so, without making still greater sacrifices in other directions.

§ 7. The incidence of various types of tax on a monopolised commodity depends on their effect upon the position of P'. If they have no tendency to alter this position, their incidence is wholly on the monopolist seller. Geometrical constructions may be elaborated to illustrate alternative types of tax and consequential new positions of the supply curve. It is, however, clear, without such elaboration, that a tax which is independent of the amount of sales—either a lump sum tax, or a tax proportionate to the maximum monopoly profits—has no tendency to alter the position of P'.

It is clear, on the other hand, that a tax which is a function of the sales, or of the price, has, in general, such a tendency. Geometry can add little here to the verbal argument of Chapter VII, § 6.

Algebraically, if $y = D(x)$ is the demand curve and $y = S(x)$ the supply curve, monopoly profits on sales $x$ are

$$x\{D(x) - S(x)\}$$

This is a maximum when

$$D(x) - S(x) + x\{D'(x) - S(x)\} = 0$$

This equation determines the most profitable level of sales, $x$, and also the most profitable price, $y$, since $y = D(x)$.

If a tax of $f(x)$ per unit is imposed on the monopolist, so that the total tax payable on sales $x$ is $xf(x)$, the most profitable level of sales will be given by the equation

$$D(x) - S(x) - f(x) + x\{D'(x) - S'(x) - f'(x)\} = 0$$

There is scope here also for mathematical manipulation, to examine how various forms of the function $f(x)$ will affect the optimum value of $x$ for the monopolist. But the verbal argument of Chapter VII, § 6, is simpler and more direct.

§ 8. I now put mathematics aside and pass from the incidence of taxes on *particular* commodities and services to that of a tax on income in *general*. This characteristic of generality in any tax has a primary importance in the theory of its incidence. For the incidence of such a tax cannot be shifted by the diversion of resources from taxed to untaxed fields. Precisely because the tax is general, no untaxed fields exist.

Most serious economists, though not all business men, agree that the usual incidence of income tax is on the income receiver, who is thus quite accurately described as the 'income tax payer'. This doctrine, according to an often quoted pronouncement, 'is true over practically the whole field and for practically the whole of the time, any exceptions being local or temporary and insufficient to invalidate it'.[1] The belief, held by many business men, that income tax imposed on them can be passed on, by way of higher prices, to the purchasers of their goods, is, apart from occasional exceptional cases, simply wrong. But, though economists agree that, in general, and certainly in the short run, income tax cannot be shifted, there has been some dispute as to what arguments establish this conclusion. The following considerations, however, appear decisive.

First, in reply to the business men who assert the contrary, income tax is not, like a tax on raw material or on finished articles, or like local rates, a true 'overhead charge' which 'enters into cost of production'. It is, as applied to business incomes, a tax on net profits, that is to say on the realised surplus of a period's trading. If there is no surplus, there is no income tax, whatever other taxes may still be payable. Income tax is not a cost of production, but a cost of success in business. As regards other kinds of income, and especially fixed incomes from property, not even business men commonly allege that the recipients of those can, as a rule, pass on their income tax.

Second, some business men may think that they actually add all their taxes, including income tax, to the selling price of their goods. But this is a delusion. They may, indeed, go through the

[1] *Report of Colwyn Committee on National Debt and Taxation, p. 119.*

form of doing such an arithmetical sum.[1] But, in fact, they have
to quote prices at which it is possible to sell. They may begin
by asking what they like; they must end by taking what they
can get.

The price which they can get is not affected by the amount of
income tax, if any, which they pay. Under perfect competition,
a seller has no power at all to alter the market price; under
perfect monopoly, he has unlimited power; under imperfect or
partial monopoly, he has some power. But in all three cases the
price which, allowing for the opportunities open to him, will
bring him in the largest profits, is independent of whether he
pays income tax or not, or of how much he pays.

Third, and this is the underlying reason for the two previous
arguments, and could, therefore, stand alone as a sufficient
logical support of the doctrine that income tax cannot be
shifted, the elasticity of supply of resources subjected to a
general income tax tends, in the short run at any rate, to be so
small as to be negligible. For no diversion of resources from
one employment to another[2] will, as a result of the tax, be
worth while, which would not have been worth while before.
And it is the possibility of such diversions, which makes the
supply of *particular kinds of resources* elastic in other cases.
Moreover, this inelasticity of supply, which is almost a certainty over a short period, may well persist over long periods,
especially if the demand for income by those who supply
resources is also, in terms of effort and sacrifice, highly inelastic.
And there are grounds for believing that this is often the case.[3]

Only on the assumption that the supply of resources, or of
some kinds of resources, is relatively elastic in the long run,
can any plausible case be made for the view that, in the long
run, the incidence of income tax can sometimes in part be
shifted. In some cases this assumption may be justified. And to
assert that the incidence of income tax cannot, in the short run,

---

[1] Though, when they price their goods, they do not know what their
subsequent liability in income tax (including, in Britain, surtax) will turn
out to be.

[2] Except, for some people, from work to leisure.

[3] See Ch. X, § 4.

be shifted by the income receivers is not, of course, to deny that the effects of income tax may include some check to work, savings and investment. This disincentive possibility will be studied in Chapter X.

Again, as was noted in Chapter VIII, § 5, a monopolist, irritated by taxation, may relax restraint and use his power more crudely. Thus, in effect, he may shift his income tax on to his customers.

§ 9. The argument that a general income tax cannot be shifted, owing to the inelastic supply of the resources on which it falls, is not invalidated by any details of graduation, differentiation between earned and unearned incomes, or abatements and allowances, which the tax may contain. For no such details diminish appreciably its attribute of generality. Substantially it remains neutral as between alternative uses of resources.

It might, at first sight, be argued that differentiation between earned and unearned incomes is a breach of this neutrality. But it is not a relevant breach, so far as incidence is concerned. For the diversion of income from unearned to earned sources, in order to escape the higher rates of tax, is not a practicable operation.

This line of argument, indeed, leads further. Where income receivers fall into 'non-competing groups', so that no appreciable diversion can occur between such groups, a special tax on the income of such a group has the same incidence as a general income tax, and cannot, as a rule, be shifted. A tax on wages, for example, such as the workers' contributions to social insurance, tends, for the most part, to be paid by wage-earners, because the supply of labour in general is highly inelastic, and no wage-earner can escape the tax by changing his trade. But a tax on wages in a particular trade can, in some measure, be shifted, since the supply of labour to particular trades is comparatively elastic, and since the demand for labour in some particular trades is comparatively inelastic. It may be added that the argument of some of the classical economists, that a tax on wages could be shifted, assumed that wages were at, or near, subsistence level and that, in consequence, the supply of labour was highly elastic. But whether this assumption was right or wrong a hundred years ago, it is not tenable today, except in very backward and poverty-stricken communities. On the other hand, as was noted in Chapter VIII, § 6, given full employment and strong Trade Unions, a tax on wages may be shifted forward on to prices.

# CHAPTER IX

## DISTRIBUTION OF THE BURDEN OF TAXATION FROM THE POINT OF VIEW OF EQUITY

§ 1. Much has been written on 'the distribution of the burden of taxation', but the range of questions usually covered by this title is narrow. Assuming that the incidence of all taxes is known, and that the necessary statistics of income, consumption, etc., are available, we can calculate how the direct money burden of any tax system is, in fact, distributed among different individuals and classes. And, even without this knowledge, we can discuss how this direct money burden *ought* to be distributed. In such discussions it is usual to take account of the direct real burdens which result from tax payments. But not of the indirect money burdens, nor of the indirect real burdens.

§ 2. Assuming that a given revenue is to be raised by taxation, the total direct real burden will be greater under some tax systems than others.[1] It is an obvious idea that the tax system should be so arranged, as to make the total direct real burden as small as possible. This has been called 'the principle of minimum sacrifice'. It has been suggested that this principle would be realised by taxing only the largest incomes, cutting down all above a certain level to that level, and exempting all below that level; by 'cutting off the heads of all the tallest poppies', as Edgeworth put it. Thus all incomes above, say, £1,500 a year would be reduced by taxation to that figure, and no one, whose income was less than this, would be taxed at all. We are led to this rough and ready plan by the conception of the diminishing marginal utility of income.[2] The chief objection

[1] Also, of course, in so far as outsiders can be made to bear any of the direct money burden of any of the taxes, the total direct real burden on members of the taxing community is reduced.

[2] Another name for the 'principle of minimum sacrifice' is 'the principle of equi-marginal sacrifice'.

to it is that, especially if it were introduced suddenly, it would probably check nearly all economic activity, beyond what was required to secure the maximum income not subject to taxation.[1] This is an objection based on grounds of economy, that is to say on the consideration of economic effects. But some people would also object to it on grounds of equity or 'fairness', and it will be found that, in most discussions of 'the proper distribution of the burden of taxation', arguments based on equity are more prominent than those based on economy.

But different people have very different ideas of what is equitable, and many of these ideas prove to be vague and unhelpful, when we try to apply them to practical problems. 'It is equitable that people in the same economic position should be treated in the same way for purposes of taxation.' No doubt; but what differences in treatment are equitable for people in different economic positions? And what is meant by the 'same economic position'? Clearly a bachelor with an income of £1,000 a year is not in the same economic position as a married man with three children and the same income. But by how much must the income of the latter be increased, in order to put him in the same position as the former?

§ 3. It is an error to object to particular taxes, as distinct from the tax system as a whole, as inequitable. For the inequity of one tax, as between different taxpayers, may be cancelled by that of another. There may be more equity in the whole tax system than in its parts. But we may sometimes approve particular taxes, as distinct from the rest of the tax system, as being especially equitable. Thus a good case may be made out, on grounds of equity, for taxes on 'windfall wealth'. This form of wealth, of which war profits and 'unearned increment' in the value of land are examples, has two characteristics. The first is 'undeservedness', in the sense that such wealth accrues to its possessor without his rendering any, or at least any equivalent, service in return, and the second is unexpectedness. The first

[1] As when the Soviet Government in 1918–20 requisitioned from the peasants all their foodstuffs in excess of the immediate requirements of themselves and their families (Dobb, *Russian Economic Development*, p. 119).

characteristic is thought by many to justify the taxation of windfall wealth from the point of view of equity, while the second, as will be argued later, justifies its taxation on economic grounds.[1] But it is not obviously equitable to tax some forms of windfall wealth, unless all forms are taxed, nor is it obvious at what rates it is equitable to tax such wealth.

When both prices and profits are falling, the holder of fixed interest securities gets a windfall; so does the holder of equities when both are rising. Thus in the nineteen thirties some thought a special tax on income from fixed-interest securities would be equitable, and in the nineteen forties special taxes on profits.

§ 4. Returning to the tax system as a whole, three alternative principles for the equitable distribution of its direct money burden have been suggested: first, the cost to the public authority of the services rendered to individual taxpayers; second, the benefit to individual taxpayers of such services; and third, individual 'ability to pay' taxation.

The 'cost of service principle' can be applied to the supply of postal services, electric current, etc., by public authorities, and the prices of such services can be fixed in accordance with this principle. But it cannot be applied to services rendered out of the proceeds of taxes, as distinguished from prices. For a tax, by definition, is a payment, in return for which no direct and specific *quid pro quo* is rendered to the payer. The services, if any, rendered to individual members of the community by expenditure on armed forces, police or public parks cannot, in fact, be determined and, therefore, the cost of rendering these services to different individuals cannot be determined. Thus the 'cost of service principle', however equitable it may seem in the abstract, is not capable of wide practical application. But consider this case, where it *could* be applied—the service of paying interest on public debt. The cost of this service is the interest,

[1] See Ch. X, § 5. But, except in a few glaring cases, the attempt to apply the test of deservedness or undeservedness to economic payments leads to great perplexities and illustrates afresh the difficulties and vagueness of the conception of equity. 'If we all got our deserts,' who should escape whipping?' as Shakespeare asks.

plus something for administration. Would it be equitable to make each holder of public securities repay, by a special contribution, his share of this cost?

The 'benefit of service principle' fails in the same way. Since the services rendered to individuals by many forms of public expenditure cannot be determined, the benefits to individuals from such services cannot be determined. But the principle can easily be applied in certain cases. For example, the benefit derived by an old age pensioner from his pension is definite enough, and the benefit of service principle would require him to repay it to the public treasury.[1] If this is equitable, it would be a simpler way of giving effect to equity to abolish old age pensions. Those who think that this would not be equitable cannot think that the benefit of service principle without qualifications is equitable. And, if qualifications are to be introduced, it is not clear, so far as equity is concerned, on what principle they are to be based, nor how far-reaching they are to be.[2]

It has, indeed, been argued[3] that from public expenditure for common benefit, as distinct from individual benefit, all citizens benefit in proportion to their incomes, and hence that such expenditure should be paid for by taxation proportional to individual incomes. But the first step in this argument is false. In general, the benefit to individuals is simply unascertainable.

§ 5. The principle that taxation should be distributed between individuals in accordance with their 'ability to pay' is, on the face of it, somewhat more practicable. But how is 'ability to pay' to be measured? It is usual, in discussions of this question, to consider the 'sacrifice' to the taxpayer of paying his taxes, and then to deduce some scheme of distribution of the burden

---

[1] Under the cost of service principle, he would be required to repay, as with interest on public debt, not only the amount of his pension, but also a small charge to cover the cost of administration of the scheme.

[2] See Ch. XIV, §§ 5-7, for a discussion of how far, on grounds of economy, the cost of service or benefit of service principles should govern the prices of services supplied by public authorities.

[3] By Professor De Viti De Marco in his *Primi Principii dell' Economia Finanziaria*.

of taxation from some principle concerning sacrifice. The three most common of such principles are those of 'equal sacrifice', 'proportional sacrifice' and 'minimum sacrifice'. To these we may add a fourth, which is sometimes expressed by the injunction, 'leave them as you find them', or, more precisely, 'do not alter the inequality of incomes by taxation'. At first sight it is not clear, on grounds of equity, which of these four is to be preferred.

According to the principle of equal sacrifice, the direct money burden of taxation should be so distributed that the direct real burden on all taxpayers is equal; according to the principle of proportional sacrifice, so that the direct real burden on every taxpayer is proportionate to the economic welfare which he derives from his income; according to the principle of minimum sacrifice, already referred to, so that the total direct real burden on the taxpayers as a whole is as small as possible; according to the principle of 'leave them as you find them', so that the inequality of incomes should be neither increased nor diminished by taxation.

In order to apply any of these four principles, we must assume some relation between money income and the economic welfare derived from it. According to the relation assumed, there will result a tax system which may be either proportional, progressive or regressive. Under proportional taxation all taxpayers contribute the same proportion of their incomes; under progressive taxation, the larger a taxpayer's income, the larger proportion which he pays; under regressive taxation, the larger a taxpayer's income, the smaller the proportion which he pays. These terms may be applied, not only to tax systems as a whole, but also to particular taxes. Thus a tax system which is proportional as a whole may contain some taxes which are progressive and others which are regressive, and a tax system which is progressive as a whole may contain some taxes which are regressive, and conversely. Again, a particular tax system may be proportional over a certain range of incomes, progressive over another range and regressive over yet another range, while there are, of course, an infinite number of possible degrees of progression and regression.

Assuming that the relation between income and economic welfare is the same for all taxpayers[1] and that the marginal utility of income diminishes fairly rapidly as income increases, the principle of equal sacrifice leads to progressive taxation, the principle of proportional sacrifice to still steeper progressive taxation, and the principle of minimum sacrifice, as already pointed out, to a relatively high level of exemption and very steeply progressive taxation of those not exempt. The principle of minimum sacrifice, indeed, gives this result, so long as it is assumed that marginal utility diminishes at all with increasing income. Both equal sacrifice and proportional sacrifice involve making all members of the community however poor (provided that they have *some* economic welfare to sacrifice) contribute something. But minimum sacrifice does not involve this. Further, the more rapidly the marginal utility of income is assumed to diminish with increasing income, the more steeply progressive must the tax system become, in order to give effect to either equal or proportional sacrifice.

Proportional taxation can only be justified by the principle of equal sacrifice, on the assumption that the marginal utility of income diminishes very slowly. It can only be justified by the principle of proportional sacrifice, on the assumption that the marginal utility of income does not diminish at all, but remains constant, as income increases. On this last assumption, the principle of minimum sacrifice would lead to no one distribution of taxation more than any other, since the total sacrifice

[1] Some economists have emphasised that this is only an assumption—none who have used it have claimed that it was more—and have pronounced it both 'unscientific' and untenable. But it is an assumption which, in civilised countries at any rate, equity demands and politicians and administrators, at least, must make. Nor is it so remote from reality as some of its critics suggest. Most of us, at given levels of income, are more like each other in our normal needs and moods, and in our reactions to variations in our income, than some theorists recognise.

It is also assumed, throughout this book, that a taxpayer's economic welfare depends only on his own income, and not on those of other taxpayers also. For an interesting study of some of the consequences of the contrary assumption see H. G. Johnson, *Macro-Economics of Income Redistribution*, in *Income Redistribution and Social Policy*, edited by A. T. Peacock (Cape, 1954).

would in all cases be proportionate to the total revenue raised by taxation.

Regressive taxation can only be justified by the principle of equal sacrifice, on the assumption that the marginal utility of income diminishes even more slowly than was required in order to justify proportional taxation by the same principle, or on the assumption that marginal utility does not diminish at all, but remains constant or actually increases. Again, regressive taxation can only be justified by the principle of proportional sacrifice, on the assumption that marginal utility actually increases, and, on this absurd assumption, the principle of minimum sacrifice would lead to exempting from taxation all incomes above a certain level, and taxing all incomes below this level a hundred per cent.

The fourth principle referred to above, that the inequality of incomes should be neither increased nor diminished by taxation, can only be applied when it has been decided how the inequality of incomes should be measured. It is often supposed by its adherents to lead to proportional taxation. But there are strong grounds for holding that, on reasonable assumptions as to the relation of income to economic welfare, this principle also leads to progressive taxation.[1]

It, therefore, appears that, on reasonable assumptions, each of our four alternative interpretations of 'ability to pay' leads to some degree of progression in the tax system. This practical conclusion is now generally accepted by modern opinion, which responds readily to the suggestion that considerably the heaviest burdens should be placed upon the broadest backs. A few high authorities of the older generation still cling with a curious fondness to the idea of proportional taxation. They have the support, for what it is worth in this connection, of Adam Smith, who held that 'the subjects of every State ought to contribute towards the support of the government, as nearly as possible, according to their respective abilities, that is to say, in proportion to the revenue, which they respectively enjoy

[1] See my article on *The Measurement of the Inequality of Incomes* (*Economic Journal*, September, 1920), reprinted as an Appendix to my *Inequality of Incomes*, and also the note to this chapter.

under the protection of the State'. But Adam Smith, though a great economist in his day, wrote more than a hundred and fifty years ago, and before the discovery of the law—or, if you prefer, before the introduction of the concept—of diminishing marginal utility.[1]

§ 6. It is important to notice that the four principles considered above, in common with all principles of equity in taxation, including the austere principle that 'everyone ought to pay something', are only matters of opinion. Failing a clearer and more generally accepted definition of equity than has hitherto been forthcoming, it cannot be proved that they are, in fact, equitable, but only that certain people at certain times think them so. And it is a fact of common observation that opinion on such questions is very liable to change. It has been truly said that current ideas of equity generally amount to little more than 'economy tempered by conservatism'. Equity often seems to say 'No', but hardly ever 'Yes', an elusive mistress, whom perhaps it is only worth the while of philosophers to pursue ardently but of politicians to watch warily.

Yet, even on grounds of equity, it may be argued very cogently that 'there is at least as good a case for taxation which makes net satisfactions equal as for taxation which makes sacrifices equal. Indeed, there is a better case. For people's economic well-being depends on the whole system of law, including the laws of property, contract and bequest, and not merely on the law about taxes. To hold that the law about taxes ought to affect different people's satisfactions equally, while allowing that the rest of the legal system may properly affect them very unequally, seems not a little arbitrary.'[2] This line of argument discredits proportional sacrifice, along with

[1] Proportional taxation has modern adherents also in Italy. In addition to Professor De Viti De Marco, already cited, Professor Einaudi, now President of the Italian Republic, argues in his *Ottima Imposta* that, since, without the aid of the State, there could be no production, every element of income is born owing a debt, and an equal debt, to the State, and that, therefore, every element of income should pay an equal share of taxation. This reasoning seems fanciful and unconvincing.

[2] Pigou, *Public Finance*, p. 60.

equal sacrifice. It is neutral towards constant inequality of incomes, and somewhat more benevolently neutral towards minimum sacrifice.

§ 7. We may indeed go further and throw doubt on all the ideas hitherto considered in this chapter. There is no special sanctity, nor any reason to expect to find equity in any pre-tax distribution of income. Nor are we likely to find equity simply by a transition, through whatever formula, to some post-tax distribution. This whole approach to justice looks too narrow. Within wide limits we can change the shape of distribution as we please. In particular, we can change it by taxation and by public expenditure combined, though it is convenient to study these two operations separately. So let us, if we can, first decide what distribution is equitable, and then make public finance produce this distribution.

It has been argued in Chapter II of this book that any system of public finance should be conceived with a view to the maximum social advantage in the long run, and it follows that any tax system, as part of this larger system, should be conceived with the same object. But it is a necessary preliminary to the consideration of any tax system from this point of view to move forward from equity to economy and consider broadly the economic effects of taxation.

## NOTE TO CHAPTER IX

§ 1. The chief purpose of this Note is to illustrate the use of mathematical methods in determining the correct distribution, on given assumptions, of the burden of taxation. As in the preceding note to Chapters VII and VIII, this discussion is designed to be illustrative, not exhaustive. Of the making of mathematical formulæ for graduating taxation, as of the making of books, there is no end. There is no logical distinction between 'theoretical' scales of graduation based on mathematical formulæ and 'practical' scales based on 'common sense'. Every scale, which is explicitly based on a mathematical formula, can readily be translated into the language of 'common sense', which here means nothing more than a series of rates of tax apparently unconnected by any formula. On the other hand, a mathematical formula, even if a long and complicated one, can always be found roughly to 'fit', and thus express, any 'practical' scale which non-mathematicians may invent.

The following argument illustrates some of the problems suggested in Chapter IX, § 5.

§ 2. Given any functional relation between income, $x$, and economic welfare, $w$, we can find a formula to give effect either to the principle of equal sacrifice or to that of proportional sacrifice.

Assume, for example, that

$$w = \log x, \text{ so that } \frac{dw}{dx} = \frac{1}{x}$$

(This is Bernouilli's Law, which is based on the proposition that proportionate additions to income make equal additions to welfare. It gives a rather slow rate of diminution of marginal utility.)

Let the rate of tax on an income $x$ be $t$, so that $tx$ is the total tax on an income $x$.

Let $w'$ be the sacrifice of welfare due to payment of the tax. Then

$$\begin{aligned} w - w' &= \log(x - tx) \\ &= \log x + \log(1 - t) \\ \therefore w' &= -\log(1 - t) \end{aligned}$$

For equal sacrifice we must have $w'$ constant. Therefore $t$ must be constant. That is to say, we must have proportional taxation.

For proportional sacrifice we must have

$$\frac{w'}{w} \text{ constant} = k, \text{ say, where } 0 < k < 1$$

$$\text{Then } k = -\frac{\log(1 - t)}{\log x}$$

$$\therefore k \log x + \log(1 - t) = 0 = \log 1$$

$$\therefore x^k (1 - t) = 1.$$

$$\therefore t = 1 - \frac{1}{x^k}$$

As $x$ increases, $t$ increases, and we have a formula for progressive taxation. Given the total taxable income and its distribution, $k$ will depend upon the total tax revenue required.

§ 3. Now assume a more rapid rate of diminution of marginal utility than under Bernouilli's Law. Assume, for example, that

$$w = c - \frac{1}{x}$$

where $c$ is a constant, so that $\dfrac{dw}{dx} = \dfrac{1}{x^2}$

(This is a formula which I have suggested elsewhere, in the *Economic Journal*, September, 1920, and in the Appendix to my *Inequality of Incomes*, as best combining simplicity and plausibility.)

Then if, as before, $w'$ is the sacrifice of welfare due to a tax $tx$ on an income $x$, we have

$$w - w' = c - \frac{1}{x - tx}$$

$$\therefore w' = \frac{1}{x - tx} - \frac{1}{x}$$

$$\therefore t = 1 - \frac{1}{1 + w'x}$$

For equal sacrifice, $w'$ is constant and, therefore, as $x$ increases, $t$ increases, so that we have progressive taxation.

For proportionate sacrifice, $\dfrac{w'}{w}$ is constant $= k$, say. Then

$$k = \frac{\dfrac{1}{x - tx} - \dfrac{1}{x}}{c - \dfrac{1}{x}}$$

$$\therefore t = 1 - \frac{1}{1 - k + ckx}$$

$\therefore$ as $x$ increases, $t$ increases, which again gives progressive taxation.

§ 4. It is, indeed, clear, without the aid of algebra, that if, any functional relation between $x$ and $w$ being given, equal sacrifice leads to progression, proportional sacrifice must lead to still steeper progression. It is a limiting case of this proposition that, if equal sacrifice leads to proportionality, proportional sacrifice must lead to progression. For consider a community consisting of two taxpayers, A and B, of whom A has the larger income. If, by certain specified contributions, they make equal sacrifices, then they will make proportional sacrifices (the sum of their two contributions remaining the same), only if A pays more and B pays less than before. This means that A will part with a larger proportion of his income, and B with a smaller proportion, under proportional sacrifice than under equal sacrifice. And this is only another way of saying that the tax system is more steeply progressive in the one case than in the other.[1] And what is true of this simple community of two persons, is true also of communities which are more populous.

§ 5. The principle of constant inequality of incomes, which to some minds seems equitable—to others merely conservative—leads, I have suggested in Chapter IX, § 5, to progressive, and not to proportional, taxation. I have supported this suggestion by a reference to an argument which I have developed at some length elsewhere. I shall not spend time repeating that argument here, but shall only recapitulate, very summarily, seven of the steps in it, which have a special relevance to our present problem.

(1) The objection to great inequality of incomes is the resulting loss of potential economic welfare. (2) It is, therefore, convenient to *define* the 'inequality' of any given distribution, as the ratio of the total economic welfare attainable under an equal distribution to the total economic welfare attained under the given distribution, the total income to be distributed being assumed to be unchanged. (3) The *measure* of inequality, so defined, will depend upon the functional relation of income to economic welfare. To every such possible relation there will

[1] For some further remarks on the degree of 'progressiveness' of a tax system, see Note to Ch. XI.

correspond a different measure of inequality. (4) But, further, common to certain wide groups of possible relations, there will be certain general tests, which all measures of inequality within the corresponding group must pass. (5) If, for example, we assume that equal additions to welfare are secured by more than proportionate additions to income (and even if we assume that they are secured by proportionate additions), all permissible measures of inequality must satisfy the condition that proportionate additions to all incomes diminish inequality. And this range of assumptions covers all probable reality, with a wide margin of safety at both ends of the range. (6) But, if proportionate additions to all incomes diminish inequality, proportionate subtractions must increase it. That is to say, the inequality of incomes will be increased by proportional taxation. (7) Therefore, if the inequality of incomes is to be left unchanged by taxation, that taxation must be in some degree progressive. The degree of progressiveness required will vary with the relation of income to economic welfare.

At the end of this Note, and of the preceding chapter, it must be frankly admitted that many of the hypotheses used are, by their nature, too exact to be true. Units of 'satisfaction', or 'utility', or 'economic welfare', are not to be caught in a butterfly net. And, apart from this, there is a spurious and inhuman precision about the various functional relationships assumed. The plain man can favour progressive taxation simply on the ground that, as it seems to him, it reduces inequality. Yet there is, I think, some value, for practice, in tracing the implications of these more precise hypotheses. They show, when all allowances for imprecision have been made, the results on distribution, in broad outline at least, of alternative principles of taxation.

# CHAPTER X

## EFFECTS OF TAXATION ON PRODUCTION

§ 1. The best system of taxation from the economic point of view is that which has the best, or the least bad, economic effects. In this and the two following chapters these effects will be considered under three heads, (1) effects on production, (2) effects on distribution, (3) other effects.

The effects of taxation on production can be divided into effects on (1) production as a whole and (2) the composition, or pattern, of production. Effects on production as a whole operate through effects on work, saving and investment. Here again we may distinguish between effects on (1) ability, and (2) desire, to work, save and invest.

Investment, if well directed, makes work more productive. It may take the form either of investment in material, or in human, capital. The first form furnishes the worker with more efficient material equipment—better buildings, machines, transport, electric power, etc. The second form makes the worker himself more efficient—stronger in health, skill, specialised knowledge and general understanding. This second form of investment, in human capital, will be further considered in Part III of this book. In this chapter we shall be primarily concerned with investment in material capital.

Such investment—and the same is true of investment in human capital—is only possible if there is saving; that is to say if not all the purchasing power of the community is spent on current consumption, but some is set aside to pay for future improvements. But savings made and investment undertaken are not, as used to be assumed, automatically equal. Indeed it is one of the principal problems of public finance to make them so. How to do this is considered in Chapter XXVII. Here it is enough to note that, if savings much exceed investment, there will be heavy unemployment, widespread business losses, rapidly falling prices and deflation; if investment much exceeds savings, there may indeed be full employment, but also widespread business profits, rapidly rising prices and inflation. Neither of these, neither a much too low nor a much too high blood pressure, are healthy conditions. Our aim should be full employment without inflation. As Stanley Baldwin once said he was, we should each seek to be, a 'non-flationist'. With full employment, at any given moment consumption and investment are alternatives. If either increases, the other must decrease. But, with less than full employment, both may increase together, and an increase in consumption may stimulate an increase in investment and a closer approach to full employment.[1]

§ 2. Let us now turn to the effects of taxation on ability to work, save and invest. Any person's ability to work will be reduced by taxation which reduces his efficiency. There is, therefore, a strong presumption against imposing any taxation upon the poorer members of modern communities, when these are still so poor that a reduction in their incomes will generally lower both the present efficiency of adults and the future efficiency of children. This argument clearly applies to direct taxes on small incomes, including deductions from wages, and to indirect taxes on necessaries and 'near-necessaries'.

It is doubtful at what level of income the line should be drawn below which taxation is likely to reduce efficiency. But it is clear that, even in the richest modern communities, the incomes of a section of the population still lie below it. Moreover, the line must be drawn at different levels for different classes of workers; higher for a coal miner or a farm worker, for instance, than for a shop assistant or a school caretaker. Public expenditure on social services may do more good to the efficiency of the poorer workers than payment of taxes will do harm. None the less, in the interests of efficiency alone—and ignoring considerations

[1] In such a situation, for example, Keynes points out that death duties will increase, and not diminish, the wealth of the country by increasing 'the propensity to consume' (*General Theory*, p. 373). This will lead to more production, more investment and more employment.

of distribution or of equity—it is a sound general rule to shield the poorer workers from taxation.

Ability to save is reduced by all taxes on persons who have any margin of income, out of which saving is possible. The only taxes, therefore, which do not to some extent reduce individual ability to save, are those which fall exclusively on people who are so poor that they have no such margin. It is plain that heavy taxes on the rich, though defensible on other grounds, substantially reduce their ability to save.

But saving is not nowadays, in advanced countries, mainly done by individuals. And much individual saving is cancelled by individual dis-saving, i.e. sales of stocks and shares and other assets, in order to spend the proceeds. Most saving is now corporate, either private or public; the undistributed profits of private enterprise on the one hand and, on the other, such items as the surpluses, in this country, of the National Insurance Fund, the sinking funds of public boards and local authorities and, sometimes, a substantial budget surplus of the Central Government.[1] Corporate ability to save is, of course, reduced by taxation, but less, in proportion to taxable income and profits, than that of wealthy individuals. In Britain undistributed profits, since my budget of 1947, pay at a lower rate than distributed profits, and surtax, as distinct from income tax, has never been applied to corporate income.

Ability to invest depends on the resources available for investment. It is clear that these are reduced by taxation. But they are increased by the use of a budget surplus to pay off debt, and by some other forms of public expenditure.

§ 3. Let us now turn from considerations of efficiency to considerations of incentive, that is to say from the effects of taxation on ability, to effects upon desire, to work, save and invest. Here we have to take account, not so much of the primary effects of actual taxation in the present, as of the

[1] In principle, from the point of view of the Government, the budget surplus is the final variable factor, whose size should be determined by the gap, which it is desired to close, between savings and investment. If, apart from this factor, savings would exceed investment, there should be a budget deficit to close the gap. See Ch. XXVII.

secondary effects of the expectation that such taxation will continue in the future. A tax which was expected to be short-lived, a special tax, for example, to meet some special emergency, such as war expenditure or the rapid extinction of a war debt, would not have important secondary effects of this kind.

It is usually assumed that taxation is disincentive, i.e. that it reduces people's desire to work and save, but on closer examination this question is found to be less simple than is commonly imagined.

First as to taxation in general. Suppose all taxation suddenly abolished, existing public expenditure being maintained. Suppose, for instance, the sudden discovery of some new and very valuable natural resource, from which the government—either by leasing the property or selling the produce or otherwise—receives enough revenue to cover all public expenditure, or alternatively that this is to be covered by some permanent arrangement for a series of gifts from outside the community. How would people react to such a change, assumed to be permanent? Most, I think, would take life more easily. Not having to pay any taxes, they would find that they had larger incomes and would be less inclined than before to work hard. They would also have a larger margin, out of which saving would be possible. Most would probably save more, but would also spend more on an improved standard of living. The proportion of increased saving to increased spending would vary widely with different individuals. And there would probably be more investment. It looks, therefore, as though, with most people, taxation is not a disincentive to work, but an incentive, leading them to work harder than they would do if there were no taxation; but that taxation may be a disincentive both to individual saving and to investment.

So much for taxation in general. But it does not follow, of course, that every increase in every tax is an incentive to work, and every decrease a disincentive. Nor conversely with individual saving and with investment. Small changes may go one way, and large changes the other. And the effects on incentive of small tax changes seem likely in most cases to be small.

The effects of any particular tax, or tax change, upon

incentives depend partly on the nature of the tax and partly on the nature of individual reactions to taxation. The latter point is most conveniently considered first.

§ 4. Any person's reaction to taxation is governed by the elasticity of his demand for income, in terms of the efforts and sacrifices which he makes in order to obtain his income.[1] His income, for the purpose of the present argument, is his net income after deduction of taxation. Suppose that, as a result of increased taxation, a given effort or sacrifice—a given amount of work or saving—produces less income than before. What is the effect upon his desire to work or save? Obviously, to strengthen it, if the elasticity of his demand for income is small, and to weaken it, if this elasticity is large. In the former case it will seem more worth while than before to work and to save, in the latter case less worth while. Taxation, or a tax increase, is an incentive with inelastic, and a disincentive with elastic, demand. The practical question, then, is to find out how the elasticity of demand for income varies with different classes of people and with different circumstances.

It is usually assumed that most people's elasticity of demand for income is large. But is it? I have already thrown doubt on this idea. Many likely cases to the contrary suggest themselves. People who have dependants to maintain, or who are saving in the hope of securing not less than a certain income at a future date, will often feel compelled by the pressure of increased taxation to work harder or to save more.[2] Such situations are common enough among those who desire income in order to satisfy ordinary human needs, or, in other words, who desire merely to be reasonably well-off. But there are many who desire not merely to be well-off, but to be visibly better-off than those whom they regard as their social rivals. Hence, along with many more innocent examples on a smaller scale, springs that ostentatious extravagance, typified by the story told of Carnegie, who kept four chauffeurs, because Astor, who lived

---

[1] Or we may speak of the elasticity of his supply of efforts and sacrifices, in terms of the income which he can obtain in return.

[2] And it is sometimes argued that a land tax, or an increase of agricultural rents, would make farmers improve their methods of production.

just across the road, kept only three. The desire to work and save, in order to indulge a sense of vainglorious vulgarity, is not likely to be much, if at all, abated by increased taxation. Again, some men, especially some of the leaders in the business world, desire wealth and an ever-increasing income chiefly as a means of power and as evidence of worldly success. The placing of obstacles, such as increased taxation, in the way of their desire to go on accumulating seems only to exhilarate such men. Thus the first Lord Leverhulme declared that 'every raising of the rate at which income tax is levied has been followed by increased efforts, successfully made, to increase incomes out of which to pay the increased tax . . . We are all inclined to say, with the Irishman, "be jabers to the tax, if you will give me the income", and having got the income we are all inclined to make increased efforts to make the income sufficiently large to stand the contribution demanded by the Chancellor of the Exchequer, in the form of income tax, without diminishing the balance remaining for the income earner.'[1] According to this view of human nature, demand for income has hardly any elasticity at all. It is, indeed, uncertain how far Leverhulme's bracing attitude towards taxation is shared by other business men, or by other sections of the community. The 'psychology of the business world' remains something of a mystery, though it occupies a central place in some economists' theories of the trade cycle. In times of trade depression it is common form in the business world to ascribe most of the economic evils of the day to the 'crushing burden of taxation', though an equal, or even a heavier, burden may have been carried without apparent difficulty through the preceding trade boom. We cannot readily accept, in the face of Leverhulme's evidence, the suggestion that business men's demand for income is so highly elastic as this, even now that taxation is so much heavier than when he wrote, and so much more steeply graduated. But it may well be more elastic in times of depression than in times of boom, and more elastic among the inefficient than among the efficient. Nor, to return to the broader question, can we readily accept the common view that most people's demand for income is so

[1] *The Six Hour Day and Other Essays*, p. 248.

elastic that taxation, or tax increases, will reduce their desire to work and save and thus check production. It seems at least as likely to be the other way. There can, of course, be no certainty about incentives; only hunches, and guesses based on limited observation in given circumstances.[1]

Looking at the same question from the other side, that of the elasticity of supply of labour in relation to net marginal pay, we may recall a point noted in Chapter III, § 4. In the short run at least this elasticity, and hence any disincentive effect of taxation, is kept small by the fact that many workers are not free to decide their own hours, or even speed, of work. These matters are largely governed by custom, or by collective agreements, or by law.

In this chapter we have considered the desire to save out of individual incomes, where the alternative to saving is individual consumption. Saving out of corporate incomes—whether through undistributed profits, or through such agencies as insurance companies, or building societies, or public or semi-public bodies—is not directly subject to the competing desire for individual consumption. Those responsible for the handling of such corporate resources are often inclined to attach primary importance to the continuance of new investment rather than to alternative uses of their funds. In this increasingly important field, therefore, desire to save may well be stimulated, rather than checked, by taxation.

§ 5. So far we have been speaking of taxation in general in relation to the desire to work and save. We must now distinguish between the effects of different kinds of taxes.

---

[1] And a change in circumstances may change the guess. A change in social habits, for example. Thus it has been suggested that the growth of hire purchase, or 'instalment selling', makes the buyers' demand for income less elastic than before in adverse, and more elastic in favourable, conditions. An alternative view is that these devices, by stimulating new desires, simply raise the whole demand curve for income, without necessarily altering its slope. I have heard it said that 'if every workman was £100 in debt for furniture and a wireless set and a motor cycle, there would be far better timekeeping and much higher output'. Or a change in social mood may change the guess. In my first budget in 1945, immediately after the war, I made large reductions in income tax, which both I and many

Whatever the taxpayer's elasticity of demand for income, there are some taxes which are neutral, in the sense that they have hardly any effect on the desire to work and save. Taxes on windfalls, already referred to in Chapter IX, § 3, are an example. From the economic, as distinct from the equitable, point of view the essential characteristic of windfall wealth is its unexpectedness. Clearly there can be no expectation of a tax on an accretion of wealth, which is itself unexpected, and as has already been pointed out, it is chiefly through the expectation of its future continuance that taxation affects the desire to work and save. In periods of great economic disturbance, or even of rapid economic change, there may be wide scope for taxes on windfalls. During both world wars, for instance, the British excess profits tax, which produced a large revenue, was substantially a tax on windfalls, at any rate for the first year or two of its imposition, though with the passage of time it gradually changed its character. 'A perfect tax for a short war', I called it in one of my budget speeches. Again, during a period of rapid expansion in a new country, windfall taxes on the value of land and other forms of appreciating property may yield large sums. But in less unsettled conditions it is not generally possible to raise much revenue by such taxes. A tax on the site value of land, or on increments of site value, is a windfall tax in some cases, but not in others, since future appreciation of value is often expected. Inherited wealth, again, is occasionally a windfall to the inheritor, though many inheritances are the subject of pleasant, or of impatient, expectation.

Another neutral tax, in this sense, is a tax on a monopolist, which gives him no inducement to alter his output or selling price. On the other hand, a tax on a monopolist, which makes a larger output and a lower selling price more profitable, will make him desire to work and save more, whatever his elasticity of demand for income.[1]

---

others believed would act *at that time* as an incentive, when we all had a fresh sense of victory, and were swinging back from war work to peace work (see Ch. XXVIII). We may have been right or wrong then. But, either way, equivalent reductions made several years later might have had quite a different effect on incentives.          [1] See Ch. VII, § 5.

§ 6. But in the majority of cases the effect of various taxes upon the desire to work and save depends on the elasticity of taxpayers' demand for income. Let us first make the assumption, which is most unfavourable to production, that his elasticity is large, and let us consider, on this basis, the comparative effect of various taxes, or rather of the expectation of various taxes, upon taxpayers' desire to work and save.

Taxes on particular commodities will be only slightly disincentive, if only a small proportion of the taxpayer's marginal income is spent on them; more disincentive if, as with alcohol, tobacco and entertainment, they absorb a large part of his marginal income,[1] provided that he clearly realises what is going on, which often he may not. A general tax on income, including saved income, will be more disincentive, especially to saving, than taxes on commodities, which fall on expenditure only and not on savings. Hence has arisen much discussion of the possibility, in the interests of production, of exempting savings from income tax, and also of taxing dis-savings, which are now exempt. With the same object in view, it has been proposed to substitute a sales tax, which is equivalent to a tax on certain sorts of expenditure, for existing income taxes. It is partly administrative difficulties which have hitherto prevented any sweeping exemption of savings from income tax, and these might in time be overcome.[2] But a more fundamental objection, as also to the substitution of a sales tax for an income tax, in

[1] See Little, *Fiscal Policy*, in *The British Economy, 1945-1950* (Oxford, 1953), pp. 183–4.

[2] Income from government securities is exempt from income tax in France and elsewhere. But in the United States the growth of tax-exempt securities has been described by serious writers as a 'menace' and has made hay of the graduated taxation of income. See Lutz, *Public Finance*, pp. 506–511. Further exemptions of savings in Britain could have been secured, without administrative difficulty, by exempting the undistributed profits of companies, which are now liable to income tax at the standard rate. But the action of certain rich men who, in order to escape surtax, formed themselves into one-man companies, distributing hardly any of their profits, raised prejudice against such an exemption, which is also open to criticism on grounds of equity. The recent tendency is in the opposite direction, i.e. increased income taxation on undistributed profits. See, for a very instructive account of methods of tax evasion a generation ago, the

countries which are sufficiently civilised to possess the latter, arises from considerations of distribution.[1]

A very steeply graduated income tax, with high and rapidly rising rates of tax in some ranges, can hardly avoid becoming somewhat disincentive in these ranges. Beyond a certain point of graduation, men, even the Leverhulmes, may feel it not worth while to make an extra effort, when so high a proportion of the income from that effort would be taken by the tax collector.[2]

More generally, progressive taxation is more disincentive, or less incentive, than proportional taxation which, in turn, is more disincentive, or less incentive, than regressive taxation. A particular case of a regressive tax is a poll tax, an equal charge on everybody, as with the employee's contribution to British social insurance. From the point of view of incentives, a poll tax is one of the best forms of tax. But from the point of view of distribution, as we shall see in the next chapter, it is one of the worst.

§ 7. A tax, which has much to commend it on other grounds, is a tax on inherited wealth. From the point of view also of its effects on production, such a tax has some advantages over an income tax.

If we compare an income tax and an inheritance tax of the ordinary type, yielding the same revenue and similarly graduated, we note that, on the one hand, as regards *the actual payment* when the tax falls due, an inheritance tax will probably be paid out of capital to a greater extent than an income tax will be paid, year by year, out of money which would otherwise have been saved. But, on the other hand, as regards the effects of the *expectation of having to pay in the future*, saving is probably more reduced, and work too, by the prospect of having to pay income tax each year, than by the remoter prospect of one's heirs having to pay inheritance tax at some uncertain future date. And there are other reasons, connected with the psychology of wealthy men, which reinforce the view that an

speeches of Mr. Winston Churchill and the late Sir Douglas Hogg, in *Hansard*, July 4th, 1927. But in my third budget in 1947, as noted above, I introduced a partial exemption of undistributed profits from profits tax.
[1] See Ch. XI, §§ 3 and 5.        [2] But note § 16 of this chapter.

inheritance tax does less damage to work and saving than a comparable income tax.[1]

The preceding argument applies to an inheritance tax of the ordinary type, whether assessed—and however graduated—on the total property passing at death or on individual inheritances, and assumes that such a tax is disincentive and checks to some extent the desire of those accumulating wealth to work and save. But, if the tax were of the type proposed by the Italian economist Rignano, the desire to work and save would be checked much less, or not at all. This proposal is that the tax on an inherited fortune should be graduated according to what one may call the age of the fortune, or, in other words, according to the number of times it has already changed hands by inheritance. The greater the age of the fortune, the heavier would be the rate of tax. In its simplest form this proposal would amount to a differentiation between what we may call a person's earned wealth and his unearned wealth, or, in other words, between wealth which he had acquired as a result of his own work and saving and wealth which had come to him by inheritance or gift from others. On his death the latter class of wealth would be taxed at a higher rate than the former, thus giving him a stronger inducement to work and save in order to provide for his heirs, and making it less easy for him to rest on his oars and allow the dead hand to propel his boat.[2]

There is a further argument in favour of inheritance taxes, as against income taxes, from the point of view of their respective effects upon production. This is their effect upon the expectations of prospective inheritors. The latter will evidently be less inclined to work and save, the more substantial the inheritance to which they look forward. They may even be tempted, by a bright and near prospect of unearned wealth, to indulge in

---

[1] The balancing of the effects of these two taxes is a recurring topic in Professor Pigou's writings. See *Wealth and Welfare* (1912), pp. 352–4 and pp. 373–7, *Economics of Welfare* (second edition, 1924), pp. 673–4, and *Public Finance* (third edition, 1947), pp. 138–46.

[2] See my *Inequality of Incomes*, Part IV, Chs. IX–X, for a fuller discussion of Rignano's scheme and of inheritance taxes in general and, for a fuller discussion still, Mr. J. Wedgwood's admirable book on *The Economics of Inheritance*.

dis-saving, living on their own capital or running into debt and borrowing on their expectations. An inheritance tax, therefore, by reducing these expectations, stimulates work and saving by prospective inheritors, and the heavier the tax, the greater the stimulus.

§ 8. The argument of the two preceding sections has been based on the assumption that taxpayers' demand for income is, on the whole, relatively elastic, and hence that various taxes are disincentive and check, in different degrees, the desire to work and save. But we have already seen that this assumption is of doubtful validity. If we assume, on the other hand, that taxpayers' demand for income is, on the whole, relatively inelastic, it will follow that taxes on particular commodities, on incomes and on inheritances will be incentive and will stimulate the desire to work and save. Without pursuing further the conflicting results of these two assumptions, we may note that, on either assumption, an inheritance tax on the Rignano plan would be among the taxes most likely to be incentive and to stimulate the productive energies of those affected by it.

A possible variant of the plan, which seems to present very few administrative difficulties, is the following. Let some proportion of every estate passing at death, in excess of a certain minimum value, be compulsorily exchanged for terminable annuities to be issued by the Treasury. These annuities might either be terminable with the life of the inheritor, or, preferably, might have a fixed term, say, twenty years from the date of issue. During this period they would carry an annual income equal to the annual value of the wealth surrendered in exchange for them. The forms of wealth which would thus be accepted in exchange might conveniently be limited to government securities, other approved securities, suitable real estate and cash. The government securities would be cancelled on receipt; the cash would be applied to debt reduction; the approved securities would either be sold and the proceeds applied to debt reduction, or held and the interest so applied. The real estate might be transferred to some appropriate public, or private non-profit-making, body. The government would thus, in effect, issue terminable annuities in exchange for the cancellation of an amount of debt of equal annual value. The proportion of the debt consisting of such annuities would gradually increase and, after a period of, say, twenty years from the inception of the scheme, a quantity of these annuities would be running off annually. Inheritors would receive these annuities as part of their inheritance. They would be stimulated, by the prospect of the annuities running out, to work and save in order to make good the prospective loss of income.[1]

§ 9. Some interesting points, recently illuminated by British Parliamentary debates, relate to 'initial allowances'. These are additional depreciation allowances, in respect of particular machines, given to their owner in the first year of their life. Thus they reduce taxation on the income or profits of the first year, and also reduce the written down value of the machines in later years. But they are not, as is sometimes said, merely 'a temporary interest-free loan from the Treasury'. Save in very exceptional circumstances, they represent a permanent tax relief to industry and a permanent cost to the Treasury. But they are only given in return for investment, e.g. the purchase of a new machine, whereas an equal tax relief, by reduction of income tax or profits tax, might go wholly, or partly, not to increased investment, but to increased dividends and increased consumption. Thus initial allowances sustain the desire to invest better than other forms of tax relief.[2]

§ 10. So far in this chapter we have been considering how taxation, through its influence on ability and desire to work, save and invest, may affect production as a whole. We have now to consider how it may affect the composition and the local pattern of production.

The undesirability, in the interests of production, of diverting economic resources from their 'natural channels', dug out by

[1] See my evidence before the Colwyn Committee, and pp. 317–18 of their *Report*. H. D. Henderson, in a pamphlet on *Inheritance and Inequality*, made a similar proposal.

[2] See *Hansard*, June 16th and July 8th, 1953, particularly the speeches of Mr. Gaitskell and Mr. Crosland and the Ministerial replies. Also, on the true nature of initial allowances, C. A. R. Crosland, *The Banker*, September, 1953. In his budget of 1954 Mr. Butler also introduced investment allowances, which are a straight subsidy to investment in the private sector.

private profitability, has been a favourite theme with many
dead economists who have argued that the resources diverted
will be less productive in their new use (or locality), than they
would have been in the old. Most modern authorities argue
that, as a general rule, such diversions tend to check production,
but that this rule is subject to a formidable number of weighty
exceptions. We may say that, in the choice of taxes, there is a
presumption in favour of those which cause the minimum of
diversion. But this presumption is often overthrown by special
arguments which apply to particular cases. It will, therefore, be
convenient to begin by considering what sorts of taxes cause, in
fact, the minimum of diversion.

§ 11. As between different uses of economic resources, taxes
which have been defended on the ground that they cause little
or no diversion, include taxes on windfalls, taxes on the site
value of land, such taxes on monopolists as offer no inducement
to alter output or selling price, and certain taxes which fall with
equal weight on all uses of wealth.

In general, the way in which diversion occurs is as follows.
A person who owns, or himself embodies, economic resources
which, in their actual use, are subject to tax, seeks to escape this
tax by diverting these resources to some other use, in which
they will either be untaxed or taxed less heavily. Such a diversion will be profitable to him provided that the loss of income,
apart from taxation, due to the change of use is less than the
gain through the payment of less taxation. The extent to which
a given tax causes a diversion of resources from the taxed use
and a reduction in the supply of its product depends, as was
shown in Chapter VII, upon the elasticity of demand for this
product and upon its elasticity of supply.

A tax on windfalls, falling unexpectedly, like a bolt from the
blue, upon accretions of wealth which are themselves unexpected, obviously gives no inducement to diversion. A tax on
the site value of land, irrespective of the use to which the land
is put, causes no diversion, since its incidence is wholly upon
the landowner,[1] and since the supply of land is fixed by nature
and, therefore, no restriction of supply is possible. A tax on a

[1] See, however, Ch. VIII, § 2.

monopolist, which gives him no inducement to alter his output or selling price and is, therefore, necessarily less than his monopoly profits, gives no inducement to diversion, because, though the monopoly becomes less profitable than it would otherwise have been, it remains more profitable than the use of resources in open competition.[1]

It has been suggested that a tax, which falls with equal weight upon all uses of economic resources, gives no inducement to diversion, because no diversion would be a source of profit. Some controversy has taken place as to what would constitute a perfect 'non-differential' tax of this kind. On the one hand, it has been maintained that a general tax on income is non-differential, while, on the other, it has been argued that such a tax, since it taxes both income when saved and income subsequently derived from savings, differentiates against saving and gives an inducement to diversion from saving to spending. If the latter argument be sound, a perfect non-differential tax would be a tax on expenditure only, or, in other words, an income tax with an exemption for income which was saved. But either an expenditure or an income tax, in so far as it falls only on marginal expenditure or marginal savings, regardless of their particular character, is evidently less differential, and tends to less diversion of resources, than taxes on particular uses of resources. For the latter fall also upon 'intra-marginal' expenditure or savings.[2]

In fact, a perfect non-differential tax would not fall at equal rates on all uses of resources. For equal rates of tax would affect unequally the supply of objects of taxation, when these had unequal elasticities of demand or supply. A tax, non-

---

[1] Though not necessarily more profitable than the use of resources in other monopolies, if these are not correspondingly taxed. But the policy of monopolists, based upon restriction of output, deliberately obstructs the entry of new resources into the monopolised field.

[2] This idea is sometimes turned into an argument in favour of direct, as against indirect, taxes. The former, it is said, impose less burden on the taxpayer than the latter, because, falling only on marginal uses, they 'destroy less consumers' surplus'. But this way of thinking does not, in my opinion, correspond to the mental processes of ordinary people, who dislike direct taxes much more than indirect.

differential in structure, would be differential in its effects, causing a diversion from objects of large elasticity, whether of demand or supply, to objects of small elasticity. Therefore, to be non-differential in its effects, a tax must be differential in its structure. Its rates must be nicely adjusted to all the relevant elasticities, falling most heavily where elasticities were smallest, least heavily where they were largest. But such a tax is only an amusing intellectual toy, not a practically useful fiscal instrument.

§ 12. It is not difficult to find cases where the presumption in favour of taxes causing a minimum of diversion is overthrown. A tax on harmful drugs, by diminishing their consumption and increasing health and efficiency, will cause a beneficial diversion.[1] So will a tax on open fires in urban areas, to help to clean the air of smoke; or a tax, like the British purchase tax, on luxuries for the home market to divert production towards untaxed export or untaxed necessaries for the home market; or, more generally, a tax on forms of production or consumption which, in countries facing serious difficulties with their balance of overseas payments, conflict with the over-riding needs of export trade.[2] So probably will a tax on a monopolist, which gives him an inducement to increase his output and lower his selling price, since the additional resources which he will employ are likely to be more productive than they would have been in some other competitive employment.

The classical example, round which debate raged in the last century and the first quarter of this, of a tax designed to divert resources from their 'natural channels', was, of course, a protective tariff. Sidgwick, in his day, said almost the last word on this subject, when he remarked that many people seem to suppose that in theory free trade is the best policy, but that in

---

[1] A diversion of economic resources, though not necessarily a diversion of money expenditure in the same direction. A tax on a commodity, by raising its price, will reduce the demand for it, and hence the resources required to meet this demand. If, however, the demand is inelastic, a larger sum of money than before will be spent on purchasing a smaller quantity.

[2] See Crosland, *Britain's Economic Problem*, for a clear and cogent discussion of this last problem in present-day Britain.

practice protection will not do much harm, and may do some good, whereas the true situation is the exact reverse of this; in theory a good case may often be made out for protection, but in practice it is wiser to stick to free trade. Since then the situation has changed. A tariff is now only one, and by no means the most potent, means of influencing international trade. Import licensing and bulk buying are much stronger. And the nature of international trade has changed, from easy facilities, convertibility of currencies and free capital movements into difficult problems of exchange control, a precarious balance of payments, discrimination and bilateral bargains. And some diversions which thirty years ago might have been sought through a tariff are now brought about by a combination of financial subsidies and physical controls.

§ 13. In the last two sections we have been considering the diversion of economic resources from one use or employment to another. But diversion may also take place, as a result of taxation, from one locality to another. The general presumption against diversions is relevant here also, though, as in the previous discussion, it is easy to find many important instances where it is overthrown.

Thus in Britain between the two world wars heavy local taxation in areas suffering from heavy and prolonged unemployment—'the distressed areas' they were then called—helped, in spite of 'derating', to ruin the existing industries in these areas and to prevent the coming of new industries. After the second world war this heavy local taxation was relieved by a new Exchequer Equalisation Grant, devised while I was Chancellor of the Exchequer. This grant made good the deficiency, in any area, of local taxable value below the national average, while under my Distribution of Industry Act, devised while I was President of the Board of Trade, special encouragements were given to new industries to come to the old 'distressed areas'—'the development areas', as they were now called. This Act by promoting full and more diversified employment in these areas, including much new employment for women, certainly helped to increase national production. The whole beneficial change was brought about by a combination

of tax changes, subsidies, physical controls and other administrative arrangements. It was beneficial both in diverting industries and other consequential employment *to* these areas, whose
social life was thus revived, and in preventing the diversion,
after lingering unemployment and physical and spiritual
deterioration, of men and women *from* these areas to big cities,
whose excessive growth in nearly every country in the world
shows the evil consequences of lazy drift down 'natural channels'.

§ 14. To sum up the main conclusions of this chapter, a
point is probably reached, as taxation increases, beyond which
any further increases will cause some check to production.
Where this point lies and how severe the check will be, in
respect of any given tax revenue, will depend both on the
character of the taxes imposed and on the character of the
taxpayers. The check may be exercised in three ways. First,
through the effects of taxation on ability to work and save;
second, through its effects on desire to work and save; third,
through diversions, due to taxation, of economic resources as
between different uses and localities. It is under the first head,
and especially as a result of reduced ability to save, that the
check is most likely. Under the second, much depends on
the character of the taxpayers, or, in technical terms, on the
elasticity of their demand for income. A check to production
under this head is not inevitable; on the contrary, a stimulus is
possible. Though some taxes may be disincentive, taxation as
a whole may be incentive. Under the third head, much depends
on a good selection of taxes. Here, again, a check to production
is not inevitable, and a stimulus is possible. Further, by the use
of subsidies and physical controls as well as taxation, other
gains, as well as increased production, may result.

If all the proceeds of taxation were spent on waste. which
contributed nothing to economic welfare, then any check to
production as a result of taxation would be a clear economic
loss. But, if the proceeds of taxation are well spent, the stimulus
to production due to this expenditure may be far stronger than
the check to production due to taxation. Public finance, viewed
as a whole, would then be responsible for increasing production. It is still true that 'the whole tendency of modern economic

reasoning is to lay less stress on the effects of this or that action in stimulating or checking the *motives* for displaying this or that kind of activity, and more stress on its effects in expanding or contracting the *sources* from which that activity emanates. A high income tax, the proceeds of which are devoted partly to debt reduction and partly to measures of public health and education, may well have a beneficial effect on the sources of both savings and business enterprise far outweighing any discouraging effect it may exercise on the incentives to display those activities.'[1]

§ 15. Since the last edition of this book of mine in 1936 many economists have written books and articles in learned journals, defining 'ideal taxes' from the point of view of production, and hence the problem of diversion, in new terms. For reasons mentioned in my Preface I have read only a small selection of this large literature.[2]

I am not sure how much of value is added by this new approach, nor how much of the old arguments is invalidated. But I am inclined to think that the answer to both questions is 'something, but not much'.

The new approach is along indifference curves. It is part of the shift from cardinal to ordinal utility systems. A new distinction is between the 'income effect' and the 'substitution effect' of a change in the price of a commodity. If the price rises, the consumers' real income falls. This is the income effect. But if, in addition, there is a change in relative prices, this may lead the consumers to buy less of the dearer commodity and, to some extent, to substitute others for it. This is the substitution effect.

[1] D. H. Robertson, *Economic Journal*, December, 1927, p. 580.

[2] Including, however, J. R. Hicks, *Value and Capital* (Oxford, 1939, second edition, 1946), I. M. D. Little, *Critique of Welfare Economics* (Oxford, 1950) and an article, 'Direct versus Indirect Taxation' (*Economic Journal*, September, 1951), in which he shows, what I sensed when Chancellor of the Exchequer, that there is no logical proof that direct taxation causes less loss of satisfaction than indirect, and D. Berry, 'Modern Welfare Analysis and the Form of Income Redistribution', in *Income Redistribution and Social Policy*, edited by A. T. Peacock (Cape, 1954). But the student will find each of these writings swarming with references to other writings on the same subject.

An ideal tax, from the point of view of production, is defined as one which causes no change in relative prices, i.e. one which has only an income effect. This means, it is said, either a poll tax or taxes on commodities with absolutely inelastic demand or supply.

An income tax is not ideal, it is argued, since it cheapens leisure, nor is a tax on one commodity which cheapens another. Both have substitution effects which are disincentive. But income effects of taxation, it is maintained, are often incentive and, at worst, neutral.

The problem of diversion is seen, according to this new approach, not, as in the language of earlier sections of this chapter, as minimising, except for good cause shown, diversion from the distribution of economic resources which would prevail if there were no taxation, or only 'non-differential taxation'. It is seen as minimising, subject to the same exception, diversion from the distribution which would prevail, if people's incomes were reduced only by ideal taxes, i.e. by taxes with no substitution effects. There is no conflict of theory here, only a new definition of a non-differential tax.

But, in practice, a tax with no substitution effects seems unearthly. A heavy poll tax, like an income tax, may make a man work hardɔr, or alternatively make him change his pattern of consumption. And so may a heavy tax on a commodity of absolutely inelastic demand or supply.

§ 16. The Second Report of the British Royal Commission on the Taxation of Profits and Income (1954, Cmd. 9105) discredits the doctrine that such taxation is seriously disincentive, either on wages and salaries, or on the largest earned incomes (see pp. 13–15, 24, 45 and 91ff.). 'The deterrent effects of P.A.Y.E. have been greatly over-emphasised', say the Commissioners, an exceptionally authoritative body of lawyers, business men, trade unionists and academic economists, and again, 'We see no evidence that the higher income earners are specially affected by disincentive'.

# CHAPTER XI

# EFFECTS OF TAXATION ON DISTRIBUTION

§ 1. It is generally agreed that we should study the effects of taxation on production, and that, other things being equal, one tax system is preferable to another, if it has less tendency to check production. It is less commonly agreed that, other things being equal, one tax system is preferable to another, if it has a stronger tendency to check inequality. The German economist Wagner deserves credit as being one of the first to insist that taxation should be used to reduce the inequality of incomes. His so-called 'socio-political' view of public finance still displeases some high authorities, but it is sound in principle, and is increasingly adopted in modern practice. For a less unequal distribution is no less desirable than an increased production of wealth.[1]

The ideal distribution, from an economic point of view, is that which causes a given amount of production to yield the maximum of economic welfare. This ideal is not, therefore, an absolutely equal distribution, but a distribution 'according to needs', or, to put the same thought in other words, according to capacity to make good use of income, i.e. to make income yield welfare. In face, however, of the great inequality of in-

---

[1] It is interesting to read in *The Statement of Objects and Reasons* accompanying the Estate Duty Bill introduced into the Indian House of the People in 1952 that, 'though the levy and collection of income tax at high rates since the war and the investigations undertaken in a number of important cases of tax-evasion have, no doubt, prevented to some extent the further concentration of wealth in the hands of those who are already wealthy, yet these do not amount to positive steps in the direction of reducing the existing inequalities in the distribution of wealth. It is hoped that by the imposition of an estate duty such unequal distribution may be rectified to a large extent.'

comes, which still prevails in most modern communities, we may be reasonably sure that any practicable reduction in inequality will give us a closer approximation to the ideal distribution. In fact, as we have already noted, the State largely settles distribution, through taxation, subsidies, etc. It is an error to suppose, as some economists do, that any actual distribution is ideal, or so nearly ideal that it should be altered as little as possible by taxation.

§ 2. It has been remarked above that the measurement of the inequality of incomes raises some difficult problems—incidentally this is also true of the measurement of production—but certain broad conclusions readily emerge.

A regressive tax system tends to increase the inequality of incomes. So does a proportional, or even a mildly progressive, tax system.[1] But a more sharply progressive tax system tends to reduce inequality and, the sharper the progression, the stronger this tendency.[2] Considerations of distribution, therefore, lead us towards the most sharply progressive tax system that is practicable. A rough approximation to such a system is that referred to in Chapter IX, § 2, in our discussion of the principle of minimum sacrifice. All incomes above a certain level would be cut down to that level, and no incomes below that level would be taxed at all. From the economic, as distinct from the equitable, point of view, and so far as considerations of distribution only are concerned, this, with certain minor adjustments, would be taxation according to ability to pay. Considerations of production may make so sharp a progression undesirable. But the case for a marked degree of progression may be taken to be firmly established.

The conflict between considerations of production and of distribution might be largely resolved, if heavy and steeply progressive rates of tax fell only on the richest individuals—a small minority of the taxpayers, including many living only on capital and income from capital—while the great majority were much

---

[1] See Ch. IX, § 5, and note to Ch. IX, § 5.

[2] Yet another tricky problem of measurement, that of the *degree of progressiveness* of a tax system, is examined in the Note at the end of this chapter.

more lightly taxed and most of them wholly exempted from direct taxes.[1]

§ 3. A poll tax, equal in amount for each taxpayer, is the simplest of all taxes. If all incomes were equal, it would be a proportional tax of great practical convenience. But, if incomes are unequal, it becomes a regressive, tax and the greater the inequality, the greater the degree of regression. It is, therefore, unsuitable to the conditions of modern communities, unless its effect on distribution is much more than offset by progressive taxes. But a poll tax is a customary form of worker's contribution to social insurance funds, and in Britain some Trade Union leaders have objected to its replacement by a graduated tax on earnings, since this, they argue, would throw doubt on the worker's right to social insurance benefits. If all pay the same, they are buying certain benefits at a fixed price.

Taxes on commodities of wide consumption are generally regressive, since, as a rule, the larger a person's income, the smaller the proportion of it which he spends on any one such commodity. Thus taxes on food are generally sharply regressive. So are taxes on tobacco and the cheaper sorts of alcohol. An *ad valorem* tax on a commodity is less regressive than a specific tax, since the former differentiates to some extent against consumers of the more expensive qualities. But taxes on luxuries, defined as articles too expensive to be much bought by the poor, are progressive, at least broadly, as between rich and poor. Since, however, expenditure on particular commodities is optional, and varies greatly from one individual to another, 'progressive' and 'regressive' have a less exact meaning with commodity taxes than with income tax.

British local rates, in so far as they fall on occupiers, are regressive, both in particular rating areas and, still more, in the

[1] In Britain it would cost only £30 millions, out of a total of £1,400 millions, of Income Tax revenue to exempt five million of the poorest, out of a total of sixteen million income-tax payers. Thus for less than 3 per cent of the yield, more than 30 per cent of the taxpayers could be set free, with large administrative savings. This could be done most simply by having a minimum, as well as a maximum, for Earned Income Relief. See a speech in the House of Commons by Mr. Douglas Jay, *Hansard*, June 11th, 1953.

country as a whole. For, broadly, the rateable value of dwelling houses is a diminishing proportion of income, as income increases, and rates in the pound are higher in poor than in rich districts.

If a tax system, which includes regressive taxes, is to be progressive on the whole, it must contain other taxes, which are themselves progressive and exercise a stronger influence on the general character of the tax system.

§ 4. Apart from luxury taxes, the most important taxes, which are easily made progressive, are income and inheritance taxes and general taxes on property.

An income tax may be made progressive by means of a graduated scale of rates, larger incomes being taxed at higher rates than smaller ones. This principle may be applied directly, each taxpayer making a return of his total income and being charged on it at the appropriate rate. But, for administrative reasons, it is more convenient to apply it to a large extent indirectly. Thus the British income tax law imposes a standard rate of tax, which is deducted 'at source' from most taxable income before it reaches its recipient, who may, however, claim some repayment, if his total taxable income is less than a certain amount. Much income tax on earned income is collected at source, and deducted at the appropriate rates under the device known as 'Pay as you earn'. The standard rate is supplemented by an additional graduated tax, or surtax, on the larger incomes only, and by a system of exemptions and allowances and reduced rates principally affecting the smaller incomes. The tax is progressive as between different sections of income-tax payers and thus helps to counter-balance the effect of regressive taxes in the rest of the tax system. But it is not, of course, progressive as between the various sections of those who are exempted, and may leave the tax system regressive as regards the latter, though progressive over the higher ranges of income.

Under the British income tax law, the incomes of a husband and wife are treated, substantially, as a single taxable income, and allowances from this taxable income are then given in respect of the wife and of any children under sixteen years of age. It is sometimes proposed that married women's incomes should be taxed independently of their husbands'. But, if this were done, a progressive income tax would fall more heavily upon a married couple, one of whom had an income of £800 a year and the other nothing, than upon a married couple, each of whom had an income of £400 a year. And it is difficult to justify, either in equity or economy, such a difference of treatment.[1] Unless, however, the income tax payable by a man with a given taxable income and no dependants is made greater than that payable out of a family income of equal size, on which two or more persons have to be supported, mere graduation of the rates of tax will not bring any close approach to taxation according to ability to pay.

§ 5. Though a sales tax, or purchase tax, of wide range tends to be regressive, it may become progressive, if its range is narrowed to luxuries and near-luxuries. Further, a progressive tax on individual expenditure might be obtained by the exemption of savings from a progressive income tax, and the assessment of dis-savings. But, as already noted, such a tax raises great administrative difficulties and, if it were thought worth while to face these, the new tax might, to begin with, be limited to the larger incomes, e.g. in Britain to surtax payers.

§ 6. An inheritance tax may be assessed and graduated in various ways. It will, as a general rule, be progressive as between inheritors, if, on the occasion of a death, it is assessed on a progressive scale on the amounts inherited by different individuals. Mill's proposal to fix a maximum sum, more than which no individual should be allowed to inherit, only implies a specially sharp progression in a tax of this kind. But, if the same individual receives separate inheritances on different occasions, complications arise. Thus a person who receives two legacies of £5,000 each will be less heavily taxed than one who receives a single legacy of £10,000. It would, therefore, be desirable, from the point of view of distribution, to graduate an inheritance tax, not only according to the amounts received by

[1] The chief reasons which are put forward for a separate, as against a joint, assessment are (1) greater inducement to both parties to work, (2) smaller inducement to 'live in sin', (3) feminist sentiment.

inheritors, but also according to the amounts of wealth which the latter already possessed. Attempts were made to apply this principle after the first world war both in Germany and in Italy, but they were abandoned owing to administrative difficulties. Many inheritance taxes are assessed on other bases. The British estate duty, for instance, which for the most part is very easy to administer, is assessed on a progressive scale on the total value of the property passing at death, regardless of its distribution among inheritors. The British legacy and succession duties, now repealed, were progressive according to the remoteness of the relationship of the inheritor to the deceased. Neither of these principles of progression necessarily leads to progression as between inheritors. In practice, the British estate duty does so in the great majority of cases, since testators generally leave most of their property to a few fortunate persons. But the duty would fall more heavily, both absolutely and proportionately, upon an estate of £50,000, to be equally divided among five inheritors, than upon an estate of £40,000 passing to a single inheritor. The legacy and succession duties, on the other hand, were often regressive on inheritors, since testators generally leave more to near than to distant relatives, and very little to persons who are not related to them.

The conclusion is that an inheritance tax, in order to contribute most surely both to the progressiveness of a tax system and to administrative efficiency, should be assessed on a steeply progressive scale on total estates passing at death; with, perhaps, a supplementary tax, also steeply graduated, either on individual inheritances, or on the total wealth of inheritors, or, best of all, on the simplified Rignano principle described in the last chapter. A heavy inheritance tax further tends slightly to reduce the inequality of incomes by stimulating gifts *inter vivos* from the old to the young, with the object of avoiding the tax.[1] But this tendency counts for less than might be supposed, since those who receive such gifts are generally those who would otherwise have inherited a little later, and since, when the tax is

[1] Harcourt, when told in 1894 that his new estate duty would lead fathers to make generous gifts to their sons, replied, 'I am on the side of the sons'.

successfully avoided, the recipients are richer than they would have been, if they had had to pay it. In principle, gifts from the living should be taxed on the same footing as gifts from the dead. But here too we meet stiff administrative difficulties.

§ 7. A general property tax may obviously be made progressive as between property owners by means of graduated rates, exemptions and allowances. The capital value of property is generally a less satisfactory basis of tax assessment than its annual value, or, in other words, than the income derived from it. But there is sometimes a strong case for a progressive tax on the value of property held by individuals, as in some presentations of the case for a capital levy.[1]

It is an argument in favour of a graduated property tax that it strikes, more heavily than an equally progressive income tax, great wealth held passively by elderly people, and strikes the young and middle-aged more lightly.[2]

In the United States taxable income is defined so as to include 'capital gains', i.e. increases in the value of the taxpayer's capital. When security prices are rising, this provision increases the progressiveness of the tax system. But, 'capital losses' being treated as a deduction from taxable income, it operates even more strongly in the opposite direction, when prices fall. Thus Pierpont Morgan was able in 1931–3 to prove to the Federal tax-collectors that he had no 'income'. His income, in the ordinary sense, was still gigantic. So was the value of his capital, which had, however, suffered some decline from the high levels of previous years.

The United States law on this subject is complicated, and I doubt if it would be worth while to imitate it in Britain. A direct 'capital levy' would be more effective for changing distribution and, as already noted, an individual expenditure tax would hit 'capital gains', if spent, though not if saved.

§ 8. The principle of progression may also be introduced into

---

[1] See Ch. XXIII.

[2] In general, capacity to make good use of income, in excess of a moderate amount, diminishes as old age sets in. I offer this concession to those who challenge the assumption that the relation of income to welfare is the same for all members of the community.

other taxes. A tax on land values, for example, may be made progressive on the total value of land owned by individuals, with a minimum of exemption. The Australians have experimented with a land tax of this type, which tends to produce a more equal distribution of land, though not necessarily of all wealth, in private ownership. For a big landowner, by selling half his land as measured by its value, will escape more than half his tax.

§ 9. It is sometimes claimed that a protective tariff might succeed, not only in increasing production, but also in improving distribution by reducing the inequality of incomes. Theoretically, it might do this in either of two ways. It might, on the one hand, tax imported commodities competing with those home industries, in which wages were comparatively high, and thus tend to divert production and employment from other industries, in which wages were lower, to these more favoured industries. And it might, on the other hand—and for this purpose it would not always need to be protective—tax imported commodities mainly consumed by the rich, and thus not only secure some revenue from the latter, but also tend to substitute for such imports others, which would be more useful, directly or indirectly, to the majority of the community.

Both these results are theoretically possible, but probably of small practical importance. If it is desired to improve distribution by taxation, more direct and powerful methods, such as have been referred to in earlier sections of this chapter, are available.

## NOTE TO CHAPTER XI

§ 1. The purpose of this note is twofold; first, to consider, in the light of some statistics, changes over recent years in the distribution of the burden of taxation in Britain and, second, to examine more closely the conception, and measurement, of 'progressiveness' in a tax system. It is interesting to notice the extent to which the British tax system has, since the beginning of the present century, become progressive. This was well brought out, for the first two decades, by Sir Herbert Samuel's (now Lord Samuel's) comparison of the distribution of the direct money burden of taxation in the three years 1903–4,

1913–14 and 1918–19.[1] His estimates excluded local rates, stamp duties and excess profits duty, but treated as a tax the profits of the Post Office. It was assumed, to facilitate the calculation, that death duties were insured against by annual premiums, which were regarded as additional income tax on incomes from property, and it was also assumed that all taxes on commodities were wholly paid by consumers.

He showed that indirect taxes were sharply regressive in each of the three years, but that direct taxes had become more and more progressive. The tax system as a whole showed the following evolution during this period.

### TABLE A

#### PERCENTAGES OF INCOMES PAID IN TAXES

| Taxpayer's annual income. £ | Incomes from work. | | | Incomes from property. | | |
|---|---|---|---|---|---|---|
| | 1903–4 | 1913–14 | 1918–19 | 1903–4 | 1913–14 | 1918–19 |
| 50 | 9·1 | 8·7 | — | 9·1 | 8·7 | — |
| 100 | 6·2 | 6·0 | 13·8 | 6·2 | 6·0 | 13·8 |
| 150 | 5·0 | 4·9 | 11·0 | 5·0 | 4·9 | 11·0 |
| 200 | 5·6 | 4·8 | 10·3 | 7·8 | 7·0 | 12·4 |
| 500 | 6·6 | 5·8 | 13·1 | 8·8 | 9·9 | 18·1 |
| 1,000 | 7·4 | 6·6 | 19·4 | 10·3 | 12·2 | 26·5 |
| 2,000 | 6·6 | 5·8 | 25·6 | 9·8 | 12·0 | 33·6 |
| 5,000 | 5·6 | 6·8 | 37·2 | 9·6 | 12·4 | 43·5 |
| 10,000 | 5·1 | 8·1 | 42·6 | 9·5 | 15·1 | 50·3 |
| 20,000 | 4·9 | 8·3 | 47·6 | 10·0 | 16·0 | 58·1 |
| 50,000 | 4·8 | 8·4 | 50·6 | 10·2 | 18·1 | 63·9 |

Taken broadly, these figures show that in the first year the tax system was, on the whole, distinctly regressive on incomes from work, regressive on incomes from property up to between £150 and £200 a year, then slightly progressive up to about £1,000 a year and then roughly proportional.

In the second year it was still regressive on incomes from work up to between £200 and £500 and on incomes from property up to between £150 and £200. On incomes from work between £500 and £5,000 it was roughly proportional, and

[1] See his paper in the *Journal of the Royal Statistical Society*, March, 1919.

above £10,000 again roughly proportional, but at a slightly higher rate. On incomes from property above £200 it was, on the whole, mildly progressive, with a proportional patch between £1,000 and £5,000.

In the third year regression was still found on incomes from work up to between £200 and £500 and on incomes from property up to between £150 and £200. Above these points the tax system had become continuously progressive on both sorts of income, and the scale of progression had been steepened to a degree which would have seemed incredible both to the Chancellors of the Exchequer and to the economists of the Victorian Age. But there was no reason to suppose that we had reached in 1918–19 the limits of practicable or desirable progression. The persistent element of regression among the smaller incomes was largely due to the maintenance of taxes on food, and was a serious blot, from the point of view of distribution, on the tax system as a whole.

§ 2. Sir Herbert Samuel's estimates were revised in 1927 by the Colwyn Committee, which added similar estimates of its own for the years 1923–4 and 1925–6. I have summarised the Colwyn Committee's estimates in the following tables.[1]

### TABLE B

#### PERCENTAGES OF INCOMES PAID IN TAXES

| Taxpayer's annual income. £ | Incomes wholly from work. | | | | |
|---|---|---|---|---|---|
| | 1903–4 | 1913–14 | 1918–19 | 1923–4 | 1925–6 |
| 50 | 8·7 | 8·0 | — | — | — |
| 100 | 5·6 | 5·4 | 9·9 | 14·1 | 11·9 |
| 150 | 4·5 | 4·4 | 9·0 | 13·5 | 11·6 |
| 200 | 4·8 | 4·0 | 7·9 | 11·8 | 10·2 |
| 500 | 5·3 | 4·4 | 10·2 | 8·0 | 6·2 |
| 1,000 | 6·1 | 5·2 | 16·9 | 14·1 | 11·0 |
| 2,000 | 5·7 | 4·9 | 24·0 | 17·9 | 15·2 |
| 5,000 | 5·5 | 6·7 | 36·6 | 28·5 | 23·2 |
| 10,000 | 5·0 | 8·0 | 42·5 | 37·1 | 31·2 |
| 20,000 | 4·9 | 8·3 | 47·6 | 42·3 | 37·5 |
| 50,000 | 4·8 | 8·4 | 50·6 | 48·0 | 44·4 |

[1] See *Report*, pp. 94–5.

## TABLE C

### PERCENTAGES OF INCOMES PAID IN TAXES

| Taxpayer's annual income. £ | Incomes half from work and half from property. | | | | |
|---|---|---|---|---|---|
| | 1903–4 | 1913–14 | 1918–19 | 1923–4 | 1925–6 |
| 50 | 9·5 | 8·8 | — | — | — |
| 100 | 6·8 | 6·6 | 11·1 | 15·3 | 13·0 |
| 150 | 5·7 | 5·6 | 10·2 | 14·7 | 12·7 |
| 200 | 6·0 | 5·3 | 9·1 | 12·9 | 11·3 |
| 500 | 6·5 | 7·1 | 13·5 | 9·9 | 8·4 |
| 1,000 | 7·8 | 8·3 | 20·6 | 16·9 | 14·4 |
| 2,000 | 7·4 | 8·4 | 28·1 | 21·5 | 19·3 |
| 5,000 | 7·5 | 9·6 | 39·2 | 32·6 | 29·5 |
| 10,000 | 7·6 | 11·8 | 46·3 | 43·0 | 40·1 |
| 20,000 | 7·7 | 13·0 | 52·3 | 51·4 | 48·7 |
| 50,000 | 8·0 | 13·6 | 58·2 | 60·7 | 57·7 |

These estimates will be seen to indicate that, as regards incomes from work, the rates of taxation on the smaller incomes, up to between £200 and £500, were increased between 1918–19 and 1923–4, while they were decreased on the larger incomes. Between 1923–4 and 1925–6 they were decreased over the whole range of incomes, but remained higher on the smaller incomes, and lower on the larger incomes, in 1925–6 than in 1918–19. The element of regression on the smaller incomes continued and its range actually increased, reaching in the two later years to incomes somewhere between £500 and £1,000.

The Colwyn Committee made no estimate, as Sir Herbert Samuel had done, of taxation on incomes wholly derived from property. They dealt instead with mixed incomes, derived half from work and half from property. Their figures show that the changes, between 1918–19 and 1925–6, in the relative rates of taxation on those mixed incomes were roughly similar to the corresponding changes in the case of incomes from work.

The broad conclusions which emerge are that the British tax system between 1918 and 1926 increased its regressive pressure on the smaller incomes, and diminished its progressive pressure on the larger, and that the range of regression widened, while the range of progression narrowed. From the point of view of distribution, therefore, the British tax system deteriorated during this period.

§ 3. It should, moreover, be noted that the effects of progressive taxation on distribution may be offset, from the side of public expenditure, by the effects of regressive grants.[1] The growth of the national debt is highly relevant here. Giving evidence in February, 1925, before the Colwyn Committee, I pointed out that 'the present annual yield of income tax and super-tax (£326 millions) is only slightly greater than the present annual interest charge on the debt (£305 millions), and falls short of the present annual charge for interest and sinking fund combined (£350 millions). In 1913–14 income tax and super-tax, yielding £47 millions, covered the total debt charges, £25 millions, nearly twice over. Now, broadly speaking, it is the income tax payers who themselves receive the interest on the debt. Leaving external debt out of account, the collection of income tax and super-tax and the payment of interest resolve themselves into mere transfers of wealth within a comparatively small section of the community. The present situation, therefore, is that income tax and super-tax payers, as such, have practically ceased to make any contribution to the current expenses of the country, as represented by the Supply Services.' The features of the situation, which I then depicted, became more marked in the next few years, owing to reductions in the rates of income tax and super-tax, without a corresponding reduction in the debt charges.[2]

[1] A system of regressive grants involves greater proportionate additions to large incomes than to small. See Ch. XVII, § 3, and Ch. XIX, § 2.

[2] In confirmation of my argument on this point, I quote the following passage from Professor Pigou's *Public Finance* (p. 244). It will be observed that he is dealing with the situation more than a year later than the date of my evidence before the Colwyn Committee, after the rates of income tax and super-tax had already been reduced by the Finance Act of 1925, that he credits the wealthier classes with their contribution to the death duties, and that he excludes from the balance sheet the interest and sinking fund on the external debt. 'In 1925–6,' he writes, 'the net produce of income tax and super-tax was £295 millions and of death duties £50 millions making £345 millions in all, while the interest on the internal debt amounted to £273 millions. When to this is added management expenses, and, say—to make allowance for foreign debt—six-sevenths of a £50

| I | | E | | I | | E | | I | | E | | I | |
|---|---|---|---|---|---|---|---|---|---|---|---|---|---|
| *s.* | *d.* | *s.* | *d.* | *s.* | *d.* | *s.* | *d.* | *s.* | *d.* | *s.* | *d.* | *s.* | *d.* |
| 0 | 4 | 1 | 4½ | 2 | 0½ | — | | 0 | 5 | — | | 0 | 4½ |
| 1 | 6½ | 3 | 0½ | 4 | 0½ | 1 | 1 | 2 | 6½ | 0 | 9 | 1 | 9 |
| 3 | 1 | 4 | 9 | 5 | 9 | 2 | 10½ | 4 | 4½ | 1 | 9 | 3 | 6½ |
| 4 | 3 | 6 | 0½ | 7 | 0½ | 4 | 3½ | 5 | 9½ | 3 | 4½ | 5 | 2 |
| 5 | 7½ | 7 | 9 | 8 | 6 | 6 | 3 | 7 | 4½ | 5 | 3½ | 7 | 1 |
| 7 | 11 | 11 | 0½ | 11 | 4 | 9 | 11½ | 10 | 5 | 9 | 7 | 10 | 3½ |
| 13 | 3 | 16 | 9½ | 16 | 10 | 16 | 5½ | 16 | 6½ | 16 | 4½ | 16 | 6 |
| 15 | 8 | 18 | 10 | 18 | 10 | 18 | 9 | 18 | 9 | 18 | 8½ | 18 | 9 |

...d world war, Sir John Anderson Chancellor

§ 4. Since 1926 there have been many changes, pointing different ways, and a second world war, with substantial increases, not only during it but after it, over pre-war levels of taxation and public expenditure. Taxation on large incomes and large inherited estates has become much more progressive and there has also been a considerable increase in indirect taxation. But no new comprehensive study of the taxation figures for this last period has been published.

For income tax and surtax alone, neglecting indirect taxes, the figures in Table D, taken from the *Annual Financial Statements*, show the progress of progression since the years covered by the Colwyn Report.

These were the average, or effective, rates. Marginal rates rose

TABLE E

| Net capital value of estate. | Percentage paid in estate duty. | | | | |
|---|---|---|---|---|---|
| £ | 1919 | 1929 | 1939 | 1946* | 1949 |
| 100 | 1 | 1 | 1 | 0 | 0 |
| 1,000 | 3 | 3 | 3 | 0 | 0 |
| 2,000 | 3 | 3 | 3 | 1 | 1 |
| 5,000 | 4 | 4 | 4 | 3 | 3 |
| 10,000 | 5 | 5 | 5 | 6 | 6 |
| 25,000 | 6 | 10 | 10 | 14 | 18 |
| 50,000 | 7 | 15 | 15 | 24 | 35 |
| 100,000 | 10 | 20 | 20 | 35 | 50 |
| 250,000 | 13 | 25 | 28 | 50 | 60 |
| 500,000 | 17 | 28 | 34 | 60 | 70 |
| 750,000 | 18 | 29 | 36 | 65 | 75 |
| 1,000,000 | 20 | 30 | 40 | 70 | 80 |
| 2,000,000 | 20 | 40 | 50 | 75 | 80 |

* After my second budget. See Ch. XXVIII, § 5.

millions sinking fund, it appears that practically the whole of the contribution to the national revenue made by the income tax paying class was absorbed in financing a debt in the main held by members of that class, nothing being left over for general government services. It is certain that, had the war been financed out of taxes, so that no aftermath of internal debt remained, the income tax paying class would have been called upon for a very substantial contribution towards those general services. Thus resort to the method of loans has enabled them to escape, at the expense of poorer persons, from a heavy burden of charges, which, had the tax method been more largely employed, they must inevitably have borne.'

to 19s. 6d. (now reduced to 19s.) in the £ on all incomes in excess of £20,000.

Likewise for estate duty, as shown in Table E.[1]

It is no longer possible to assume, as Sir Herbert Samuel and the Colwyn Committee did, that death duties can now be completely insured against by annual payments out of income. To make this impossible, and to ensure that large estates passing at death really *are* diminished, quite substantially, has been the firm intention of most British Chancellors of the Exchequer since 1945. The equalising effects of the most recent scales will only appear gradually. But the march towards greater equality of fortunes is very slow. It has been estimated[2] that in England and Wales two-thirds of the privately owned wealth belonged to one per cent of adults just before the first war, to two per cent just before the second, and to three per cent just after it; the next sixth to two, five and seven per cent at the respective dates, and the remaining sixth to the poorest ninety-seven, ninety-three and ninety per cent respectively.

§ 5. Turning from statistics to theory, it is a simple idea that, if a rate of tax $t$ falls upon an income $x$, the progression, or 'degree of progressiveness', of the tax may be measured by $\dfrac{dt}{dx}$. According as this is positive, zero, or negative, we have progressive, proportional, and regressive taxation respectively. If it is both large and positive, we shall naturally speak, thinking in terms of a graph, of 'steeply' progressive taxation.

But this idea only relates to progression *at a particular point* on the tax scale. It throws no light on the degree of progression of the tax scale *as a whole*.

This more general conception may be approached from several angles. Begin, once more, with a community consisting of two taxpayers only, A and B, of whom A has the larger

---

[1] Part of the increase of estate duty in 1949 was to offset the repeal of the legacy and succession duties, but the scale of estate duty was steepened. Since 1949 there was no change in the scale till 1954, when on my proposal the exemption limit was raised from £2000 to £3000 and the rate between £3000 and £4000 reduced from 2 to 1 per cent.

[2] By Miss K. Langley (*Oxford Bulletin of Statistics*, 1951).

income. Let the rates of tax falling upon their incomes be $t_1$ and $t_2$ respectively. Then $p$, the degree of progression of this elementary tax system, may be conveniently measured either by $p = k(t_1 - t_2)$, or by $p = k \dfrac{t_1 - t_2}{t_1 + t_2}$, when $k$ is a positive constant.

The second of these two formula is to be preferred, following the rule that relative are better than absolute measures of dispersion. Here again, if $p > 0$, we have progression; if $p = 0$, we have proportionality; if $p < 0$, we have regression.

We have now to generalise this formula for a more populous community. Of what more general measure of dispersion is it a particular case? Obviously of many. Two of the simplest are the relative mean deviation and the relative mean difference. (The former, for $n$ quantities, is the average of their deviations, all taken positively, from the arithmetic mean, divided by the arithmetic mean itself. The latter is the average of the differences, all taken positively, between all possible pairs selected from these $n$ quantities, divided by the arithmetic mean.)

If then, we have $n$ incomes, $x_1$, $x_2 \ldots x_n$, arranged in descending order of magnitude, and if the respective rates of tax are $t_1$, $t_2 \ldots t_n$, the degree of progression of the tax system may plausibly be measured either by the relative mean deviation, or by the relative mean difference, of $t_1$, $t_2 \ldots t_n$. Between these two alternative measures, there is *prima facie* nothing to choose. Usually they will corroborate each other's evidence.

These measures are only directly applicable, if $t_1$, $t_2 \ldots t_n$ likewise fall either into a continuously descending, or into a continuously ascending, order of magnitude. In the former case we have continuous progression in the tax scale, in the latter case continuous regression.[1] In both cases a simple measure, either positive or negative, of the degree of progression of the tax scale as a whole can be obtained. But, if the tax scale contains one or more ranges both of progression and of regression, no such simple measure can be applied. The progression or regression of each range must then be measured separately.

[1] And, if $t_1 = t_2 = \ldots = t_n$, continuous proportionality.

Here again we may rest content with a series of such separate measures over defined ranges of income, or we may seek to combine them in one single measure for the tax scale as a whole. What formula for combination will be appropriate?

The answer depends upon the relative weight to be attached, in formulating a single measure, to the component measures for the separate ranges. And this suggests a further distinction.

When we speak of the degree of progression of a tax system, we may mean either the degree of progression of the *tax scale itself*, regardless of the distribution of incomes along the scale, or the degree of progression of the *incidence of the tax scale*, taking account of the distribution of incomes along it. This distinction is a particular case of that between an unweighted and a weighted index-number. Clearly the second meaning is the more significant, for parts of the tax scale will be more densely populated by taxpayers than other parts, and some parts may be wholly unpopulated, so that the scale is, to that extent, inoperative and merely hypothetical. But clearly, also, the first meaning is often the only one which it is practicable to adopt, owing to inadequate knowledge of the distribution of taxable incomes.

If $x_1, x_2 \ldots x_n$ are actual individual incomes, our measure of progression bears the second meaning; if they are only representative income levels, it bears the first. In fact, the Samuel and Colwyn enquiries do not reach beyond representative income levels; they take no account of the number of dwellers at each level.

A few easy sums in arithmetic will illustrate the preceding argument. Take the five tax scales of the Colwyn Committee set out in Table C above, affecting mixed incomes, half from work and half from property, and calculate the corresponding measures of regression and progression. Let the measure applied be the relative mean deviation.

The first scale, for 1903–4, divides into no fewer than four ranges, regressive below £150, progressive between £150 and £1,000, regressive between £1,000 and £2,000, progressive above £2,000. The measures of progression for these four ranges are $-\cdot2$, $+\cdot1$, $-\cdot03$ and $+\cdot002$ respectively. The scale as a whole is not far from proportionality, with regression on the smallest incomes as the most marked departure from this general feature.

The second, third, fourth and fifth scales all divide into two ranges, regressive below, and progressive above, a certain dividing line. This dividing line is at £200 for the second and third, and at £500 for the fourth and fifth. The measures of progression for these two ranges respectively work out as follows:

| | |
|---|---|
| Second scale (1913–14) | —·17 and + ·28 |
| Third scale (1918–19) | —·07 and + ·47 |
| Fourth scale (1923–4) | —·14 and + ·46 |
| Fifth scale (1925–6) | —·13 and + ·48 |

These are rough and ready calculations applied to a mere handful of tax rates. They illustrate method rather than establish secure conclusions. They illustrate also the distinction between changes in the *general level* of a tax scale and changes in its *shape*. Thus there were substantial reductions, between 1923–4 and 1925–6, in the general level of the tax scale. But there was no substantial change in its shape. The element of regression was only fractionally diminished, while the element of progression was fractionally increased.

How should these pairs of measures be combined to give a single measure of the progressiveness of the tax scale as a whole at the different dates? Combining on an 'unweighted' basis, we shall simply set the progressive plus against the regressive minus. This makes each of these four scales progressive on balance, their respective measures of progression being +·11, +·40, +·32 and +·35. The first scale, that of 1903–4, is, however, regressive on balance, its measure of progression being—·13. If, on the other hand, we aim at combination on a properly 'weighted' basis, how shall we weight? The fact that many more individual incomes fall within the regressive, than within the progressive, range points to a heavier weight for the former. The fact that much more taxation is collected within the progressive range points in the opposite direction.

§ 6. This question suggests another line of approach to the general conception of the degree of progression of a tax scale as a whole. Since the interest of this conception is purely distributional, it is not unreasonable to measure the intensity of progression directly, by its effect on distribution, that is to say by its effect on the inequality of incomes. The degree of progression of a tax system might then be measured by some such formula as

$$p = \delta - \delta' + k$$

where $\delta$ is the inequality of incomes before, and $\delta'$ the inequality of net incomes after, the payment of taxation, and $k$ is a positive constant, so chosen as to allow for the fact that inequality is increased, not only by regression and proportionality, but even by the milder degrees of progression.[1] Inequality, in other words, will only be diminished, if $p$ is positive *and greater than k*.

§ 7. Another suggested approach is to define 'progression'—with particular reference to comparatively small changes in taxation—in terms of absolute changes in incomes. Thus Mr. I. M. D. Little argues that in Britain, 'although the 1949–50 income and surtax structure can be seen to be much more progressive than that of 1938, it is somewhat less progressive than that of 1945. Between 1945 and 1950 income tax concessions resulted in greater absolute gains for the better off', except 'in the very high income ranges where there was no change in progression'.[2] But this runs counter to the commonly accepted definition of 'progression'. For if, as Mr. Little suggests, progression is diminished by tax reductions, which increase large incomes absolutely, but not relatively, more than small, then progression is increased by tax increases which take more absolutely, but not relatively, from large incomes than from small. But, if such tax increases are applied to pre-tax incomes, this, by definition, is *regression* or, in the limit, proportionality. This suggestion, therefore, does not seem acceptable.[3]

[1] See Note to Ch. IX, § 5.        [2] *Fiscal Policy*, loc. cit., p. 174.

[3] Mr. Little, in a footnote to his discussion of this point, says 'this is what is here meant by "less progressive", although it could be taken to mean that the proportionate increase in large incomes exceeded the proportionate increase in small ones. Both definitions can be paradoxical, and both are persuasive.' The alternative in his footnote is more consistent with usage and, I think, less paradoxical than his suggestion in the text, and not more 'persuasive', in the pejorative sense in which this word is used by some philosophers.

§ 8. The simplest approach of all and the most empirical is through the drawing of graphs. Draw comparable graphs of two tax scales and look at them. Sometimes, though not always, it will be possible to judge, from mere inspection, that the general slope of one is 'steeper', that is to say more progressive,[1] than the other. This simple procedure is only applicable, of course, to the unweighted tax scale.

But such pictorial representations, relating incomes to average (or 'effective') rates of income tax, including surtax, show for each British budget from 1945 to 1951, whenever changes were made in income tax or surtax, a steepened slope.[2]

[1] Or more regressive, if the slope is reversed.

[2] See some acute and interesting comments on progressiveness and inequality by A. H. Conrad, 'Redistribution through Government Budget in the United States, 1950' (in *Income Redistribution and Social Policy*, edited by A. T. Peacock, 1954).

# CHAPTER XII

## SOME OTHER EFFECTS OF TAXATION

§ 1. To complete our study of the economic effects of taxation, there is a little more to say. A tax may serve some other purpose than merely raising revenue, or minimising the loss of production, or improving distribution. It may be used for planning, as has been claimed for the British purchase tax—either by stimulating certain exports, since this tax falls only on goods made and consumed at home and not on exports, or by stimulating one industry relatively to others, by taxing it more lightly than others, or even by exempting it altogether. And other taxes, besides purchase tax, can also be used in this way, so that the pattern of production may be greatly changed by taxation.

§ 2. Connected with the more general effects of taxation on production are considerations of the cost of collection of taxes. Unnecessarily high cost of collection involves a waste of labour and materials, which is equivalent to a loss of production. Other things being equal, the best tax system is that in which the cost of collection, in proportion to the revenue collected, is a minimum.[1]

As a rule, the cost of collecting a tax on a commodity is the same, per unit of commodity, whether the rate of tax is high or low.[2] Provided, therefore, that the rate of tax is not so high as to reduce the revenue yield below the maximum, the cost of collection, in proportion to the revenue yield, is less for a heavy tax than for a light one. This points to fairly heavy taxes on a

[1] An advantage of raising revenue by currency inflation, which is discussed in Ch. XV, is that there is practically no cost of collection, the cost of printing even very large supplies of paper money being quite small. But there are other costs and disadvantages.

[2] Unless the rate of tax is so high as seriously to stimulate attempts at evasion. Thus high import duties may encourage attempts at smuggling, the prevention of which may be expensive.

small number of commodities rather than lighter taxes on a larger number. Again, cost of collection is generally greater for *ad valorem* than for specific duties, and for duties which differentiate between commodities from different sources of supply than for duties which tax all alike.

So too, as a rule, the cost of collecting an income tax, or an inheritance tax, at a flat rate is the same, per taxpayer, whether the rate of tax is high or low. It is, therefore, cheaper to collect a given revenue at a high flat rate from a small number of taxpayers than at a low flat rate from a larger number. And, when rates are not flat, there is an additional cost of collection in administering exemptions, allowances and graduated rates. The taxation of small incomes presents special difficulties. An income tax on wages must either be paid at intervals of some months, which may inflict great hardship on the taxpayer and is difficult to assess owing to weekly variations in wages, or in a larger number of instalments during the year, an arrangement which further increases the cost and trouble of collection, while not altogether avoiding the difficulty of wage variations. The cheapest way to collect an income tax on wages is to require employers to deduct the tax weekly. And this is now the British practice, both for wages and salaries, under P.A.Y.E. But, even so, the cost of collection is large, though much of it falls on employers and not on the Inland Revenue. British experience shows that, in proportion to the revenue collected, cost of collection is smaller for income and inheritance taxes on the relatively rich than for taxes on commodities, and smaller for the latter than for income tax on the relatively poor. Income tax on wages, based on quarterly assessments, was found to be extremely expensive to collect.[1] This experience

[1] In 1920–1, the cost of collecting £754 millions of inland revenue, chiefly income tax and death duties on the relatively rich, was £8,500,000, or 1·13 per cent of the yield (*Report of Inland Revenue Commissioners*, 1920–1, p. 4). With the reductions in the rates of tax in subsequent years, the total cost of collection also fell, but the cost per cent of the yield steadily rose, and reached 1·61 per cent in 1926–7 (*Report*, 1926–7, p. 10). On the other hand, in 1920–1 it cost £800,000 to collect £5 millions of income tax from wage-earners, or 16 per cent of the yield (answer by Sir Hilton Young to a Parliamentary question on February 14th, 1922). By

P.P.F.—I

supports the view that it is best to tax the rich principally through their incomes and inheritances, and the poor, in so far as they are taxed at all, through a few commodities of wide consumption, such as alcohol and tobacco. This applies to all communities which are highly developed industrially and fairly thickly populated. But in communities which are more primitive industrially, such as India, or more thinly populated, such as Canada, the cost of collection of income tax may be relatively higher as compared with taxes on commodities, and especially as compared with customs duties. For it is often cheaper and more convenient to tax commodities as they cross political frontiers, than as they are produced or sold within these frontiers. Thus the cost of collection of import and export duties is generally lower than that of a sales tax, or turnover tax, yielding the same revenue.

The British method of collecting a large part of the income tax at the source is cheap and efficient and makes evasion more difficult. Other governments, which have been less successful in checking evasion, would be wise to adopt it. And it may be argued that the subjective burden of taxation is less, if one never receives the money, than if one receives it, spends it and then has to repay it to the tax collector.

§ 3. It is also important to keep the cost of collection to the persons from whom the taxes are collected as low as possible. The olive growers in Turkey, who used to be forbidden to dispose of their olives, even though these should go bad through keeping, until the tax collector had called and counted them, would have appreciated this precept. And in many countries taxpayers are subjected to needless trouble in filling up a number of different forms, where one would be enough, and in

1928, Mr. Churchill informed me in answer to a Parliamentary question, the cost had risen to about 33 per cent. For 1934–5 the cost of collecting £667 millions of revenue of all kinds was £12,500,000, or 1·89 per cent (*Financial Statement*, 1934–5, p. 19). For 1952–3 it cost £30·7 millions, or 1·12 per cent to collect £2,753 millions of inland revenue, and £12·5 millions, or ·71 per cent, to collect £1,764 millions of customs and excise (*Reports*, pp. 18 and 17 respectively). Ministers have said in Parliament that no separate figures can be given for the cost of collecting income tax under P.A.Y.E.

replying to the demands of a number of different tax collectors, whose activities are not properly co-ordinated. It has been said that, just as a prudent man visits his dentist once a year, so a prudent and honest taxpayer should pay an annual visit to his Surveyor of Taxes, so that his affairs shall be kept in good order with a minimum of inconvenience.[1] Again, some taxes involve much cost and trouble to those from whom they are collected, even though the latter may be able to pass the tax on to others. So far as it goes, this is an argument against such taxes. An example is the Italian tax on visitors' hotel bills, which compels hotel keepers to keep meticulous accounts in triplicate, on prescribed forms, for every visitor, to plaster these with stamps, to make periodical returns and to submit their books to frequent and prolonged examination by inspectors. The cost of collection of this tax to the Italian Treasury must also be considerable.[2]

§ 4. The effects of taxation upon the steadiness of employment are often misunderstood. It is sometimes suggested that taxation, especially of the rich, increases unemployment. But many of those who entertain this idea seem to suppose that the money collected in taxation is put into a stocking or thrown into the sea. In fact, of course, it is spent by the public authorities concerned. A transfer of purchasing power takes place from the taxpayer to the public authority, and therewith a transfer of the power to 'give employment'. As a result of this transfer, there may be a change in the character, but not necessarily in the total volume, of the demand for labour. Taxation, considered jointly with the corresponding public expenditure, has no general tendency to cause unemployment. And often it may increase employment. If 'marginal propensity to consume', in Keynesian language, is nine-tenths, then £100 raised in taxation initially reduces private expenditure by £90, but public expenditure increases by £100.

Some taxes, however, tend, by their nature, to diminish

---

[1] And those whose affairs are complicated do wisely to consult private experts in tax law.

[2] So all this was explained to me by hotel keepers in Italy between the wars. It may be quite different now.

employment. An obvious example is a tax on employers, in proportion to the number of workers they employ, a common feature in the finance of 'contributory' social insurance. For this is simply a tax on employment. Similarly, any tax imposed on employers, regardless of the amount of business they may be doing, or of the amount of profit or loss they may be making, tends to diminish employment in marginal businesses. The heavier the tax, the wider the margin affected. Local rates, as distinguished from income tax,—and especially heavy local rates—operate in this fashion, being insensitive to variations in employers' 'ability to pay'. For this reason it is legitimate to regard local rates, and also employers' contributions to social insurance, as a 'burden on industry', in a sense in which income tax is not.

It has been suggested that we might reduce unemployment, almost to vanishing point, by giving a sufficient subsidy to employment through the medium of changes in the income tax.[1] Employers might be given, in respect of each of their employees, an allowance in relief of income tax, and the loss in revenue made good by an increase in the standard rate of tax. This would redistribute income tax in favour of those who employed much labour at the expense of those who employed little, and would redistribute industry in favour of concerns employing a high proportion of labour to capital at the expense of those employing a low proportion. From the point of view of employers it would be equivalent to a reduction of wages, though wages would not, in fact, be reduced. There would be an increase in profits and a saving, both to the budget and the Insurance Fund, on unemployment relief. The effect on unemployment of a given subsidy would depend on the elasticity of demand for labour. With ten million working and two million unemployed—approximately the situation in this country in 1935—a relief to employers equivalent to a 10 per cent reduction in wages would absorb one million unemployed if this elasticity was equal to one, and the whole two million if it was equal to two. Owing to the lack of mobility, both

[1] This interesting suggestion was made to me many years ago by Mr. Nicholas Kaldor.

geographical and occupational, of many of the unemployed, this ingenious plan, though it might greatly reduce, could not, in fact, abolish unemployment.

Unemployment, within the institutional framework of capitalism, is not so simple nor so static a problem as this line of approach suggests. It is, in part, a consequence of fluctuation in new investment and in other forms of economic activity. How the budget can be used to promote full employment will be discussed later.[1] But here we may note that unemployment can be reduced by tax reductions, public expenditure remaining the same, or by increased public expenditure, taxation remaining the same. In each case purchasing power, and hence the demand for labour, is raised.

## NOTE TO CHAPTER XII

§ 1. The habit of concentrating attention on the effects of taxation, to the complete exclusion of the effects of the corresponding public expenditure, has led many eminent persons into error.

Thus Mr. McKenna, speaking with the double authority of a Bank Chairman and an ex-Chancellor of the Exchequer, once estimated the 'taxable capacity' of the country, and alleged that it was being 'exceeded', on the assumption that no money, which is taken in taxation, is available for investment in industry.[2] But what, to take only one example, of taxation devoted to the reduction of public debt? If A is taxed £100 in order to pay off £100 of B's War Loan, B will probably reinvest a larger proportion of this amount than A would have invested if it had not been taken from him.

§ 2. 'Taxable capacity' is a common phrase, but a dim and confused conception. The purpose of this Note is to examine it more closely.

We may begin by distinguishing two possible senses in which the phrase may be used: (1) the absolute taxable capacity of a single community, and (2) the relative taxable capacity of two

---

[1] See Ch. XXVII.

[2] In a speech at the Annual Dinner of the National Union of Manufacturers on June 14th, 1920.

or more communities. Thus we may ask (1) how much can a particular community be taxed, without producing various unpleasant effects? When these unpleasant effects result from the operation of the tax system, it is possible to say that 'taxable capacity has been exceeded' in an absolute sense. Or we may ask (2) in what proportions should two or more communities contribute, by taxation, to a common expenditure? If one of these communities is contributing more than its due proportion, it is possible to say that its 'taxable capacity has been exceeded' in a relative sense. But, though it is *possible* to use these forms of words, they do not promote clear thinking. Some of the problems, in connection with which they have been used, are quite unreal, while others, though real and important, are better handled in other terms.

§ 3. Let us first examine the conception of absolute taxable capacity. I have deliberately begun by stating it vaguely in terms of 'unpleasant effects' which follow, if it is 'exceeded'. But exactly what 'unpleasant effects' shall be taken into account? All taxation has the unpleasant effect of reducing the taxpayer's real income in the first instance, though it may sometimes stimulate him to make good the loss, and though his loss through taxation may be outweighed by his gain through the corresponding public expenditure. Much ambiguity has resulted from confusion between two extreme ideas, namely capacity to pay without suffering and capacity to pay regardless of suffering. In the one case taxable capacity is nil, except for the very rich, in the other it is limited only by the taxpayers' total resources. It is plain that the path of practical wisdom lies somewhere between these two extremes, but not that this path can be illuminated by any more precise definition of this elusive conception.

If we go back to first principles, we may define the unpleasant effects of 'exceeding taxable capacity' merely as a diminution of economic welfare. But, as has been pointed out more than once, it is futile to look only at taxation and to ignore the corresponding public expenditure, or to assume that this expenditure brings no benefit to anyone, but represents simply a subtraction from wealth, which is destroyed or thrown into the sea. Yet this seems to be the view of Mr. McKenna in the speech which has already been quoted, for otherwise it is impossible to make any sense of his remarks. Sir Josiah Stamp, later Lord Stamp, commenting upon this speech, says that Mr. McKenna was 'doubtless fully alive to' other considerations, but 'it would be quite unfair to expect, in an after-dinner statement, on a hot evening in June, any exact review of all the issues involved'.[1]

How much public expenditure we can 'afford', and hence how much taxation we can advantageously pay, obviously depends upon the character of the public expenditure. Further, the character of the public expenditure being given, we could, perhaps, 'afford' it, if the taxation was raised in one way, but not if it was raised in another. For the effects of tax-systems, on production, on distribution and in other directions, vary, and the gain from a given expenditure might be greater than the loss from one tax-system, but less than the loss from another which raised the same revenue. These considerations are elementary and have already been set out in earlier chapters of this book. But they lead to a very simple and important negative conclusion. It is quite impossible to fix any definite sum, or any definite proportion of a community's income, which could be said to represent the limits of its taxable capacity at any particular time. For any such estimate would necessarily leave out of account almost every factor relevant to a practical decision on policy.

§ 4. The British Association asked a number of economists and others in 1921, 'How is the taxable capacity of a nation ascertained? Has it been reached and passed, as Mr. McKenna suggests, in the case of Great Britain?' The best and shortest answer to the first question was given by Edwin Cannan, who replied, 'Nohow'. Others were less good. Thus Sir Drummond Fraser, a banker, exclaimed that 'the taxable capacity of a nation is surely reached when taxpayers are forced to borrow from the banks to pay their taxes'. But what about those taxpayers who have no banking accounts? On this criterion, there would be no limit to the taxable capacity of most wage-earners.

[1] *Wealth and Taxable Capacity*, p. 125.

Stamp's discussion,[1] since he was regarded in his day as a high authority on such matters, is worth brief notice. The first approximation, he thinks, to taxable capacity is total production minus the amount required to maintain the population at subsistence level. But he points out that, if all this margin were taken away, for example from Germany for the payment of reparations, future production, and hence future taxable capacity according to his definition, would be diminished. This is certainly true. He then argues that taxable capacity depends also on distribution and will be greater, the greater the inequality of incomes. For this argument I can find no justification. If total production and population are given, and if subsistence level is fixed, and if none are below it, distribution is irrelevant to taxable capacity as defined above. But on the next page Stamp defines it differently, as the margin of total production over total consumption. On this criterion, taxable capacity has very seldom been exceeded anywhere. Then, shifting his ground again, he considers the effects of taxation on work and saving and finds two alternative 'limits to taxable capacity' in (1) the check to total production, and (2) the check to the total revenue yield, as a result of increasing taxation. Finally he gives five good reasons why the 'limit of taxable capacity' is not an absolute or fixed amount. This last conclusion is admirable, but it seems to make nonsense of nearly everything which precedes it. What residue is left at the end of all this and a number of other discussions of this subject? Nothing but a slipshod muddle. But the muddle, though it might have been less slipshod, is inherent in all such enquiries into the absolute taxable capacity of a community. The thing is an illusion. Cannan's 'Nohow' is the last word.[2]

[1] In Ch. IV of his book *Wealth and Taxable Capacity*.

[2] Mr. Colin Clark has argued in the *Economic Journal*, December, 1945, and in his *Welfare and Taxation* (Catholic Social Guild, Oxford, 1954) that the 'safe limit' for taxation is 25 per cent of the national production and that, if taxable capacity thus defined is exceeded 'for more than two or three years', prices will rise and production stagnate. I do not find this convincing. Just to add up taxation and ignore expenditure is a false track. Mr. Clark admits (*Welfare and Taxation*, pp. 8-9) that a great many families are quite unaware of how much, especially of indirect, taxation

§ 5. Relative taxable capacity, on the other hand, may be given an intelligible meaning. Principles, as we have seen, may be laid down to govern the distribution of a given burden between two or more persons according to some criterion of their 'ability to pay'. Similar principles may be applied to two or more communities sharing a common expenditure. 'Ability to pay' may, if we choose, be renamed 'taxable capacity', but the substance of the problem remains unchanged. If the common expenditure increases, the proportions paid by the richer contributors should increase and those paid by 'the poorer should diminish. Conversely, if the common expenditure diminishes. And so forth. Examples of this general problem are furnished by the financial relations between Federal Governments and the State or Provincial Governments below them. And by the problem of distributing the cost of international organisations between the Member States, though the cost of most of these is so trivial that States have been known to take offence at a proposal to diminish their relative contribution, which they regarded as a measure of their international importance.

§ 6. There is no logical connection between relative and absolute taxable capacity. A community may be contributing, in excess of its relative taxable capacity, towards some common expenditure with other communities. But it does not follow that its absolute taxable capacity, according to any of the definitions which we have examined, is being exceeded. Similarly, its absolute taxable capacity, according to some definition or other, may be exceeded, but it does not follow that its relative taxable capacity is being exceeded in any of its common expenditures with other communities. My general conclusion is that relative taxable capacity is a reality, which can, however, be equally well expressed in other terms, while absolute

they are paying. This spoils his disincentive argument. And much public finance works out merely as price rearrangements. You may tax beer and subsidise milk. There is no necessary limit to such rearrangements, which have no uniform effect either on capacities or on incentives, and no bearing on anything which can plausibly be called 'taxable capacity'. Nor does the rate of increase of production in Britain and other heavily taxed countries since 1945 justify Mr. Clark's pessimism.

taxable capacity is a myth. In the interests of clear think-ing, it would be well that the phrase 'taxable capacity' should be banished from all serious discussions of public finance.

# CHAPTER XIII

# THE TAX SYSTEM FROM THE POINT OF VIEW OF ECONOMY

§ 1. The last three chapters have been devoted to a discussion of the economic effects of taxation. It is upon the aggregate of such effects that tax systems must be judged from the point of view of economy. How far taxation should be carried, and how great use should be made of particular taxes, can only be decided, as was said in Chapter II, by considerations of the maximum social advantage to be derived from the operations of public finance as a whole. There is no desirable limit to the increase of any particular tax, except that the social loss, if any, from such an increase should not be greater than the social loss from an equivalent increase in any other practicable tax. There are no desirable limits to the increase of taxation in general, except that the social loss from such an increase should not be greater than the social gain from the corresponding increase of public expenditure, nor greater than the social loss of raising further public income by some other method than that of taxation.[1] The chief of such other methods, apart from borrowing which is discussed in Part IV, will be considered in the next two chapters.

§ 2. As to the ideal distribution of the direct money burden of taxation, considerations of economy lead us to no such simple solution, as do formulæ based on considerations of equity. Nor can we ignore the indirect burdens and other more remote effects of taxation. We may, indeed, still say that taxation should be distributed according to 'ability to pay'. But we must now interpret this last phrase more broadly. We must measure the relative ability of individuals to pay by the relative effects

[1] All this subject also to the qualifications in the footnote on p. 14 above.

123

of their payments, not only upon distribution, but upon production and, indeed, upon the whole economic welfare of the community. Thus A's ability, as compared with B's, to pay a given sum under a given tax system, depends upon the relative economic loss resulting from payment in the two cases, account being taken, not only of the direct loss of economic welfare to A and B respectively, but also of any indirect loss, or gain, to others. Taxation according to ability to pay means, therefore, taxation with the minimum of economic loss to the community as a whole.

But one important practical conclusion, which emerges clearly from the argument of the preceding chapters, is that there is no reason, on grounds of economy, why all, or even the majority of, the members of a community, in which great inequality of incomes prevails, should contribute to taxation. No equitable doctrine, such as equal or proportional sacrifice, which presupposes some contribution, however small, from all who have any economic welfare to sacrifice, finds any strong support in considerations of economy.[1] We are rather drawn towards the doctrine of minimum sacrifice, with widespread exemptions for the poorer sections of the community, and steep progression for the richer. But this doctrine too must be interpreted more broadly by economy than by equity, so as to mean minimum sacrifice in the long run, when all economic effects, including effects on production, are taken into account. And this is much the same thing as maximum social advantage on a long view, so that we return to the general principle from

---

[1] The plausible argument that everyone ought to pay something, in order that a sense of political responsibility shall be widely diffused and a check imposed on public extravagance, does not seem to me to be a strong one. For (1) much taxation, especially taxes on commodities, which are the most convenient method of securing a contribution from the poor, is not clearly realised by the taxpayer; (2) a sense of political responsibility is often found, independently of the consciousness of paying taxes, and, where it is absent, conscious taxpaying will seldom be sufficient to create it; and (3) where a dislike of taxation is keenly developed, especially if its development is provoked by the undiscriminating irritant of press campaigns, etc., false economy, rather than true, is likely to result. Compare Ch. VI, § 5.

which we started. It cannot be claimed that the last three chapters have amplified the principle itself, for its very simplicity and comprehensiveness make this impossible. But they should have thrown light upon its practical application.

# CHAPTER XIV

## INCOME FROM PUBLIC PROPERTY AND PUBLIC ENTERPRISES

§ 1. All public authorities, in varying degrees, own property and conduct economic enterprises. Net money income derived by a public authority from such property or enterprises is a part of its net income. If the finances of the property or enterprise are regarded as part of, or closely linked with, the authority's budget, the receipt of such income makes marginal taxation less, and marginal expenditure more, desirable than would otherwise be the case. Thus the public authority is justified in taxing rather less and spending rather more than it should otherwise do. Often a public authority's property and enterprises are burdened by debts to private persons incurred in respect of their acquisition or development. In such cases debt charges, both for interest and sinking fund, must be deducted from receipts before the public authority's net money income from these sources can be estimated.

§ 2. The relation of the finance of a public enterprise to the budget may take several forms. It may be wholly merged in the budget, any surplus being treated as part of the public authority's revenue, and any deficit as part of its expenditure. Or it may be wholly separate from the budget, any surplus being at the disposal of the enterprise, and any deficit met by borrowing. Or it may be partly merged, in the sense that the public authority receives an agreed contribution, the equivalent of a tax, from the enterprise.

Thus in many countries, including Britain, the accounts of the Post Office are wholly merged in the budget, and so are those of the State Forests.[1] So in Britain are those of the Public

[1] The British Forestry Commission, now the largest landowner in this island—it owned one and a half million acres in 1952, of which 800,000 acres were already under State Forests—was established in 1919, when

Boards responsible for Civil Aviation. But the accounts of the British Public Boards responsible for Coal, Electricity, Gas and Transport (other than by Air) are wholly separate from the budget. Whatever the relationship to the budget, the pricing policy adopted by the public enterprise may have important effects, both on production and on distribution.

§ 3. Mere passive ownership by a public authority, as compared with passive private ownership, will generally not much affect production. If the terms of his tenancy are the same, it makes no great difference to a tenant whether his landlord is a public authority or a private person. In some cases it may be argued that the development of natural resources would have been more effective, and productive methods less wasteful, under public than under private ownership, especially when the latter is much sub-divided among proprietors, whose co-operation is essential to efficient production, but in practice is not forthcoming. Passivity may degenerate into stupid obstruction. There is often a strong argument for the public ownership of minerals on these grounds.[1] In other cases it may be argued that private, rather than public, ownership gives the greater stimulus to development.

Active ownership, on the other hand, which soon merges into actual conduct of enterprises by a public authority, may have

public opinion was shocked, after the fellings of the first world war, to find that we had hardly any timber, and that much of this had little commercial value. Private landowners had planted too few trees and most of these, commercially, of the wrong kind, since 95 per cent of current demand is for soft wood. We could not cover 5 per cent of our total annual timber requirements from the annual produce of our woodlands. The Commission, partly through its own planting and partly by stimulating private planting, is working to a programme designed to enable us ultimately to cover two-thirds of our annual requirements from our own woodlands. It is financed by a direct grant from the Exchequer, supplemented by the steadily increasing sale of forest produce. As its forests mature, it will show a financial surplus, and will give our overseas trade balance a most helpful tilt.

[1] Thus in South-West Durham in the nineteen-thirties seventy million tons of the best coking coal in Britain were 'drowned out' and many pits closed, because private owners would not co-operate in pumping out water. In the nineteen-fifties, under public ownership, pumping has made much of this drowned coal workable, and it is now being reached through new and modern workings.

very great effects on production. A public authority may be either more or less efficient in the present than a private individual or corporation; it may make better or worse provision for the future; it may make greater or less use of monopoly power to restrict output and raise prices. But this large argument—as to the desirable width of the 'public sector'—applied to particular cases, lies outside the field of public finance.[1]

§ 4. As regards effects on distribution, public ownership of property, provided that the latter is free, or at least partly free, from private mortgage, will generally be better than private ownership. For, the larger the proportion of property which is publicly owned in any community, the less unequal is distribution likely to be. The reason for this is that the benefits from public property are likely to be more equally distributed than the benefits from private property.[2] The same argument favours the conduct of enterprise by public authorities. But effects on distribution are partly dependent on the price policy which a public authority pursues.

§ 5. The most appropriate price policy will vary with circumstances. Payment may be made for services rendered by

[1] But some particular cases are interesting. In Norway since 1948 there is a State football pool, with a legal monopoly. It runs nearly all the year round, with Norwegian games in summer and English League games in winter. Only half the money staked goes in prizes; the rest, after deducting expenses, is clear profit. Profits are divided between sport—chiefly for laying out playing fields and running tracks—and science. The Norwegian Atomic Institute's uranium reactor, the first to be built by a small power, was financed partly by football pools. 'The Norwegian public appear perfectly happy with the present arrangement. They believe that the pool is efficiently run, and that running costs have been pared to a minimum; and they know that the only profit-takers are sport and science. Nor do they think it improper that the Ministry of Church and Education should run what is virtually a gambling institution. For many years the Ministry of Social Affairs has, through another State Corporation, had a monopoly of the wine and spirits trade, and the general view seems to be that in gambling, as in drink, a public monopoly is the best safeguard against abuse' (*Economist*, March 20th, 1954).

[2] See my *Inequality of Incomes*, pp. 276–8. But if in Britain we had not nationalised the railways, income from private property would be slightly less unequal, for private railway shares would now be worth very little. The case for this change was in its effects on production.

a public authority according to any of three alternative principles, or according to some combination of these.

Payment may be made, in the first place, out of general taxation, collected from individuals without reference to the cost of the service rendered to them. This is the principle adopted as regards the cost of the military forces, the civil service, free education, national assistance, etc. We may call this the general taxation principle.

Payment may be made, in the second place, by compulsory charges, collected from individuals in proportion to the cost of the services rendered, or presumed to be rendered, to them. This is the principle usually adopted as regards the supply of water by local authorities, as regards the cost of road repair, when it is debited to owners of motor vehicles by means of a tax based on their weight or horse-power, and as regards such services as street cleaning and dust collection, paid for out of local rates. We may call this the compulsory cost of service principle.

Payment may be made, in the third place, by voluntary purchases by individuals at prices fixed by the public authority. This is the principle usually adopted, for example, as regards the cost of postal services and publicly operated transport agencies. We may call this the voluntary price principle.

§ 6. In this third case the further question arises whether prices should be so fixed, as to result in a profit or a loss to the public authorities, and in either case, how much. Where a price is charged, but a loss is incurred and made good out of general taxation, we have a combination of the voluntary price principle and the general taxation principle.

Taking, first, passive ownership of property by a public athority, it is reasonable, as a general rule, to make the same charges to private users of such property as a private proprietor, not possessed of monopoly power, would make. There is, for instance, no general reason for making a gift of any of the economic rent of publicly owned land to the tenants for the time being.[1]

---

[1] Though in Canada much public land was handed over free to settlers, as an inducement to, and on condition of, its speedy development.

Turning to the conduct of public enterprises, i.e. to the supply of services which involve the public authority in appreciable costs, three cases may be distinguished.

Where considerations of social advantage do not require that the services in question should be either specially stimulated or specially discouraged, these should be supplied at a price which will agree, as closely as possible, with that charged for similar services by private traders without monopoly power. Thus surplus stores, or timber from State Forests, should as a rule be sold on the open market at competitive prices, though large fluctuations in such prices should be prevented by suitable marketing arrangements. Unless management is very inefficient, or unless prices are falling rapidly, such competitive prices should at least cover cost. They may also prove a useful weapon for restraining the power of private monopolists to keep prices too high.

But where considerations of social advantage require that the use of the services in question should be specially discouraged—the supply of alcohol, for example—higher prices should be charged, which, as has been pointed out above, must be regarded as containing an element of tax.

The less elastic the demand for such services, the greater the profit which a public authority can obtain by raising their price. But if it is desired to make a publicly supplied service or commodity a large source of revenue, it is practically necessary to establish a legal public monopoly, as various European governments have done with tobacco, matches and other commodities. For otherwise private traders will undersell the public authority and steal away the revenue. Thus the French Government has not only established a State match monopoly, but legally prohibits the private sale of mechanical lighters and other substitutes for matches.

Where, on the other hand, considerations of social advantage require that the use of the services in question should be specially encouraged, lower prices, or even no price at all, may reasonably be charged and the resulting loss made good out of taxation. This policy involves public expenditure and the circumstances, in which it should be adopted, will be discussed later.[1] But free supply is only practicable, without the risk of causing great waste, if demand is inelastic or rationing is easy.[2] Sometimes, however, free supply is adopted simply because it is the most convenient arrangement. This explains, for example, the free use of roads, turnpike gates being inconvenient, and the free postage allowed to the British Army in wartime, where the practical difficulty of selling stamps in the trenches, or during rapidly moving warfare, reinforced sentimental considerations. In all cases of free supply the voluntary price principle disappears and the general taxation principle takes its place.

The general effect upon distribution of these alternative methods of charging, within the voluntary price principle, for services supplied by a public authority is fairly clear. If a service is supplied at a loss, those persons benefit who make most use of it; if it is supplied at a large profit, based on high prices, those persons lose who make most use of it. Thus the supply of a particular service at a loss will make for a more equal distribution, if it is chiefly used by the poor than if it is chiefly used by the rich.[3] And the reverse is true of a service supplied at a large profit. Distribution may also be slightly affected, if the same service or commodity is supplied at different prices to different persons according to their wealth. But price discrimination of this kind is not often practicable.

§ 7. As between the general taxation principle, the compulsory cost of service principle and the voluntary price principle, the choice often depends, as has already been pointed out, largely upon practical convenience. But there are some cases in which, the voluntary price principle being ruled out as too inconvenient, the compulsory cost of service principle is preferable to the general taxation principle, in view of effects on production. An example is the cost of road repair, already mentioned, in so far as this is necessitated by damage done to

---

[1] See Ch. XVIII, § 8, and Ch. XIX, § 2.

[2] See Pigou, *Public Finance*, pp. 25–9.

[3] Obviously also, in considering the effect upon distribution of supplying a service at a loss, account must be taken of the general character of the tax system, which will make good the loss.

road surfaces by motor vehicles, or the cost of new road construction, or road widening, necessitated by the excessive congestion of traffic on existing roads. If such costs are wholly covered by general taxation, there will be a tendency to an excessive diversion of economic resources from other channels into the development of motor road transport, which will, in effect, be receiving a large subsidy from the general taxpayer and, incidentally, from other transport agencies. For reasons discussed in Chapter X, there is a presumption that such a diversion will check production, and there is, therefore, a case for a special tax on motor vehicles, sufficient to cover at least part of the special costs which they would otherwise occasion to the public. On the other hand, this presumption is weakened by the fact that better transport facilities bring many indirect social gains.

§ 8. The effects of alternative pricing policies on the pattern, or composition, of production—and hence on the 'best use of resources'—have been much studied by economists in recent years, particularly the pricing policies of public enterprises. As yet no general agreement has been reached, though a number of interesting ideas have been put into circulation, and some familiar precepts discredited.[1] This is a battle still in progress.

§ 9. Returning to public property and enterprises as a source of public income, we may repeat that such income is of two kinds, first, the equivalent of taxation, where a public authority deliberately charges monopoly prices for its services, and

[1] Notable contributions to this debate include Mr. I. M. D. Little's book *The Price of Fuel* (Oxford University Press, 1953) and Mr. C. A. R. Crosland's article 'Prices and Costs in Nationalised Undertakings' (*Oxford Economic Papers*, January, 1950). Mr. Little condemns the present pricing policies both of the National Coal Board and the British Electricity Authority. He would raise substantially the price of coal consumed at home and would use the resulting surplus, most of which would be handed over to the Treasury as a 'tax on coal', (1) to subsidise, or even supply free, solid-fuel-saving appliances, (2) to increase miners' wages, and (3) to increase child allowances, pensions, etc., so that, for the poorest and largest families, any rise in the cost of living, through dearer coal, would be more than offset. Coal saved at home would swell coal exports. He would revise electricity prices, introducing time-of-day or seasonal tariffs. This would

second, the equivalent of profits from ordinary competitive prices, such as a private proprietor or business firm might charge, under competitive conditions, for the use of property or the supply of services. A large public income of the second kind is easily obtainable, without any serious risk of economic loss to the community, by public authorities which retain the ownership of minerals and other natural resources and, subject if necessary to long private leases, of land, both agricultural and urban. If such obvious opportunities, not to speak of others which are more debatable, had been taken in the past, modern communities would be able both to spend more freely on desirable public objects, and to escape part of their present heavy burden of taxation.

divert much of the demand for electricity to gas and solid fuel. It would heavily cut down space heating by electricity, which is most wasteful of coal and raises peak demands. If these peaks were lowered, great savings could be made in the vast capital programme of the B.E.A. These recommendations have had a mixed reception. Mr. Crosland, in a wider and more abstract treatment, demolishes, both on theoretical and practical grounds, the proposition, previously accepted by many economists, that under public ownership price should equal marginal cost. He proposes instead (1) for public utilities, either a two-part tariff or price to equal average cost, (2) for an industry with many plants and one product, price to equal average cost in marginal plant, marginal costs in all plants being then equated to this price, and (3) for an industry with many plants and many products, average cost to equal average revenue both for individual plants and individual products, marginal costs in all plants being then (as a rule) equated to marginal revenue. He claims that these directives can be couched in familiar commercial language and will give good results in the use of resources.

# CHAPTER XV

# INCOME FROM THE PUBLIC
# PRINTING PRESS

§ 1. A special form of enterprise, which can be made to yield a large income to a public authority, is the use of the printing press to manufacture legal tender paper money.[1] The printing press may be used for this purpose either directly or indirectly; directly when a public authority pays its creditors with new paper money specially printed for the purpose; indirectly when a public authority pays its creditors out of loans to itself from the central bank and issues new paper money to the bank in order, as it is sometimes put, 'to support the additional credit thus created'. Otherwise the bank would have to raise its rates of interest to inconvenient heights, or to restrict credit in other ways, or see its reserves dangerously depleted.[2]

There is no essential difference between the economic effects of the two methods, except that the indirect method, besides mystifying simple minds, involves the public authority in the additional expense of paying interest on its loans from the bank. If, therefore, either method is to be adopted, there is something to be said for the direct method, though it is now unfashionable,

[1] It was pointed out in Ch. I, § 1, that an important distinction among public authorities is between those, generally central or federal, which have the legal right to issue currency, and those, generally local or provincial or state (in the United States, or Australian, or Indian, or Brazilian sense), which have not. Only the former can have a monetary policy. In the province of Alberta the Social Credit party won an election in 1935 on the monetary policy of Major Douglas linked with the ethics of the Gospel. But the courts held that no Canadian province could adopt a monetary policy of its own. The Social Credit Government of Alberta thereupon followed a provincial policy of rather conservative, though still slightly messianic, individualism. They have been in power ever since, much helped by sensational discoveries of new natural resources.

[2] And, of course, even if the government is not borrowing, a bank may need more currency. But this is not an incident of public finance.

134

on the ground both of economy and of intelligibility to the public.

§ 2. Either method, if used to excess, causes an undesirable currency inflation. As to the measure of excess, and even as to the proper definitions of 'inflation' and 'deflation', there is some dispute among economists. We shall return to these questions later, in Chapters XXVI and XXVII, when we consider budgetary policy as a means of stabilising economic life. Here it is enough to note that, if the printing press is so freely used as to cause a substantial fall in the purchasing power of money, this result, at least, may properly be called inflation.[1]

§ 3. It is sometimes said that the issue of a given amount of new paper money by a public authority is equivalent to the levying of a forced loan, free of interest, to that amount. It is more correct to say that it is equivalent to the levying of taxation to that amount—a sort of turnover tax on the use of money. But the purchasing power, in the hands of the public authority, of successive equal additions to the supply of paper money decreases as the value (per unit) of the money falls. If all internal prices, including the prices of services and interest on loans, rose equally, this taxation would fall upon individuals exactly in proportion to their incomes. But, in fact, all prices do not rise equally. Wages generally lag behind the prices of commodities during an upward movement, while investors in gilt-edged securities and other recipients of fixed money incomes, including old age pensions and the recipients of all similar social service benefits, suffer the full force of the fall in the value of money. Inflation, therefore, causes a redistribution of income in favour of business men, who secure windfall profits, at the expense of wage-earners and, still more, at the expense of the recipients of fixed money incomes and of sticky salaries. On balance, inflation seems likely to increase the inequality of incomes and to operate, not as a proportional, but as a regressive tax, supplemented by a subsidy to business men, ordinary shareholders and many speculators. On the other hand, in conditions of full employment, wages need not lag much, if at all,

[1] But, as is pointed out in Ch. XXIV, § 6, an increase in the quantity of money does not necessarily reduce its purchasing power at all.

behind prices, and full employment itself, which may be partly due to inflation, reduces inequality. Further, in so far as great fortunes are held predominantly in forms yielding fixed money incomes, inflation eats them away. But, on the whole, from the point of view of distribution, it is a bad means of raising much revenue.

§ 4. The effect of inflation upon production is sometimes thought to be stimulating, since business men are encouraged by unwonted gains to undertake new enterprises. But it has often been only a temporary and unhealthy stimulus, carrying within itself the seeds of subsequent severe relapse. Doped by inflationary prosperity, many business men become first light-hearted and then light-headed, miscalculate prospects, misdirect resources, and launch enterprises which cannot prosper. The mere cessation, sometimes even a mere slackening in the rate, of further inflation is enough, without any positive deflation, to break the illusion, to destroy 'business confidence', to disappoint anticipations of demand, and to put out of action, sometimes for a long time, a large part of the productive power which these business men control. On the other hand, the continued growth of inflation, and the expansion, even at a constant rate, of the currency, sooner or later destroys the confidence, not only of business men, but of the whole community, in the future value of this currency. Then comes the stage known as 'the flight' from the currency, everyone trying to get rid of it, in exchange for goods and services and other currencies, as quickly as he can, and to conduct transactions, as far as possible, without making use of it at all. There is a sharp fall in the demand for this discredited money, and an increase, more than in proportion to the increase in the total supply, in that part of the supply which is offered for exchange in successive short periods. Hence the fall in its value is continuously accelerated. Under such hectic conditions, which prevailed soon after the first world war in a number of European countries, organised production becomes impossible and all economic transactions, other than by primitive barter, are reduced to a wild gamble. Economic chaos, political upheavals and, perhaps, violent revolution are then not far away.

After the second world war there were fewer examples of 'runaway inflation' of this kind, though there were some drastic devaluations of currencies in terms of gold and dollars.[1] But how to prevent runaway inflation was better understood and by means of controls, over prices and the use of economic resources, the purchasing power of money was much better sustained. In these conditions a moderate degree of inflation may sometimes have helped to create, and to maintain, full employment.

The revenue yield of high inflation rapidly dries up. For, as has already been noted, not only does the value of money tend to fall as its supply increases, but, after a certain point, when the flight from the currency begins and becomes gradually more and more precipitate, the value per unit falls much faster than the supply increases. Well before this point is reached, an impression will have been created of a weak government, whose financial policy is out of control. And this will sap confidence, both in the government and in the currency.

§ 5. Deflation cannot be, like inflation, a source of public revenue. It leads, indeed, to a shrinkage of the revenue. The effects of severe deflation on production are most adverse. For rapidly falling prices, combined with the increasing pressure of fixed money charges, bring losses and even ruin to producers, and thus not only check production but lay resources, both human and material, idle.

The effects of deflation on distribution do not merely cancel out those of inflation, though they tend to enrich the recipients of fixed money incomes at the expense of other classes. But these fixed money incomes themselves may, under extreme pressure on the budget, be reduced by law, or through the insolvency of debtors, public or private, may even cease to be paid at all. Moreover, by causing heavy unemployment, deflation brings extreme poverty to many. And just as inflation, pushed to great lengths, may precipitate political

[1] Or in terms simply of the new currency now introduced. In Czechoslovakia in 1953 one new unit was exchanged for five old, up to a total of two hundred old. Beyond this, one new unit was exchanged for fifty old, thus combining devaluation with drastic redistribution.

upheavals and violent revolutions, so may deflation. In Germany, indeed, in 1933 it did so.

But, though large and rapid changes in the value of money, in either direction, are generally very harmful, moderate and gradual changes may do little harm and even sometimes some good.

# PART THREE

# PUBLIC EXPENDITURE

★

## CHAPTER XVI

## OBJECTS AND CLASSIFICATION OF PUBLIC EXPENDITURE

§ 1. English economists as a body have had surprisingly little to say concerning the principles of public expenditure. As an American critic observes, 'the older English writers did not need a theory of expenditures, because the theory of government which they held implied a fixed limit to governmental functions'.[1] Typical of such writers was Sir H. Parnell, an early nineteenth-century pundit, who maintained that 'every particle of expenditure beyond what necessity absolutely requires for the preservation of social order and for protection against foreign attack is waste and an unjust and oppressive imposition on the public'.[2] On this pronouncement the comment has been made that, if so, we must give up growing crocuses in the public parks, unless it can be proved that they preserve social order, for they are certainly no protection against foreign attack. This barren and negative view of the proper economic activities of the State still finds some support, even if it is seldom expressed in such extreme terms.[3]

[1] Adams, *Science of Finance*, p. 53.
[2] Quoted by Adams, *ibid.*, p. 50.
[3] Not all social expenditure, of course, could be at once retrenched. But some of Parnell's descendants are masters of emotive and question-begging language. 1 take a typical example and have placed the more emotive words in italics. 'The severe *distortion* implied by the *huge* central Budget. . . . A

139

Modern economists have been slow to correct vulgar prejudices on this matter and to place the whole question, from the point of view of principles, upon a rational footing.

Clear thinking is sometimes hindered by the doctrine that 'the State has needs of its own', which can only be satisfied through public expenditure. Taken literally, this is a piece of Hegelian nonsense; taken metaphorically, it is a woolly phrase which leads us nowhere. The truth is, of course, that only individuals have needs, but that some of these needs can be most effectively satisfied through the agency of the State and by means of public expenditure.

§ 2. But what needs are these? How shall they be classified, and distinguished from those needs which can be most effectively satisfied by means of private expenditure? A full answer to this question would be long. I must content myself, in this place, with a few simple propositions and references.

Wagner's 'law of increasing State activities' is as nearly universally true in modern times as any inductive generalisation of this type can hope to be. Wagner maintained that there is a persistent tendency both towards an 'extensive' and an 'intensive' increase in the functions of the State. New functions are continually being undertaken, and old functions are being performed more efficiently and on a larger scale. The evidence of facts supports both these statements. They are true, even if we leave out of account the functions of preparing for war,

system of State finance with *colossal* taxation and expenditure; a parallel system of controls and subsidies, and a *steadily creeping inflation*. . . . Food subsidies are the key. There are other *distortions* of at least equal gravity, such as rent restriction, but . . . if people paid for their food more nearly what it costs to produce it, they would at once have a *saner, clearer* view of the world in which they live; and if at the same time they were allowed to *keep more of their own money*, instead of having it taken from them to pay for the cheap food, the *double incentive* would have a stimulating effect. . . . This line of thought has been *blackguarded* by its opponents as a policy of squeezing the poor to relieve the rich. . . . Those best able to pay, and to suffer the sacrifices, of whatever class, must bear their burden. The vital question is whether it should be done by the old formula of *heavy taxation for taxation's sake*, which has failed, or whether we are to begin to move *decisively* towards a *balanced* and *natural* economy' (*Sunday Times*, leading article, March 9th, 1952).

waging war, and paying for war long after it is over. They are still more obviously true, if these grim functions are included. 'Economy campaigns', in spite of the influential forces behind them, produce only temporary fluctuations in the growth of State activities. They do not reverse the continuous upward trend.

It is a fallacy to explain Wagner's law, as some have done, simply in terms of increasing division of labour. It is true that the individual tends to satisfy fewer and fewer of his own needs without the assistance of others. But the alternative to unassisted individual action is not only collective action through the agency of the State. There is also the alternative of collective action through the agency of private association. Given the increasing division of labour, we have still to explain the fact that the State continually undertakes new functions and strengthens its grip upon old functions, when both might conceivably have been performed by private enterprise.

Modern developments have tended, in many fields, to increase the efficiency of public authorities, relatively to that of those private associations which are the alternative instruments of action. The choice of public, rather than private, agencies is often, therefore, wise today, though it might have been foolish yesterday.[1] And in other cases, though still foolish today, it may be wise tomorrow.

Modern developments, moreover, in other fields, have made it necessary for public authorities to assume new functions, which could not, in fact, have been assumed by private enterprise at all. Functions of public health in modern cities illustrate this. The hygienic conditions of life in London, for example, and hence the risks of disease and ill-health, are in large

[1] 'There are many things,' said Edwin Cannan in 1908, 'which we can trust Edward VII to do for us, which we should not have expected from Edward VI. There is no reason to suppose that the process of improvement (in the efficiency of public enterprise) will not continue, and we may even hope to accelerate it greatly if we take in hand the education of officials, and perhaps even of legislators. While great things may thus be expected of corporate management in the future, there does not seem the same reason for expecting improvement in private enterprise' (*Economic Journal*, September, 1908, p. 417).

measure common both to rich and poor. 'When the rich man dies, his lungs will be as black from London smoke as those of any other city dweller.'[1]

Public expenditure, again, can provide a communal and inclusive use of many goods, where private expenditure tends only to provide an individual and exclusive use.[2] Parks and open spaces, museums, art galleries and public libraries are cases in point.

§ 3. Returning, after this digression, to the main line of our discussion, we may recall the principle, stated in Chapter III, §§ 2–3, that public expenditure should be carried just so far that the marginal social advantages of expenditure in all directions are equal, and just balance the marginal social disadvantages of all methods of raising additional public income; that this is a difficult calculus, but that statesmen must handle it as best they can, since there is no practical alternative.[3] Many objects of public expenditure are not wholly, or even mainly, economic, though most have economic effects and all have economic costs.

[1] W. A. Robson, *The Relation of Wealth to Welfare*, p. 39. This book contains a good discussion of the superiority of public over private expenditure, as a means of securing many of the chief gains of modern civilisation.

[2] Though private expenditure, if impelled by a sense of public duty, both could, and sometimes does, achieve results comparable here to those of public expenditure.

[3] Dr. F. C. Benham in an article on 'The Pure Theory of Public Finance' (*Economica*, November, 1934) makes a brave attempt to construct an alternative, based on a conception of 'neutrality' in a system of public finance. This would 'translate into effect the voluntary judgments and preferences of the citizens'. Each would pay as much as he felt disposed for whatever public expenditure he fancied. But the practical difficulties of such a system are insuperable. Nor, even if they were not, would such a system commend itself to anyone who regarded great inequality of incomes as an evil, which public finance can help to remedy. Mr. Colin Clark in his provocative pamphlet *Welfare and Taxation* proposes to make the use of all social services voluntary, to detach them from the State and to attach them—education to the Churches, health to the Friendly Societies, unemployment to the Trade Unions, old age and widowhood to a National Co-operative Society, etc. This, he argues, would greatly reduce taxation and stimulate production.

A broad distinction may be drawn between public expenditure designed, on the one hand, to preserve the social life of the community against violent attack, whether internal or external, and, on the other, to improve the quality of that social life. In other words, the object may be either to keep social life secure and ordered, or to make that secure and ordered life better worth living.

§ 4. Turning to the actual expenditure of modern public authorities, the following is an obvious catalogue:

(1) The maintenance and equipment of armed forces and police (*a*) in peace, (*b*) in war.

(2) The administration of justice.

(3) The maintenance of the ceremonial head of the State—in monarchical countries, the Royal Family and Court—and of diplomatic representatives abroad.

(4) The maintenance of the machinery of civil government, including ministers, legislators and civil servants.

(5) Public debt charges, including interest, repayment of principal and cost of management.

(6) Expenditure directly devoted to 'fostering industry and commerce', such as the maintenance of consuls abroad and the performance of industrial and commercial functions, such as the supply of currency, conduct of postal services, transport services, etc.

(7) 'Social expenditure' on health, education, child allowances, pensions and other forms of social security, price subsidies, etc.

This is an empirical catalogue rather than a scientific classification. For example, the salaries of the Minister of Education and his staff come under (4), whereas they should, perhaps, come under (7). But such points are unimportant. Net expenditures, and not gross, are significant. For example, postal services are only an object of net expenditure, if the gross expenditure exceeds the receipts, and the administration of justice should be credited with the court fees paid by litigants. Broadly speaking, we may say that (1), (2) and (3) are expenditures designed, at least ostensibly, to keep social life secure and ordered. So is part of (4). So, if we look to its origin, is most of

(5), for the great bulk of outstanding public debts have been incurred for purposes of war. On the other hand, (6) and (7) together with part of (4)—the salaries of factory inspectors, for example—and that part of (5) which covers debts incurred for purposes of economic development, are designed to make a secure and ordered life better worth living. Within this latter group of expenditures, however, the aims of economic and non-economic improvement are often mixed. Expenditure on health and education are examples. It is not the only, or indeed the chief, advantage of being healthy or educated, that one is thereby enabled to produce more wealth or make more money.

§ 5. Classifications, as distinct from catalogues, of public expenditure may follow several alternative principles. We may construct, if we please, a 'functional classification' of expenditure, based on a classification of the various functions actually performed by public authorities. Or, if we prefer, we may adopt a 'departmental classification', based upon the expenditure of the actual administrative departments of government. Even where the range of functions is given, these two methods may yield different results. For the distribution of functions between departments is not invariable, nor logically predetermined. It is often due to historical accident, or to the ambition of influential politicians to magnify their office, or to the mutual jealousy or vested interests of officials. But to pursue this matter further, even by way of illustration, would be to drift too far into descriptive detail.

We may, however, notice here some further distinctions which throw light on particular problems. Thus we may distinguish between optional expenditure, which the public authority is free to increase or diminish at its pleasure, and obligatory expenditure, in respect of which, owing to past contracts and other legal commitments, it is not free. But this distinction, though valid in a limited way, is only one of degree. For, on the one hand, contracts and other legal arrangements may be revised to the advantage of the public authority—this has been a common practice with governments embarrassed by unbalanced budgets—and, on the other, expenditure, which is legally optional, may be obligatory from the point of view of political expediency.

Again, we may distinguish between real, or 'exhaustive', expenditure on the one hand, and mere transfer expenditure on the other. Real expenditure implies the actual using-up of commodities and services, which would otherwise have been available for some other purpose.[1] Transfer expenditure implies, in itself, no such using-up, but only a transfer, from one person to another, of command over commodities and services. Expenditure on armaments and on education are examples of real expenditure; expenditure on debt interest and on pensions are examples of transfer expenditure.[2] Real expenditure determines, so far as it goes, both the amount and the character of production. Transfer expenditure does not directly influence either, though it has direct effects on distribution and indirect effects upon production.

Again, a classification, which is adopted in many text-books, distinguishes expenditures according as they confer divisible or indivisible benefits, or, in other words, particular benefits on individual members of the community, or common benefits on all (or most) members. To this distinction, which is relevant to a discussion of the effects of public expenditure upon distribution, we shall return in Chapter XIX. There is, however, another which it is convenient to consider first. This is the distinction between grants and purchase prices.

[1] The nature of the distinction is illustrated by Smart's observation (*Studies in Economics*, pp. 269–70), that 'society involves in the same condemnation the man who spends his income in gambling or speculation and the man who wastes it in foolish eating and drinking, although the world as a whole loses nothing by the former and loses everything by the latter'.

[2] Assuming that the recipients of debt interest and of pensions are members of the same community as the taxpayers who provide the funds for those payments. If, however, the recipients belong to one community and the taxpayers to another, the payments are real expenditure from the point of view of the second community.

# CHAPTER XVII

## GRANTS AND PURCHASE PRICES

§ 1. The division of public expenditure into grants and purchase prices, corresponds to that of public income into taxes and selling prices.[1] An individual, who receives public money or money's worth, may or may not render in return a direct *quid pro quo* to the public authority. In the former case the public authority makes a purchase from him; in the latter case it makes him a grant. This grant may consist either of money, or of services, such as medical treatment or education or the security presumed to be derived from armed forces or police. Payments by a public authority to any of its employees, by way of salaries and wages, or to contractors whom it employs, are purchase prices. On the other hand, payments of old age pensions, or contributions out of general revenue to schemes of social insurance, are grants.

Just as there are costs of collection of taxes, so there are costs of administration of grants. These are, from the public authority's point of view, purchases incidental to grants. Thus a teacher's salary is a purchase incidental to the grant of free education, and a policeman's pay is a purchase incidental to the grant of security.

Payments of interest on public debts, if we look to their origin in the past, may be represented to be purchase prices, paid for the investment of money in public securities. But, if we look to their character in the present, they are grants. For

[1] Compare Ch. IV, § 2. What I here call 'grants' are often called 'subsidies' and in what follows I shall use these two words indifferently. Many payments by the British Government are officially described as 'grants', e.g. to local authorities, to Universities and to individual students and researchers. 'Grant' is shorter, by two syllables, than 'subsidy' and on this ground to be preferred. But 'subsidise' is shorter by one syllable (though 'subsidises' is not) than 'make a grant to'.

the receivers of interest are not rendering any present *quid pro quo* to the public authority.[1] It is proper, therefore, in a study of things as they are, to treat these interest payments as grants. But sinking fund payments, to redeem public securities, are purchases. Pensions of all kinds, paid from public revenue, are best classed as grants, though in some cases they may be regarded as deferred payments for past services rendered by the recipients.

§ 2. The parallel between taxes and grants on the one hand, and purchase and selling prices on the other, may be carried a good deal further. Just as a selling price may include an element of tax, when a public authority is selling above the price which a non-monopolist private seller would charge, so a purchase price may include an element of grant, when a public authority is buying above the price which a non-monopolist private buyer would offer. This may be the case if higher salaries or wages are paid in public than in comparable private employment. But if the higher pay results in proportionately better work, the element of grant disappears and the whole payment is a purchase price. Again, a public enterprise run at a loss covered by taxation makes grants, in proportion to their purchases, to all its customers. So too when food or rent subsidies keep food prices or rents below what they would otherwise be.

The distinction between grants and purchase prices may be compared with that between transfer expenditure and real expenditure, which was noticed in the last chapter. All grants of money are transfer expenditure and, in general, purchase prices represent real expenditure. But, where a purchase price includes an element of money grant, it includes a corresponding element of transfer expenditure. Moreover, grants of particular services or commodities presuppose a real expenditure in these particular directions.

---

[1] This proposition is repugnant to those who hold that all interest is a price paid for 'the service of waiting', no matter how long. But note the joint dictum of Bowley and Stamp, two very respectable authorities (*The National Income*, 1924, p. 41), that 'the most important transfers of purchasing power, for which the recipient renders no current economic services, are interest on war debt and pensions'.

§ 3. A grant is a negative tax and, therefore, to every proposition regarding taxes, there corresponds a proposition regarding grants. Thus grants, like taxes, may be classified as direct and indirect.[1] If we base the distinction between direct and indirect on incidence, a grant may be said to be direct, when the whole benefit accrues to the person to whom the grant is made. It may be said to be indirect, if the benefit is passed on, in whole or in part, from the person to whom the grant is made to some other person, owing to a consequential change in the terms of some contract or bargain between them. Thus an old age pension is a direct grant.[2] A subsidy to a private enterprise is an indirect grant, in so far as part of the benefit is passed on to consumers through lower prices or to workers through higher wages, but direct, in so far as it increases profits.

The incidence of grants is similar to that of taxes.[3] The incidence of a (money) grant is upon those who receive the direct money benefit of the grant. The incidence of a direct grant is, by definition, wholly on the person to whom the grant is made. The incidence of an indirect grant, or subsidy, in respect of any commodity is divided between the buyer and the seller in the ratio of the elasticity of supply of the commodity to the elasticity of demand for it.

§ 4. Parallel to the proper distribution of the burden of taxation is the proper distribution of the benefit of grants.

Take, for instance, the conception of 'ability to pay' taxation. Corresponding to this we may formulate a conception of 'ability to receive' grants. But, just as 'ability to pay' should be interpreted to mean ability to pay *with a minimum of economic loss*,[4] so 'ability to receive' should mean ability to receive *with a maximum of economic gain*. From the three alternative applications of the principle of ability to pay, namely minimum

[1] Compare Ch. V, § 2.

[2] Relatives or friends, who are supporting an old person, will benefit through his receipt of a pension, in so far as they reduce the amount of assistance which they were previously giving. But this benefit is best classified as indirect and not as part of the incidence of the grant of the pension.

[3] Compare Ch. VII, and especially § 2.

[4] See Ch. XIII, § 2.

sacrifice, proportional sacrifice and equal sacrifice, we may derive three alternative applications of the principle of ability to receive, namely maximum benefit, proportional benefit, and equal benefit. Maximum benefit would be attained, as a first approximation, by making no grants to anyone whose income was above a certain level, and by raising all smaller incomes, by means of grants, to exactly this level. This plan may seem too crude for practice, but it is an approach to the excellent principle of a national minimum standard of economic conditions below which no member of a civilised community should be allowed to fall.[1] There is nothing to be said for adopting the principle of either proportional or equal benefit in the distribution of grants, nor, corresponding to the precept that the inequality of incomes should not be altered by taxation, for the precept that this inequality should not be altered by grants. From this last precept, which is no more acceptable than its mate, it follows that the richer of two old men should receive the larger old age pension. The same consequence follows both from proportional and from equal benefit—the difference in favour of the richer old man being larger in the former case. Equal *grants*, as distinct from equal *benefit*, can often be defended on grounds of administrative simplicity. And such grants are progressive.

Just as a particular tax, or a tax system as a whole, may be either proportional, progressive or regressive, so may a particular grant, or a grant system as a whole. Under a progressive grant system, the larger the recipient's income, the smaller the proportion which is added to it by grants, while under a regressive grant system, the larger the income, the larger the proportion which is added.

§ 5. Finally, just as, with taxation, incidence is only part of the wider question of effects, so it is with grants. The next three chapters, therefore, will be devoted to a discussion of the

[1] And it is exactly the plan adopted (reading 'rateable value per head' for 'income'), on the joint initiative of myself when Chancellor of the Exchequer and Mr. Aneurin Bevan when Minister of Health, in the British Local Government Act of 1948 for the distribution of the Exchequer Equalisation Grant among local authorities.

economic effects of grants, and of public expenditure generally. As in the corresponding case of taxation, more light is thrown upon the practical desirability of various policies by such a study in economy than by considerations of equity.

# CHAPTER XVIII

## EFFECTS OF PUBLIC EXPENDITURE ON PRODUCTION

§ 1. The distinction between grants and purchase prices is less prominent in this chapter, on the effects of public expenditure on production, than in the next, on the corresponding effects on distribution. In this chapter the essential fact is that public expenditure, combined with taxation and other methods of raising public income, causes large diversions of economic resources, from the channels into which they would otherwise have flowed (or in which they might have stagnated in unemployment), into channels determined by public policy. And this may cause large changes both in the character and in the total volume of production.

Just as taxation, other things being equal, should reduce production as little as possible, so public·expenditure should increase it as much as possible.

§ 2. Some people still do not seem to realise that public expenditure can ever increase production. Consider, for example, the following pronouncement, which, though more than thirty years old, has quite a modern ring. 'The proportion of government expenditure to national income is several times as great as it was before the war, which means that a far smaller proportion of that income is available for provision for old age, for saving and business enterprise.'[1] It is here assumed that ·government expenditure' may be simply subtracted from ·national income', and that the result of this subtraction

---

[1] From a letter on 'Prodigal Public Expenditure' (*Manchester Guardian*, July 16th, 1920), bearing the following signatures: 'Askwith, Chalmers, Cowdray, A. Herbert Dixon, R. A. Hadfield, Inchcape, Islington, Godfrey Locker-Lampson, Walter Leaf, Midleton, John Denison Pender, W. Peter Rylands, Salisbury, Selborne, Arthur Steel-Maitland, Richard V. Vassar-Smith.' And all these were well-known political, financial or industrial names in their time.

represents, in large measure, what 'is available for provision for old age, for saving and business enterprise'. But this misses two simple points. First, much public expenditure involves mere transfers of purchasing power within the community. But the purchasing power, after transfer, may still serve, largely, the same purposes as before. As we have seen, payment of interest on internal public debt and payment of old age pensions are obvious examples of such transfers. The authors of the pronouncement just quoted seem to suggest that no dividends on War Loan are ever saved, and that old age pensions are not a provision for old age. Second, much public expenditure, on education and health for example, increases the productive power of the community, and hence the resources available for the purposes to which the authors refer. Public 'expenditure', in short, includes public savings, and may promote much investment in human, as well as in material, capital, as well as much enterprise, both public and private.

A correct view of the effects of public expenditure on production can only be reached by following a line of enquiry parallel to that of Chapter X on the effects of taxation on production. It is necessary to consider successively (1) effects upon ability to work, save and invest, (2) effects upon desire to do these things, and (3) effects of diversions of economic resources as between different uses and localities.

§ 3. Before taking up these lines of thought, we shall make a digression. A large part of modern public expenditure is devoted to purposes which make no direct contribution to economic welfare. Provision for national defence, either by nations acting independently or as members of some international group—that is to say expenditure on armaments and armed forces—is the most striking example of this, and it is often said that such expenditure is economic waste. For men cannot eat guns or explosives. And the multiplication of warships is not an economical solution of the housing problem.

The economic waste and destruction of modern warfare need no emphasis, though many of the most overwhelming evils which war brings with it—pain and terror, anxiety and bereavement, hatred and moral degradation—lie outside the economic sphere. But it is undeniable that war expenditure, which results in preventing or limiting invasion or in bringing military victory, diminishes the economic (as well as the non-economic) loss which invasion or defeat would otherwise have caused. It is even possible that, in exceptional circumstances, a short and successful war may bring to a community as a whole a balance of economic gain, while nearly every war brings gain to a favoured few, even among the vanquished. But, if the speeches of statesmen are the key to history, such possibilities of gain play no part in the diplomacy which from time to time launches a multitude of lives upon a sea of death.

Yet the simple economist, unversed in these diplomatic mysteries, cannot deny that the services of soldiers, sailors and airmen, and even of arms manufacturers, may, under favourable conditions, contribute to his security and so be in principle entitled, no less than the services of plumbers, scavengers and fire brigades, to a place in the aggregate of national 'production' in its widest sense. Best of all, they may prevent, rather than help to wage, a war. But here, as elsewhere, there is need for true economy, and a danger that the resources used for defence may be either too great or too small. They may be too great to be borne without a serious weakening of production for civilian needs, or too small to serve their primary purpose of preventing war, or their secondary purpose of averting defeat if war comes.

Every defence programme subtracts economic resources from other uses in which they might have made a direct contribution to economic welfare. It subtracts, in particular, the services of a picked body of men, above the average in physical and not below it in mental powers—in the case of scientists, some of the pioneers of new thought. And it subtracts large quantities of important commodities, such as iron, coal, oil and many of the rarer minerals. The communities concerned certainly have less economic welfare and they may have no greater security. For security is not only material but psychological. And the greater the part which armed forces and armed habits of thought play in the life of a nation, the smaller is the psychological security against war. It is fear of the armed forces of other

nations which has often pushed nations into war. Few propositions are more obvious than that the cutting down of armed
forces, all the world over, to the level of an international police
force would be a condition both of maximum security and of
maximum economic welfare. What is required here is an international agreement for the limitation of output, and for the
policing of its use. Distrust hinders this. But science does not
slumber nor sleep and if, indeed, another war should come, in
which the greatest powers in the world took part, this would
not be just 'another war'. It would be a colossal chemical
catastrophe, which little that we value would survive.

§ 4. I now return to the effects of public expenditure upon
people's ability to work, save and invest.

Just as taxation will reduce a man's ability to work, if it
diminishes his efficiency, so public expenditure will increase it,
if it increases his efficiency. This opens a wide field for socially
desirable expenditure, which will be further considered below
under the head of diversion of economic resources. Some grants
in money may increase the efficiency, not so much of the direct
recipients, as of their children in the future. This is an important
part of the case for widows' pensions, family allowances and
similar payments. Further, certain grants in kind, such as
educational and medical services and house accommodation,
even at 'uneconomic rents', will do more to increase efficiency
than equivalent grants in money, which would often be spent
to less good purpose.[1] Such reactions of grants upon efficiency
are one measure of the recipients' 'ability to receive', which is
analogous to taxpayers' 'ability to pay'.[2]

Again, just as all taxation will reduce the victim's ability to
save, if he has any margin out of which saving is possible, so

[1] Not only because the recipients might spend less wisely from their own
point of view, but also because communal provision. e.g. of education and
health, is often far more efficient and economical than any alternative
method of providing the same services. See Tawney, *Equality*, pp. 127–32.

[2] Ability to work is sometimes limited by law. A grant, e.g. a 'retirement
pension', may be conditional on the pensioner not working, or, as under
the present British law, not earning more than £2 a week. The case against
such conditions is well set out by Mr. Brian Abel-Smith, *The Reform of
Social Security* (Gollancz, 1953), pp. 29–32.

all public expenditure will increase the beneficiary's ability to save, in so far as it gives him any additional margin of this kind. If £100 is taken from A by taxation and handed over to B— it matters not whether as dividends on War Loan, or in payment of a civil servant's salary, or on any other pretext— the increase in B's ability to save exactly offsets the decrease in A's.

Ability to invest will be increased if public expenditure places investible funds in the hands of any agency, either public or private, whose business it is to undertake capital expenditure.

§ 5. Turning from effects upon ability, to effects upon desire, to work, save and invest, it was argued in Chapter X, § 3, that here the expectation of future taxation is more important than the fact of present taxation. The expectation of future benefits from public expenditure has, likewise, an important influence. In many cases the amount of these future benefits, by way of grants, is independent of the amount of the recipient's future work and saving. War pensions and interest on War Loan are, once more, good examples. The expectation of such fixed, periodical and, so far as the future is concerned, unconditional receipts will seldom[1] increase desire to work or save, and, where demand for income in terms of effort is very inelastic, will decrease this desire so much that the effort put forth will produce an income smaller by nearly the full amount of the grant. Generally, such grants will be disincentive. But not all grants are thus fixed and unconditional. The prospect of a conditional grant, which will be paid only in the event of sickness or unemployment, will not decrease present desire to work.[2] In some cases, by raising morale, it may even increase it, and thus be incentive. Again, the prospect of a grant which is not fixed, but increases, the greater the future efforts of the recipient, such as a subsidy to his earnings or savings, would,

---

[1] Though the expectation of a small fixed minimum income in the future may, by creating a foundation of security, make it seem more worth while to build on this foundation than it would have been to start building without it.

[2] Unless the grant is larger than, or almost as large as, the earnings lost through sickness or unemployment.

unless demand for income was very inelastic, increase his desire
to work or save. But grants of this kind are not often feasible
in practice.[1] On the other hand, the prospect of a grant which
diminishes with the future efforts of the recipient (i.e. the
greater the efforts, the less the grant) will be disincentive.
Similarly a grant which diminishes in proportion to his past
efforts, as when, under a 'means test', an unemployed man with
savings gets less than one without. Thus 'thrift is penalised'.

§ 6. We may now go on to consider the effects on production
of diversions, due to public expenditure, of economic resources
as between different uses and localities. Taking first diversions
as between different uses, the special case of expenditure on
armed forces has already been discussed. Akin to this are all
other cases of expenditure designed, according to the classification adopted in Chapter XVI, § 2, to keep the social life of the
community secure and ordered. All that can be said of such
expenditure, in this connection, is that it should be governed
by the principle of economy. The advantage of a little more
security and order must be balanced against the disadvantage
of doing without those other commodities and services, which
would otherwise have been produced.

Let us now turn to that other broad category of expenditure,
which is designed to make the secure and ordered life of the
community better worth living. Sometimes the diversion,
through public expenditure, of economic resources into particular uses will increase production.

§ 7. Many examples might be given, but it is to obtain a better
economic provision for the future that the most far-reaching
diversions may be justified. The economic institutions of
capitalism are such that, apart from the intervention of public
authorities, too little provision of this kind is made, and what
is made is badly composed. Too little provision is made, because there are very few people who do not to some extent

[1] The proposals of the Millard-Tucker Committee on the treatment for
taxation of financial provisions for retirement (Cmd. 9063 of 1954) may
be defended as encouraging saving. They are, in effect, a series of subsidies, through tax relief, to some sorts of saving. But they are open to
objection on grounds of distribution, and of equity between pensioners.

discount the future, and especially the more distant future.[1] Most people would prefer to spend £100 now rather than to have £105 to spend a year hence. Many would prefer £100 for themselves now rather than £1,000 for themselves, or, in the event of their death, for some other person, thirty years hence. Again, what provision is made is badly composed, in the sense that too large a proportion takes the form of material capital and too small a proportion the form of human capital and of knowledge. For the return obtainable by an individual from a wise investment in human capital or in knowledge is generally smaller than that obtainable from an equally wise investment in material capital. But, for this very reason, the return to the community as a whole is generally greater from an increase in the former type of investment than from an increase in the latter.[2]

There is thus a large field for the intervention of public authorities to increase economic provision for the future and to create a better balance between its component elements. These two objects furnish the key to nearly all public expenditure designed to increase productive power.

From the point of view of production, those forms of public expenditure are socially desirable which will increase productive power more than it would be increased, if the funds required were left in private hands. To this category belongs expenditure on (1) debt redemption, where most of the money repaid will generally be reinvested;[3] (2) many projects of transport development, especially in new countries, irrigation, afforestation, etc., which may be expected to yield large returns in the long run, but not in the immediate future, and which do not, therefore, attract the private investor; (3) the increase of

---

[1] See Ch. III, § 5. 'Posterity was a chilly thing to work for, no matter how much a man happened to love his own, or other people's already-produced children' (T. E. Lawrence, *Seven Pillars of Wisdom*, p. 191).

[2] For a discussion of these important points see Pigou, *Economics of Welfare*, pp. 24–7 and 773–81; Cannan, *Wealth*, pp. 138 and 199–201; and my own *Inequality of Incomes*, pp. 264–8.

[3] In the financial sense. But it must also be invested in the real sense, if employment is to be maintained and production increased. See § 9 of this chapter.

knowledge, by the encouragement of research and invention and, as regards opportunities of employment, by the maintenance of employment exchanges; (4) education and training; (5) public health; and (6) expenditure in aid of social security schemes, in so far as these promote efficiency and hence increase production.[1]

Under (2) above, which is a broad category, fall many cases in which the State can take a more confident view about future uncertainties than the private investor, largely because it can itself influence the future, e.g. by encouraging new towns to grow up along a new railway, and many cases where external benefits, of interest to the State but not to the private investor, result from the expenditure, e.g. where irrigation or afforestation favourably influences climate and rainfall over a wide area.

There are, of course, limits to the amount that can be advantageously spent by public authorities on any of these objects, but there are strong grounds for believing that many of these limits still lie well ahead of most actual expenditures. Hence increased public expenditure in many of these directions is desirable in order to bring about that distribution of the community's resources between different uses, which will give the best results, balancing without bias the present and the future.

In Britain we have established a national educational service and a national health service, both free, subject to some minor exceptions, and paid for out of public funds. Likewise a wide-ranging system of social security. Payments are also made from public funds for food subsidies on selected foodstuffs and for rent subsidies on houses built to let by local authorities.

Some argue for curtailment of some of these social expenditures, others for their extension. In each case we must balance the effects of a change, in either direction, in social expenditure against the effects of a corresponding change in taxation.

§ 8. Public expenditure to encourage the use of selected

[1] But even if a particular social security system were adverse to output, maximum production should not be the sole objective of public policy. Squeezing extra output out of our population at the cost of undue strain on particular groups would be an abysmal confusion of means and ends' (Abel Smith, *loc. cit.*, p. 11).

commodities and services may thus greatly increase productivity. But this policy, when it takes the form of the supply of such commodities and services free, or much below cost price, raises some further questions. Since a lowering of price leads to an increase of demand, a public authority must be prepared either to increase correspondingly the supply of the commodities and services concerned, or to ration the supply, if the increased demand exceeds it. But a very large increase of supply would sometimes mean an excessive and wasteful diversion of economic resources. On the other hand, rationing, though often a sound and popular policy in war time, seems less appropriate and is less popular in time of peace. The policy of free, or very cheap, supply is, therefore, better suited to commodities and services with an inelastic, than for those with an elastic, demand at low prices. Thus free education is, in this sense, more economical than free railway travel or free clothing. Some have thought that the demand for medical services is very inelastic at low prices. But this seems doubtful. Probably the truth is that health services in general, even when free, are, in fact, rationed by the shortage of doctors and the length of surgery queues.

§ 9. It follows from the preceding argument that to promote the growth of material capital, at the expense either of human capital or of knowledge, is a mistaken policy which will tend to diminish, and not to increase, production. But to promote the growth of material capital, at the expense of consumption which does not add appreciably to human efficiency, is a policy which will increase production. Broadly, such a policy will substitute saving, either by public authorities or private persons, for spending. There are very large possibilities here, which modern governments have hardly yet begun to explore. The Government of the Soviet Union is an exception. Under its successive Five Year Plans provision for the future has been made, by means of public investment, on an enormous, possibly even on an excessive, scale. There has been no discounting of the future here; rather the contrary.

But it is not less important to provide new enterprise to absorb new savings than to provide new savings to sustain new enterprise. The volume of new investment, in any given period, need not coincide with the volume of new savings. The lack of this coincidence is one of the causes of instability in the price level, of inflation and deflation, and of unemployment. To create and maintain such a coincidence public intervention is often required, partly through programmes of public enterprise financed by loan, partly through the organisation and stimulus of new investment by private enterprise. But public enterprise can also be financed by taxation. This method has indeed been used by many governments in many parts of the world. The magnitude and speed of achievement of such a programme is limited, not by the obstacle of the rate of interest, as sometimes with programmes of public or private capital development by loan, but by the obstacle of the rate of taxation which, if it were raised above a certain point, or if it were raised too rapidly, would arouse effective opposition.

The effects of financing public development by loan and by taxation differ in several respects. Finance by taxation causes only a transfer, and changed use, of purchasing power, not an addition to it. But finance by loan may increase purchasing power through an expansion of credit. And sometimes such an increase is desirable, in order to stimulate production and dispel depression. On the other hand, just because it makes no addition to purchasing power, but only transfers it and changes its use, finance by taxation may have an advantage over finance by loan in checking an unhealthy boom. This point is dealt with in Chapter XX. The effects of the two methods on distribution also differ, as is explained in Chapter XIX. Even when funds for public development are raised by taxation, they may, of course, be lent, and interest charged, to public enterprises. For this purpose a public loan fund for development, fed by taxation, may be created.

Similarly, a budget surplus, instead of going automatically to debt reduction, might be lent either to public bodies, or to selected private enterprises, in which the Treasury, or some public agency created for the purpose, would become a shareholder. The case for such loans to private enterprise is strengthened, if there is evidence of a shortage of risk capital.

§ 10. Diversions, through public expenditure, of economic resources as between different localities will sometimes increase productive power. A distribution of grants from a central exchequer to local authorities, in such a way as to stimulate the latter in the efficient performance of their functions, may do this. Further, special grants in aid of public services in the poorer areas—such as the British Exchequer Equalisation Grant already referred to—will enable the public authorities in these areas to make a better provision for these services, many of which may greatly improve the economic efficiency of their areas, than could have been made, if a given total of grants had been less unequally distributed. Of even greater importance has been the deliberate steering, by geographical planning and financial inducement, of new industries, public and private, into the pre-war 'distressed areas' of Britain. By establishing arms factories, later converted to civilian production, in these neglected areas, and other factories, with the aid of the Distribution of Industry Act of 1945, a much greater diversity and stability of employment has been created. Unemployment among men, often above 50 per cent before the war, has fallen almost to the national average, and there is now a large employment of women in these areas, particularly in light industries, which before the war did not exist at all. In these 'development areas', as they are now officially named, as compared with pre-war years there has been a spectacular social transformation and a remarkable increase in production.

§ 11. The preceding argument has assumed a framework of private property and private enterprise, within which we have studied the diversion of economic resources in consequence of public expenditure, and in an earlier chapter in consequence of taxation, from that distribution between uses and localities which would otherwise have come about. This method of study is most appropriate when the range of public authorities' economic activities is narrow. It becomes less and less appropriate as this range widens, since the basis ·of comparison becomes more and more remote and unreal. In the Soviet Union, for example, Public Finance merges into Public Economy as a whole, and is dominated by a central planned direction of all the economic activities of the community towards certain deliberately chosen ends. Thus in the first Five Year Plan light industry was stiffly taxed to promote the growth of heavy industry and electrification, and this tendency seems to have continued until very recently. With the abolition of private property in the means of production, and with the disappearance of all large inherited fortunes, though not of all large earned incomes, private saving becomes of small importance. The individual taxpayer fades into the background and the public enterprise becomes the chief taxable subject. The form of any useful discussion of public finance must, therefore, be adapted to the current economic institutions.

§ 12. To sum up the main conclusions of this chapter, whereas taxation, taken alone, may check production, public expenditure, taken alone, should almost certainly increase it. Expenditure on police and armed forces, if not overdone, and on the other apparatus of order and security, creates the conditions under which alone organised production can take place at all. Expenditure of other kinds acts on production in three ways, first, through its effects on ability to work, save and invest; second, through its effects, incentive and disincentive, on desire to do these things; third, through diversions of economic resources as between different uses and localities. Under the first head, the stimulus to production is clear, just as the corresponding check due to taxation is clear. Under the second head, much depends, as in the case of taxation, on the character both of persons and of policy. There are cross currents, and it is difficult to be sure which flows strongest. Under the third head, there are great possibilities, hitherto not fully exploited, of stimulating production, more especially through wise expenditure on health, education and the increase of knowledge, and through a stimulus to saving, both public and private, provided adequate opportunities for investment are created. Such expenditure, in turn, will indirectly increase ability, and perhaps also desire, to work, save and invest.

Striking a balance between the two sides of the account, there can be little doubt that the stimulus to production afforded by a wise system of public expenditure should far outweigh the check, if any, to production resulting from the taxation and other devices required to finance this system, provided that these too are well chosen. But the actual public expenditure of many modern communities, largely on armed forces and war debts, is a melancholy spectacle, on which the shrill and undiscriminating clamour of 'economists', in the vulgar sense of the word, is an inadequate commentary.

# CHAPTER XIX

# EFFECTS OF PUBLIC EXPENDITURE ON DISTRIBUTION

§ 1. A study of the effects of public expenditure on distribution requires a discussion, on parallel lines to that in Chapter XI, of the effects of taxation on distribution. The parallelism is complete as regards that part of public expenditure, which consists of grants conferring special benefit on individuals. We may, therefore, begin with public expenditure of this sort.

Those who find Wagner's 'socio-political' view of taxation hard to swallow, may find it a still harder saying that, other things being equal, that system of public expenditure is best, which has the strongest tendency to reduce the inequality of incomes. Yet this follows logically from the view that a less unequal distribution is desirable.

§ 2. As was pointed out in Chapter XVII, § 4, a particular grant or subsidy, like a particular tax, may be regressive, proportional or progressive. A grant is regressive if, the smaller the recipient's income, the smaller the proportionate addition made by the grant; progressive if, the smaller the recipient's income, the larger the proportionate addition; proportional if, whatever the size of the recipient's income the proportionate addition is the same. Thus a universal and equal old age pension payable to all who attain a certain age would be progressive as between the recipients, while interest on public debt is, on the whole, regressive.[1] More generally, a system of grants, like a system of taxes, may be regressive, proportional or progressive either over the whole body of citizens, or over particular groups of grant recipients.

A progressive grant system tends to reduce the inequality of

---

[1] Most obviously with individual holdings, but also when the benefit of corporate holdings, e.g. by banks or insurance companies, is traced through to individual shareholders.

incomes. So does a proportional, or even a mildly regressive, grant system. But a more sharply regressive grant system tends to increase inequality. On the other hand, the sharper the progression, the stronger the tendency to reduction of inequality.[1] Considerations of distribution, therefore, lead us toward the most sharply progressive grant system that is practicable. The principle of minimum sacrifice in the distribution of taxation runs parallel to the principle of maximum benefit in the distribution of grants. As pointed out above, a rough approximation to the latter principle would be a grant system which brought all incomes below a certain level up to that level, and added nothing to any income above that level. But, whereas the policy of the National Minimum embodies the first part of this idea, the second part is not practically attainable, at any rate while large public debts remain, with interest payments regressively distributed. Moreover, considerations of production limit the height at which national minimum standards can be set. But the case for a considerable degree of progression may be taken to be firmly established.

The question of subsidies, referred to in the last chapter from the point of view of production, may also be looked at from the point of view of distribution. Thus a bread or a milk subsidy which lowered prices would operate as a progressive grant, while a subsidy on private savings would be regressive. If there is great inequality of incomes, the case for progressive subsidies is strengthened.

Food subsidies are progressive, in so far as the subsidised foods form a larger proportion of the expenditure of the poor than of the rich. But these subsidies may be either general or special. They are general if they reduce the price of any particular food no matter who eats it. They are special if they concentrate on protective or nutritional foods eaten or drunk by selected groups, such as expectant and nursing mothers, babies and young children, or by children having meals at school. The case for general subsidies on food is often strong, but depends on political and psychological considerations, and on what alternatives are open, through increased social

[1] See Ch. XI, § 2, and Note to Ch. IX, § 5.

expenditure, to compensate those who gain most from the subsidies. The case for special subsidies of the type mentioned above is always very strong. It illustrates the principle of distribution of benefits according to ability to receive.

If the purpose of a subsidy on a particular food is to increase its consumption, then foods with elastic are more suitable than foods with inelastic demand.

§ 3. The effect of grants on distribution may be modified by their reactions on individual incomes. If the prospect of a grant causes a person to work or save less than he would otherwise have done, the effect of the grant in increasing his income will be diminished; in the opposite case its effect will be increased.

Again, distribution would be indirectly affected, and the inequality of incomes reduced, by educational expenditure on a scale sufficient to enable the younger generation to move in large numbers from the worse paid to the better paid occupations and thereby to reduce considerably the differences between the higher and the lower rates of pay.[1]

Again, the free provision of some service for all members of the community, such as a free health service, 'narrows', in Professor Tawney's phrase, 'the area of inequality'.[2] And this is one road of approach to a less unequal society.

§ 4. Grants may improve distribution simply by diminishing the inequality of incomes. But they may also improve it by adjusting individual incomes more closely to individual, or family, needs during different periods of life. The latter sort of improvement is the aim of much modern legislation for social security, including the provision, wholly or partly out of public funds, of old age pensions, sick benefit, unemployment benefit, industrial injury benefit, maternity benefit, widows' pensions, child allowances, national assistance, free health service, and so forth.[3] There is some parallelism here with

[1] See my *Inequality of Incomes*, pp. 264–7.
[2] *Equality*, pp. 250–1.
[3] Much social provision of this sort is often called 'insurance', an emotive word which creates a friendly reception for these arrangements. But they differ widely from 'insurance', in so far as entry into such schemes is compulsory, there is no adjustment of premium to risk, and a heavy

the adjustment of taxation to the changing domestic circumstances of the taxpayer.

From the point of view of distribution, expenditure according to ability to receive, the correlative of taxation according to ability to pay, is achieved, when, corresponding to a given expenditure, the maximum addition is made to economic welfare.

§ 5. We may now turn from grants conferring special benefit on particular persons to grants conferring common benefit on all members of a particular class. The effects of the latter upon distribution are difficult to trace, and the dividing line between the two sorts of grants is not clear cut. But common benefit is sometimes clearly traceable to particular groups, as, for example, when grants-in-aid from the central exchequer benefit local ratepayers, when local expenditure increases the value of fixed property and thus benefits local landowners, when expenditure on roads benefits motorists, or when expenditure on a public park confers a common benefit on all who use it.

Again, the benefit of security is common to all members of the community, except a few criminals. But this benefit cannot be accurately allocated as between different people. At first sight it seems clear that, the greater a man's wealth, the greater the benefit which he derives from security of his material possessions. But the relative advantage, which accrues to people of different degrees of wealth, from the protection of life and property and the prevention of military invasion or bombardment from the air cannot, in fact, be estimated.

Improvements in public health confer a common benefit on all classes. But the greatest benefit on the poorest. For they

subsidy is paid, in addition to the workers' and employers' contributions, from general taxation. Nor are the reserve funds of the schemes, in this country at least, separate from other public funds controlled by the Treasury. All this is well brought out by Mr. A. T. Peacock in his *Economics of National Insurance* (Hodge, 1952) The whole thing is just a part of the budget. Once this is perceived, even dimly, large ideas of simplification, both on the revenue and the expenditure side, and of sweeping administrative economies, are very tempting, and a number of writers have propounded them. But on close examination there are many snags.

attack what Professor Tawney has called 'the fundamental inequality' of the early nineteenth century in Britain, 'that one class lived and another died'.[1] In some parts of the world this attack is not yet launched.

§ 6. In the last chapter we compared the effects of financing public development by taxation and by loan. From the point of view of distribution, finance by taxation has the advantage that it creates no new private unearned income. New publicly owned capital assets are created, free from any interest charge in favour of private persons. But if public development is financed by loans from publicly owned banks, so that no interest on the loans is paid to private persons, there is little difference, in respect of distribution, between the two methods.

§ 7. The extent of redistribution, that is to say the combined effects on distribution of the raising and spending of public revenue, varies greatly from one public authority, and from one period of time, to another. In those modern communities which have adopted both progressive taxation and a large expenditure on social services, it is likely that the combined effects of taxes and of grants or subsidies—of positive and negative taxes—has been substantially to reduce inequality. But the answer, in particular cases, can only be given by statisticians. And even they must tread warily. For, of course, no distribution of income can be absolutely independent of the intervention of the public powers, and it is unreal to imagine a community in which there is no public finance. What we must compare is one actual distribution, with an actual scheme of public finance, and another distribution, with another scheme of public finance. These may relate to the same community at different times. But we must not lightly assume that any change in inequality is due to a change in public finance.[2]

---

[1] *Equality*, p. 137.

[2] The question of how to *define* redistribution of income through public finance, and the further question of how to *measure* this redistribution, when defined, are considered in the volume of essays, edited by A. T. Peacock, on *Income Redistribution and Social Policy* (Cape, 1954). Particularly interesting is the essay by A. H. Conrad. As to definition, several con-

There can also be redistribution by law, outside public finance, e.g. rent restriction, which transfers income from land-lords to tenants of privately owned houses, thus, on the whole, reducing inequality, but discouraging repairs. For this difficulty more than one remedy has been proposed.

tributors follow T. Barna, the author of a pioneer study of this problem, *The Redistribution of Income through Public Finance in 1937* (Oxford, 1945). They take public expenditure as it is, then assume that each taxpayer pays for the benefits he gets and no more, and then compare the actual, with this hypothetical, tax system. The trouble is that the indivisible benefits of public expenditure cannot be divided, and it is difficult to allocate even some of the benefits common to groups. We can only skirt round this trouble by making further arbitrary assumptions. More work on this tricky problem is worth while.

# CHAPTER XX

## SOME OTHER EFFECTS OF PUBLIC EXPENDITURE

§ 1. In this chapter we shall conclude our study of the economic effects of public expenditure.

Just as the cost of collection of taxes is an important test of the efficiency of a tax system, so the cost of administration of policies involving public expenditure is an important test of the success of such policies. If the cost of administration is greater than it need be in order to obtain a given result, this is equivalent to a loss of production, through waste of labour and materials. Many accusations of waste and inefficiency made against public departments are based on ignorance and prejudiced exaggeration. But there is no doubt that the cost of public administration is sometimes excessive in relation to the results obtained. This opens up questions, too large to be pursued here, of the most efficient methods of organisation of public departments. But it is very desirable that the latter should cultivate to the full what may be described as a marginal sense, and should balance the advantage of a small increase in their activities against its cost. Sometimes such considerations will point to the need for an increase, rather than a decrease, of expenditure. It may well be, for example, that a small increase in the staff of the Inland Revenue Department would yield a large additional revenue.

§ 2. On the relation of public expenditure to unemployment something further may be said here, not so much from the point of view of increasing production, which was considered in Chapter XVIII, as from that of steadying employment.

Until recent years, this aim was generally conceived as that of steadying employment at some level which allowed for considerable, though much more nearly constant, unemployment. With this aim in view policies were proposed by which public authorities would vary their activities, and their demand for labour, inversely with the activities and demand of private enterprise. This was not very ambitious.

Now, however, the aim is generally conceived as that of full employment, steadily maintained. Thus in 1944 the British War Coalition Government declared that 'the Government accepts as one of their primary aims and responsibilities the maintenance of a high and stable level of employment after the war'.[1] Later, in 1950 and on a British initiative, the Council of Europe adopted full employment as the aim of all the member countries, and an interesting report on how this could be achieved without inflation was published at the Council's request in 1951.[2]

Broadly what is required, in order to move from substantial unemployment to full employment, is an increase both in consumption and in investment, both public and private.

And clearly full employment, or a close approach to it, will make possible higher production than could be got from a community much of whose labour force was idle. Full employment (in the sense of not more than 1·5 per cent of workers unemployed) has been achieved in Britain almost continuously since the second world war ended in 1945. And some other countries have done as well, or nearly as well.

§ 3. There are many other ways in which well directed public expenditure may do good. Some of the most important of these are linked with planning the best use of land. Thus the concentration of a high proportion of the population in great cities is an almost universal disease of modern communities; as severe in Australia and Argentina as in Britain. One of its worst consequences, apart from much increased vulnerability to air attack, is the creation of a needless transport problem. Millions of workers waste time, money and nervous energy,

[1] Foreword to *Employment Policy*, Cmd. 6526, 1944 'Full employment', as the aim of public policy, particularly in relation to international conventions, was first formulated by Australian Labour Governments between the two world wars.

[2] *Full Employment Objectives in Relation to the Problem of European Co-operation* by N. Kaldor, C. A. R. Crosland and others (Council of Europe, Strasbourg, 1951).

travelling long distances, often most uncomfortably, twice a day, between home and work.

Lord Beveridge recalls that in a leading article for the *Morning Post* in 1906 he wrote: 'We are bound as a community to choose between having great central aggregations of factories, surrounded by work people making considerable journeys to and fro, and having our factories in small groups immediately surrounded by their working population, with the bulk of the necessary travelling falling on the product, not on the producer. . . . We cannot doubt for a moment that Garden Cities rather than an ever-growing accumulation of monster suburbs should be our ideal.' But, he adds, 'what seemed so obvious to the young man seeking to influence opinion in 1906, did not appeal to anyone who had power then. . . . The 4,000,000 houses built between the two wars were allowed to be built largely in the wrong places. The New Towns Act of 1946 came forty years too late.'[1]

None the less the British New Towns, all built with public money, are a brave attempt, not only to create small new communities, better laid out, more spacious, more beautiful and more convenient than the old, but to redistribute population, homes and employment away from the big towns into smaller, more dispersed centres, closer to the life of the countryside. Public expenditure on New Towns differs from public expenditure in Development Areas, mentioned in Chapter XVIII, in that the latter is designed to *increase* employment for workers living in old areas of heavy unemployment, the former to *transfer* employment, and employed workers as well, to new areas. Akin to both are the new Forest Villages, built with public money by the Forestry Commission, primarily for their own workers, in the midst of the growing national forests—the only case where rural depopulation in the Scottish Highlands, and in parts of England and Wales, has been effectively countered by the deliberate creation of new rural settlements with an assured future. Likewise a comparatively small public expenditure in aid of National Parks, and Long Distance Public Routes for walkers and horsemen, brings large returns in health and

[1] *Power and Influence*, p. 54 (Hodder and Stoughton, 1953).

happiness, and is another instance of a planned, good use of land.

§ 4. These are a few British examples, which could be matched by comparable examples from many other countries. But the discussion contained in this and the two preceding chapters indicates the wide range of objects which wise public expenditure may serve. We may bring this part of our enquiry to an end by emphasising once more the fundamental proposition, which in different aspects has been emphasised several times before. The central problem of public finance is no less, and no more, than the problem of securing the best use of the economic resources of the community, in so far as public authorities by their financial policies can influence this use.

# PART FOUR

# PUBLIC DEBTS

★

## CHAPTER XXI

## GENERAL CHARACTERISTICS OF PUBLIC DEBTS

§ 1. One method by which a public authority may obtain income is by borrowing. The proceeds of such public borrowing form part of public receipts. On the other hand, the payment of interest on, and the repayment of the principal of, the public debts thus created form part of public expenditure. The correlative of public debts is public assets. The debts of most national governments greatly exceed their assets, chiefly because most of these debts are war debts. But some public authorities, especially local authorities, most of whose debts have been incurred in order to finance local capital developments, have assets in excess of their debts.

A distinction is often drawn between 'reproductive debt'—an absurd phrase—and 'deadweight debt'. The former is debt which is fully covered, or balanced, by the possession of assets of equal value; the latter is debt to which no existing assets correspond. The interest and sinking fund on reproductive debt is normally paid out of income derived by the public authority from the ownership of its property or the conduct of its enterprises, and here it is a good working rule that the debt should be repaid within the physical lifetime of the corresponding asset. The interest and sinking fund, if any, on deadweight debt must be obtained from some other source of public income, generally from taxation, and since there is no corresponding asset, there is no good working rule for the period of repayment. It is significant of the usual relation of public debts to public assets in the modern world that there is no commonly recognised distinction between public assets which are subject to, and those which are free from, a mortgage of debt to private persons. If the assets of public authorities often exceeded their debts, such a distinction would be familiar.

§ 2. Public debts are incurred through public loans, which may be classified in various ways. In the first place, a loan may be either voluntary or compulsory. A compulsory, or forced, loan is a rarity in modern public finance, since it combines the disadvantages, while lacking the advantages, of both a tax and a voluntary loan. The chief advantage of a voluntary loan, as compared with a tax, is that different lenders are free, according to their circumstances and inclinations, to subscribe as much or as little as they please. But this disadvantage is lacking in a forced loan, which must be compulsorily subscribed on the same basis as a tax. The chief advantage of a tax, as compared with a voluntary loan, is that it leaves behind it no trail of charges for interest and repayment of principal. But this advantage is lacking in a forced loan, though the rate of interest on the latter may be lower than on a voluntary loan.[1]

In the second place, a loan may be either internal or external. A loan is internal, if subscribed by persons or institutions within the area controlled by the public authority which raises the loan; external, if subscribed by persons or institutions outside this area. An internal loan may be either voluntary or forced; an external loan must, except under military or other coercion, be voluntary. An internal loan only involves transfers of wealth within the borrowing community—which in this case is the same as the lending community; an external loan involves, first, a transfer of wealth from the lending to the borrowing community, when the loan is made, and second, a transfer in the reverse direction, when interest is paid or principal repaid. An external loan may be gradually transformed into an internal loan through the purchase by members of the debtor community of public securities held by outsiders. Similarly, an

[1] Or even zero, as with British Post-War Credits.

internal loan may be gradually transformed into an external loan by sales to outsiders of public securities held by members of the debtor community.

§ 3. In the third place, a loan may be for a long, or for a short, term. This is a distinction of degree. The extreme example, in British practice, of a long-term loan is a so-called 'undated stock', of which there are a number of examples. Such stocks *may* be repaid at the option of the government at or after some fixed date, but there is no date at which the government *must* repay. The extreme example, in British practice, of a public short-term loan is the Treasury Bill, repayable after three months. It is common, in intermediate cases, to fix two dates, after the earlier of which the public authority *may*, and at the later of which it *must*, repay the principal. Alternatively a single date may be fixed for repayment. Under both these alternatives the loans are called 'dated stocks'. Long-term debt, in the form of dated stocks, gradually turns into short-term, as its final date of repayment approaches. Like a boat which seemed securely beached on the shore, it is sooner or later floated off on the rising tide of time. But undated stocks lie securely above time's high-water mark.[1]

Hence the distinction often drawn between 'funded' and 'floating' debt, which is roughly equivalent to that between long and short term debt.[2] The near approach of the obligation to repay large sums is often a disturbing factor in the calculations of Finance Ministers. The process of 'funding the floating debt' is designed to remove this factor by borrowing for a term of years, in order to repay part at least of the floating debt which is 'maturing' in the immediate future.

There is, indeed, another form of public debt which relieves Finance Ministers from any such preoccupation. This is the

[1] The United States Government issues no undated stocks, *Economics of Public Finance*, p. 465, by E. D. Allen and O. H. Brownlee (New York, Prentice-Hall, 1948). This is an excellent American textbook, wide in scope and modern in tone.

[2] But the use of the terms 'funded', 'unfunded' and 'floating' is often confusing. Thus the British Funding Loan, issued in 1919 to fund part of the floating debt and repayable between 1960 and 1990, has always been classed officially as 'unfunded' debt!

terminable annuity, involving a series of predetermined payments to a lender for a term of years, but no further repayment of any capital sum at the end of the term. This costs the borrower more per year during the term of the annuity than an ordinary loan, since annual payments include capital repayments, but less in the total.

§ 4. The fact that a debt is not repayable before a certain date does not, of course, prevent a public authority from purchasing its own securities on the Stock Exchange at any time at their current price, and cancelling them. The phrase 'not repayable' means not *compulsorily* repayable at par, or at whatever the price fixed for repayment when the debt was contracted. To make debts not repayable, in this sense, before a distant date is an additional inducement to lenders, if they anticipate that the rate of interest will fall. For the public authority is then binding itself not to take advantage of this fall in order to convert the debt into another at a lower rate of interest. On the other hand, to make debts repayable at an early date is an additional inducement to lenders, if they anticipate that the rate of interest will rise. For they will then be protected against capital depreciation and will be able, when repaid, to reinvest their money at the higher rate.

There are other special inducements which may be offered to lenders by a borrowing public authority, such as exemption from its own taxation of the income from its own securities, the right to tender these securities at a price above the market price in payment of taxes, the right of conversion into subsequent loans, if issued at a higher rate of interest, the right to repayment at a premium, and so on. Special inducements of this kind are substitutes for a higher rate of interest. And most of them are bad substitutes. In particular, so far as internal debt is concerned, the exemption of public securities, or the income from them, from all future taxation is most undesirable, hampering the discretion of future Finance Ministers, making it more difficult to apply progressive taxation, and introducing tiresome complications into the tax system.

§ 5. As a rule, public debts bear interest at a fixed rate. If subsequently rates of interest or prices fall, lenders secure an unearned increment. There is a case, on grounds of promoting stability, for making the rate of interest on new public debts vary in accordance with changes in the general rate of interest, or with changes in the general level of prices, or with these two sets of changes taken in combination.

But there is also a case the other way, since there is no clear reason why the holders of government securities should be insulated, when other important sections of the community are not, against the effects in either direction of changes in these two most vital variables.

§ 6. It has already been remarked that, with most national governments, particularly in Europe, the bulk of their public debt is deadweight debt incurred for purposes of war. This is not a new development since 1914. The British Government for several hundred years has increased its debt by a large percentage at each successive war, by which our history is illuminated, and has never succeeded in wiping out these increases before the outbreak of the next war in the series. The British national debt of 1914 was, in part, incurred during the wars against the French more than a hundred years before.[1] Nor was the British Government alone in thus preserving from generation to generation financial mementos of 'old unhappy far off things, and battles long ago'. Others did the same. But since 1918, many, especially if, unlike the British, they have lost their wars, have shrugged off their internal war debts by inflation. Thus they have escaped heavy burdens, which we victorious and faithful British still carry. Of external war debts I shall speak in Chapter XXV.

[1] The British national debt was only reduced from £850 millions in 1817 to £840 millions in 1842, £800 millions in 1867, £660 millions in 1895 and £707 millions in 1914. The net reduction in these ninety-seven years was thus only £143 millions. Of the £707 millions outstanding in 1914, some £210 millions represented new borrowings since 1817, including £35 millions for the Crimean War and £140 millions for the Boer War. But there remained some £496 millions of the debt of 1817, which had not been paid off in 1914. Moreover, if account be taken of the increase in the value of money during this period, both the real value of the annual interest charge in terms of commodities, and the real value of the principal of the debt, were actually greater at the end than at the beginning. This is a remarkable fact which seems to have escaped the notice of historians.

# CHAPTER XXII

## BURDEN OF PUBLIC DEBTS

§ 1. The nature of the burden of a deadweight public debt is often misunderstood. The direct burden of an external debt is a simple matter. During any given period the direct money burden is measured by the sum of money payments, for interest and repayment of principal, to external creditors, and the direct real burden by the loss of economic welfare, which these payments involve, to members of the debtor community. If the direct money burden is given, the direct real burden will vary according to the proportions in which various members of the community contribute to the required money payments. If these are made mainly by the rich, the direct real burden will be less than if they are made mainly by the poor. Putting it another way, the money payments are used by the external creditors to obtain goods and services, which would otherwise have been at the disposal of members of the debtor community. The latter are, therefore, deprived of goods and services to this amount, and the resulting direct real burden will depend on the way in which this deprivation is distributed. If creditors' demand for debtors' exports is inelastic, debtors will pay by importing less from creditors, unless they pay from gold and currency reserves.

The indirect burden of an external debt, whether money burden or real burden, arises from any check to production due, first, to the taxation required to meet the debt charges and, second, to any economies in forms of public expenditure which would promote production. This indirect burden is like that of an internal debt and can best be discussed under that heading.

§ 2. In the case of an internal debt we are dealing, not with a debtor community in relation to a body of external creditors, but with debtors and creditors within the same community. Thus all transactions connected with an internal debt resolve themselves into a series of transfers of wealth within the community. It follows that there can never be any direct money burden, or direct money benefit, of an internal debt. For all the money payments cancel out. A, as a taxpayer, makes certain payments, for interest on the debt or repayment of principal, and these payments, minus a small proportion to cover the expenses of management of the debt, are received by B, who is a public creditor by reason of his holding of public securities. Often A and B are the same person.

The debt will involve a direct real burden or a direct real benefit to the community, according to the nature of this series of transfers from taxpayers to public creditors. Primarily it will bring burden or benefit, according as the transfers increase or decrease the inequality of incomes. The question, therefore, depends upon the distribution of taxation on the one hand, and of public securities on the other, among different members of the community. Roughly speaking, there will be a direct real burden, if the proportion of taxation[1] paid by the rich towards the cost of the debt service is smaller than the proportion of public securities held by them. There will be a direct real benefit if it is larger. If the British debt consisted only of Savings Certificates held by wage-earners, and if British taxation consisted only of income tax and death duties on the wealthy, the British debt transactions would involve a large direct real benefit to the community. But the actual facts are very different from this, both in Britain and elsewhere. Owing to the large inequality of incomes, which is a feature of nearly all modern communities, the bulk of public securities are generally held by the wealthier classes, either directly, or indirectly in the form of shares in companies which themselves hold public securities among their assets. On the other hand, taxation, even if progressive, is seldom likely to be so sharply progressive as to

[1] We cannot, in fact, separate the taxes which go to pay debt charges from the taxes which go to pay for armaments or education. But we can calculate the proportion of the debt charges to the total expenditure, and can then assume that this same proportion of the taxes paid by any individual goes to pay debt charges. For another basis of calculation see Note to Ch. XI, § 3.

counterbalance, among the wealthier classes, the income derived from public securities.[1] In most actual cases, therefore, an internal debt is likely to involve transfers from poorer to richer, and hence a direct real burden.

Nor is this all. The transfers of income involved in the service of an internal debt are not only transfers from poorer to richer. They are also transfers, on balance, from the younger to the older generations, and from the active to the passive elements in the economic life of the community. There is a general presumption, on grounds of distribution, against making the old richer and the young poorer, thus widening the gap, often too wide already, in favour of the old. This presumption is much strengthened when the instrument of enrichment is a War Loan, to which the old have subscribed in comparatively safety, while the young have been risking their lives in battle. Here, if nowhere else in the sphere of public finance, the voice of equity rings loud and clear.[2] There is also a general presumption, on grounds of production, against the enrichment of the passive at the expense of the active, whereby work and productive risk-taking are penalised for the benefit of accumulated wealth.[3]

§ 3. Again, as a general rule, an internal debt is likely to involve an additional and indirect burden on a community and, as already observed, an external debt does the same. One reason for this is that the taxation required for the service of the debt may check production, if it reduces taxpayers' ability and desire to work and save. Another reason is that short-

---

[1] In other words the progressiveness of the tax system is not likely to be greater than the regressiveness of the grants paid, in the form of interest, to the holders of public securities. Repayments of principal are not grants, but purchase prices, and do not enter into the expenditure side of this calculation. But the corresponding tax payments do enter into the taxation side.

[2] On the morrow of cease fire. But the voice fades, as time passes and the old die off and the young grow old; and as the new techniques of war equalise risks as between age-groups and increase destruction.

[3] It has been objected to this analysis that similar injurious transfers are found elsewhere in modern economic systems, and that these evils are not, therefore, peculiar to the finance of public debts. This is true, but it cannot be regarded as an objection. It is rather an invitation to seek to remove these evils elsewhere, as well as here.

sighted 'economies' in desirable social expenditure are likely to be made, when heavy taxation is required to meet debt charges.

It might be supposed at first sight that the evil effects of taxation would be balanced, in the case of internal debt at any rate, by the good effects of expenditure to meet the debt charges. But this is not so.

In the case of an external debt, any effect of taxes in checking taxpayers' ability to work and save is clearly irremediable, so far as the debtor community is concerned. For it is the external creditors, and not members of the debtor community, whose ability to work and save will be increased through the receipt of the debt payments. In the case of an internal debt, the position in this respect is better. For, against the reduction of taxpayers' ability to work and save, must be set the increased ability of internal creditors. But even here there may be a net loss to the community. For, where the debt involves a direct real burden —as in practice it probably will—it is also probable that taxation will reduce personal efficiency more than the receipt of debt payments will increase it. There would thus be a net loss in ability to work, while ability to save would be unaffected by the transfer of income.

When we turn from effects upon ability, to effects upon desire, to work and save, the prospects are still worse. It has been argued in Chapter X that it is the taxpayers' elasticity of demand for income which determines whether taxation will, or will not, check this desire. Any loss to production through this cause is, again, clearly irremediable in the case of an external debt. Loss is not certain, but it is not unlikely. In the case of an internal debt, we have to consider the effect, upon the desire of internal creditors to work and save, of the prospect of receiving year by year an addition to their incomes, irrespective of any work or saving which they may perform. Whatever their elasticity of demand for income, this prospect will not be an incentive. On the contrary, it will almost certainly be a disincentive and thereby cause a further loss to production and a further increase in the indirect burden of the debt.

It is, of course, possible that taxation may be an incentive to taxpayers more than offsetting the disincentive to creditors.

But, in general, the chance seems slender. On the other hand, if the poor are taxed to pay interest to the rich, one result may be more saving.

§ 4. The preceding argument points to the conclusion that deadweight public debts should not be lightly created. 'The evil that men do lives after them' is a fit motto for those statesmen who, following tradition and the path of least resistance, choose loans rather than taxes as the chief means of financing war. Yet inflation, which usually accompanies loans in war time, will operate as a most arbitrary, even if unintended, tax.

But for the carrying out of schemes of economic development in time of peace, finance by internal loans stands on a better footing. For public debts, which are the means of creating public assets yielding an income sufficient to cover the debt charges, throw no burden on the community. But even in such cases it would often be best to rely more on taxes and less on loans, so as to avoid the needless breeding of unearned income, and in order that, as the schemes matured, there should result, not merely no burden but an additional positive benefit due, in effect, to compulsory collective saving. Where, however, the total new expenditure on such schemes is large and very variable from year to year, the inconvenience of correspondingly large annual variations in taxation justifies the use of loans, provided these are repaid within a reasonable time, in order to diminish such variations. Likewise, as has been argued earlier, when an expansion of credit is desired, loans for public works are often the best means to this end.

The justification of external loans rests on different grounds. In time of peace external debts may reasonably be contracted, subject to suitable safeguards for their own sovereignty, by governments controlling large, undeveloped natural resources, the rapid development of which is too big a task for their own citizens to perform, unaided, out of their own resources. And in time of war an external loan is often the only practicable means of financing imports on the scale required.

§ 5. We may conclude this discussion by examining a misconception, which has occasionally found influential support. This is the idea that the burden of a public debt can be shifted, wholly or in substantial part, from the present to future generations.

It is often suggested that we can 'make posterity pay' the debts of our own generation. Even if we can, it does not follow that we should. For 'posterity' will have had no share in the responsibility for those policies which have created our present debts. And we are inclined, in any case, unduly to discount the future and thus evade the moral obligation to leave the world better than we found it. But, ignoring moral issues, *can* we 'make posterity pay'?

The suggestion is that we can do this by paying only the interest on present debts, but making no repayment of the principal. But whom, if this is done, will posterity pay? Not us, who will be out of sight and out of mind in the days of posterity, but part of itself. Some members of posterity will pay other members. Future taxpayers will pay future bondholders and, unless some new cause intervenes to stop it, this process will continue indefinitely. The process will, however, be brought to an end at some point in the future, if the debt is repaid, and this will mean that, over a given period, taxpayers, present and future, will pay bondholders, present and future, not only interest, but principal also. The burden of a public debt is not something which can be thrown backwards and forwards through time and made to fall, at will, wholly on one generation or wholly on another.

And generations overlap. If a young fighter pilot of the Battle of Britain saves part of his service pay, or of his pay in civil life, and puts it in Savings Bonds, and draws his pension, and lives to be old, the next generation, most justly, will pay *him*. 'Those who have borne the heat and burden of the day should be fanned in the evening'.

§ 6. The case so far deployed against a large debt is that, as a rule, it worsens distribution and discourages production. And this, so far as it goes, is a strong case. But it is confronted by another case, which, if we approach the question from another angle, seems equally strong. To maintain full employment, it may often be necessary to have a budget deficit, that is to say to increase the debt. And it may well be that, if the aim is continuing full employment, the debt should be allowed to continue to increase. This approach to the question will be examined in Chapter XXVII, where I shall suggest that capital taxation and low rates of interest may help to reconcile the two approaches.

# CHAPTER XXIII

## REPAYMENT OF PUBLIC DEBTS

§ 1. One way of escape from the burden of a public debt is to repay it. Another, which may seem even more obvious, is to repudiate it. Let us begin by considering this second possibility. If contracts between a public authority and its creditors are repudiated, while other contracts remain in force, a particular group of property owners is penalised, while all other groups are unaffected, and may even gain through subsequent reduction of taxation. There is a clear argument from equity against such a discrimination. If, on the other hand, all contracts involving payments to property owners are repudiated simultaneously, there is no discrimination against any particular group and the previous argument from equity loses its force. But we are now contemplating a social revolution, the results of which might be held to be inequitable to property owners as a class. Some hold, however, that a *régime* of private property, especially if it involves great inequality, is itself inequitable towards those without property.

Turning from considerations of equity to probable economic consequences, a public authority which repudiates its debts, whether as a mere incident in a social revolution or as an isolated act of policy, will find it difficult, at any rate for some time, to raise new loans. This is an argument against repudiation, except where the debt to be repudiated is larger than the loans likely to be required in the near future.

There are many weapons, ranging from propaganda, through various forms of economic and financial pressure, up to overt military action 'to collect debts', which have been used by creditors, particularly against governments repudiating external debts. Taking account of all these possibilities, there seems, on economic grounds alone, to be a strong *prima facie* case against repudiation.

But this case sometimes weakens with the lapse of time. Old memories may grow faint, new lenders on tolerable terms may be forthcoming and the government, which repudiated old debts years ago, may, if it pays new debts faithfully, regain its 'credit' and the goodwill of its neighbours. It is pretty obvious, nearly forty years after the event, that, on a long view, the Soviet Government was wise in its early repudiation of all Tsarist debts. So too with the repudiation of debts owed to British citizens by a number of the American States before the American Civil War.

§ 2. In recent times there have been interesting developments both in the terminology and the technique of repudiation. This has been renamed 'suspension of payments', 'transfer moratorium', etc. 'Repudiation' sounds provocative, wilful and unnecessary. These softer synonyms suggest inevitability, honest and regretful inability to pay, a chance of payment soon, though not yet. A 'transfer moratorium' is a particularly soothing conception. The creditors' money is quite safe; it has been collected by the debtor government and lodged in a bank; unfortunately, for the moment, difficulties connected with foreign exchange make it impossible to pay it over.

As regards internal debts, some governments in the slump between the wars reduced the rate of interest on existing debts, either by compulsory conversions, as in Australia and New Zealand, or merely by decree, as in France. Strictly this was a partial repudiation. But it usually formed part of a programme of economies, designed to balance the budget by deflation. There was, therefore, no special discrimination against public creditors, but an attempt to make these share the sacrifices imposed on other classes. And this attempt was defended on grounds of equity.

Inflation, far more thoroughly, has destroyed the value of fixed money claims, including public debts both internal and, where the debt is measured in the debtor's currency, external. This, too, some have called 'repudiation'. But, as in the preceding case of deflationary revision, there is no special discrimination against public creditors. All with fixed money incomes are hit equally hard, and all with sticky money incomes nearly as hard. And, unlike the preceding case, there is no change in the form of the debt contract, but only in its practical meaning.

Except in settled economic weather, loans, even to the most respectable governments, carry risks, and sudden storms may wash away even the most reasonable expectations of creditors. But it is surprising how little, in most cases, and for how short a time, the public credit suffers.

§ 3. We may now turn from repudiation, a topic the mere discussion of which may seem disturbing, to the more comfortable theme of the repayment of public debts. This is a fair weather theme. But there is not much immediate comfort here for taxpayers, who are confronted with various disagreeable alternatives. Leaving 'reproductive debt' aside, all ways of escape from the burden of a deadweight debt are themselves burdensome. To the burden of interest must be added the burden of repayment of principal.

The chief decision to be taken is how fast repayment shall proceed. For the purpose of this decision, an external debt is analogous to the debt of a private person, but an internal debt is not. The rate, that is to say, at which an external debt should be paid off, depends on the wealth of the debtor community in relation to the amount of the debt. The greater the wealth, and the smaller the debt, the faster should the debt be paid off, and conversely. The rate at which an internal debt should be paid off, turns on different considerations. In this case repayment involves not a subtraction from the wealth of the community, for the benefit of outsiders, but only a transfer of wealth within the community.[1] The total burden, however, and particularly the indirect burden, of interest plus even a slow rate of repayment, may seem so heavy as to make it seem less burdensome to tolerate an internal debt until eternity than to repay it. To postpone payment altogether may, in some conditions and for a

[1] The one, in the language of Ch. XVI, § 5, is real, or exhaustive, expenditure, the other transfer expenditure. For this reason a learned British Judge (Mr Justice Younger) was too summary when he remarked some years ago that the national debt was 'eating up a large part of the income of the country'.

time, be justifiable, and may suit the requirements of full employment. But there are some strong arguments for quick repayment, as against either slow repayment or no repayment at all.

With no repayment till eternity the debt remains an eternal bad influence both on production and distribution. With a slow rate of repayment, and a comparatively small sinking fund, the burden of interest payments will only decrease slowly and there will be, in addition, a long continuing burden due to the sinking fund payments. There is likely, therefore, to be a long sustained check to productivity and to beneficial public expenditure. If, on the other hand, the debt, or at any rate a large fraction of it, is repaid quickly, by means of special but short lived taxation, the burden of interest payments will diminish quickly, while the additional burden of taxation for repayment will be heavy while it lasts, but will not last long. The check to productivity and to beneficial public expenditure will, therefore, be greatly lessened in a short time. For, in general, the effect upon the budget of large reductions in the debt charges will be to make possible considerable reductions in taxation, simultaneously with considerable increases in desirable forms of public expenditure. Where, however, there is heavy and sharply progressive taxation on large incomes and fortunes, a reduction in the debt charges will be offset, to a substantial extent, by a consequential loss of tax revenue. And this weakens the argument for rapid repayment.

Further, as against rapid repayment, it has been argued that the heavy taxation required, even if short lived, would demoralise the Stock Exchange and the financial world, would ruin many businesses and would be impossible to collect.

In favour of rapid repayment is the argument that it is the *expectation of the continuance* of heavy taxation, rather than its actual impact, which is often disincentive.[1] When heavy taxation is compressed in time, even though for a short time it may be much heavier, and is afterwards lightened, then disincentive expectation is diminished.

§ 4. The proposal to institute a special debt-redemption levy,

[1] See Ch. X, § 3.

or 'capital levy' as it was often called, led, in several countries, to one of the major political controversies of the early nineteen-twenties. On this issue competent economists were divided among themselves, and some changed sides at short notice. A similar division, and instability, of opinion was shown in other circles, political, administrative and industrial, no less than academic. Of those who ventured to be vocal, most British economists, following in the footsteps of Ricardo,[1] were in favour of a capital levy immediately after the first world war. But later most declared against it. In two British general elections, those of 1922 and 1923, it was the most favourite subject of debate. But with the appointment of the Colwyn Committee on National Debt and Taxation in 1923, and still more with the Report of that Committee in 1927 and the coming of the Great Depression in 1929, it faded out of the foreground of public interest.

Most expert British opinion judged in the nineteen-twenties that a capital levy was administratively practicable in this country, though some added a proviso that there must be a reasonable measure of co-operation by the banks and the general body of contributors. Some, especially in the earlier stages of the controversy, attached great importance to the reduction of our then unprecedentedly high annual taxation, which the carrying through of the levy would make possible, and to the removal of the risk that a heavy fall in prices would

[1] Ricardo, who cannot be accused either of revolutionary opinions or lack of business experience, strongly supported a capital levy after the Napoleonic Wars. He held that 'a country which has accumulated a large debt is placed in a most artificial situation. . . . A country which has involved itself in the difficulties attending this artificial system would act wisely by ransoming itself from them, at the sacrifice of any portion of its property which might be necessary to redeem the debt. . . . This scheme has been often recommended, but we have, I fear, neither wisdom enough, nor virtue enough, to adopt it' (*Works*, p. 149). Ricardo was right in his estimate of the wisdom and virtue, as he conceived them, of the politicians of those days. No capital levy was imposed. But the Victorians, even if they lacked wisdom and virtue, had a surprising run of luck, which Ricardo could not have foreseen. The real burden per head of the national debt was greatly reduced during the next hundred years by the unprecedented growth of wealth, population and gold production.

greatly increase the real burden of the debt. In later stages of the controversy the following arguments combined to change the minds of several high authorities who had previously supported the levy, and to create an adverse majority among the experts.

First, the evil effects of high annual taxation on business enterprise and production in general had been much exaggerated. Second, annual taxation had already been much reduced, without the aid of a capital levy, since 1918. Third, the fall in prices, and the consequent increase in the real burden of the debt, against the risk of which the capital levy would, a few years earlier, have been a partial safeguard, had actually taken place.[1] Fourth, there was a serious danger of organised opposition to the collection of the levy. Such organised opposition by the banks and the wealthy classes generally would make the levy administratively unworkable. Fifth, the net saving from the levy on the scale hitherto proposed would not be more than about £50 millions a year. The consequential loss of revenue would be much higher than was at first supposed. In view of this, the levy would hardly be worth while. Sixth, the prolonged trade depression, in which we still found ourselves, made the time inopportune for a levy. Seventh, psychologically the time for the levy had passed. As the war receded, and public opinion became accustomed to the debt and its more obvious consequences, it was increasingly difficult to arouse sufficient interest or political driving force to put the levy through.

This was a formidable cumulative case. But I continued to hold the view, through the inter-war years, that the capital levy remained the best policy, on merits and on the balance of the argument, for dealing with the debt.

§ 5. I attached, I think, more weight than most economists to the argument from equity already cited in the previous

---

[1] 'Between March, 1920, and March, 1925', owing to the fall in prices, 'the value of every pound paid in interest upon the debt increased by about 87 per cent' (*Colwyn Report*, p. 365). After March, 1925, first as a result of the return to the gold standard, and later, in the course of the depression, prices fell still further.

Chapter. I held that one of the chief advantages of a substantial debt-redemption levy would be, not only the abolition
of heavy burdens and the conferring of a net benefit upon the
community as a whole, but also the shifting of a burden from
the shoulders of the young, the enterprising and the oncom-
ing, on whom taxation and the lack of educational and other
opportunities pressed heavily, to the shoulders of the old, the
comfortable and the established, in whose ranks most of the
largest contributors to the levy would be found. And that, if
this good deed was not delayed until the generation of fighters
in the First War grew old, and until most of those, who were
too old to fight, were dead, would be an act of rough justice
as between the generations. But, with each year that passed,
even such delayed part payment of a moral debt became more
difficult to accomplish.[1]

§ 6. Now, after the Second World War, when public debts
have everywhere risen to new heights, from which in some
countries inflation and 'currency reform' have pulled them
down again, the question must be considered afresh. Debt
interest, thanks to low interest rates as well as to inflation, is
often not a much increased percentage of the national income.
But in many countries a substantial debt-redemption levy
would still bring substantial easement to the budget. In Britain
and some other countries this would not be so. Changes in our
tax system, during and since the last war, rendering it heavier
and more progressive, have much increased the loss of revenue
consequential on a levy. The consequential gain to the budget
would thus be slight. The argument for a substantial levy now

[1] I took a prominent part in the capital levy controversy in the nineteen-
twenties and set out my views on this subject in my *Capital Levy Explained*
(Labour Publishing Company, 1923), long out of print, and in my evidence
before the Colwyn Committee in 1925. For an expression of other views
I recommend the reader to study the Report of the Colwyn Committee
and the evidence of other witnesses before it, especially Professor Pigou,
Professor Scott, Lord Keynes and Lord Pethick Lawrence. Professor Pigou
pointed out that a debt-redemption levy, to yield a given sum, might be
assessed on the basis, not of a person's capital, but of his income.
Administratively this would be easier. This was the basis adopted by Sir
Stafford Cripp for his Special Contribution in 1948.

is that it could substantially reduce the inequality of private property, and hence the inequality of pre-tax incomes. It would leave fewer taxpayers exposed to the highest, and often most disincentive, marginal tax rates. It could also be used, if desired, to pay off part, or all, of the compensation debts of nationalised industries, though this, of course, might lead to a net loss to the budget.[1] In 1947, when I was Chancellor of the Exchequer, I was considering the possibility of a capital levy in 1948.

§ 7. I now turn to the consideration of more gradual and less dramatic methods of reducing the burden of the debt. Barring out inflation, which has been considered above, and conversion, which will be considered in the next chapter, these alternatives consist of a number of varieties of the sinking fund. The phrase 'sinking fund', the meaning of which is not self-evident, signifies simply a debt-redemption fund. The creation and maintenance of a sinking fund implies that some part of the public revenue is devoted to the repayment of debt. A sinking fund which is fed, not from revenue, but from new borrowings, is not a true sinking fund at all. For in this case no net redemption of debt is taking place, but only a replacement of old debts by new.

A special debt-redemption levy, which paid off the whole debt at one blow, would be the limiting case of a sinking fund with a very short period. Even where such heroic measures are for various reasons excluded, strong arguments, as we have seen, remain in favour of a comparatively short period of repayment. As already noted, in the case of 'reproductive debt', where a debt is incurred for the creation or acquisition of tangible assets, in the form of capital goods, it is common for a legal condition to be imposed, e.g. by the British Parliament upon British local authorities, that the debt must be repaid within a fixed period, which has some relation to the natural life of the capital goods. The sinking fund is, therefore, in such cases, equivalent to a depreciation fund. The principle, which in general is a sound one, is that, by the time the capital goods are worn out, the debt should be paid off. But war debts have few tangible assets, if any, to be set against them. It would seem

---

[1] But it would give greater freedom in pricing, and other, policy to Public Boards and would raise morale in the public sector.

to follow that the appropriate period for their repayment is shorter than that appropriate to a debt incurred for productive purposes. The appropriate period for the repayment of the British war debt might, perhaps, be put, on this basis, at about thirty-five years.[1] Mr. Churchill proposed a plan in his budget speech of 1928 for repayment by a cumulative sinking fund in fifty years, while the United States Government was then paying off its debt at a pace which, if maintained without any cumulative element, would have extinguished the whole remaining debt in another twenty years.[2]

A cumulative sinking fund implies a constant debt charge for interest and sinking fund together, so that what is saved each year in interest is added to the sinking fund. The annual sinking fund, therefore, increases at compound interest.[3]

[1] So Edwin Cannan argued in evidence before the Colwyn Committee, estimating that a cumulative sinking fund starting at £100 millions a year would do the trick. In Victorian days it was sometimes said that our national debt should be paid off before our coalfields were 'exhausted'. A vague conception, but based on the depreciation fund analogy.

[2] The United States Federal Government debt was reduced in the year 1927-8 by $907 millions, i.e. from $18,511 millions to $17,604 millions. A continuance of annual repayments at this level would have cleared the whole debt by 1948. In fact, it was reduced to $15,922 millions in 1930. But from that year onwards it rose rapidly again, owing to a series of budget deficits. In 1945, at the end of the Second World War, it stood at $247,000 millions. Mr. Churchill's plan broke down, with a budget deficit, in 1929! In 1945 our debt had climbed from £7,500 millions in 1928 to £23,000 millions. In the Nationalisation Acts of 1946 to 1950 the period for repayment of the initial compensation debt was fixed at fifty years, except for the Bank of England, where the period is eternity and need never start.

[3] It is interesting to notice, as a legal and psychological curiosity, the creation in this country in 1927 of the National Fund, started by an anonymous gift of £500,000 to accumulate, together with any other gifts which might subsequently be made, for the eventual redemption of the National Debt. To make this gift legally valid, the law against 'perpetuities' and long accumulations was amended in 1927. On March 31st, 1954, the Fund stood, with accumulations, at £2,118,000. Two other Funds were created later, in 1929 and 1932, each to accumulate for fifty years and then be applied to debt reduction. Starting with £534,000 these two Funds stood, with accumulations, on March 31st, 1954, at £1,442,000. The trustees of the two later Funds were limited to Trustee securities, those of the first were not (Cmd. 9188 of 1954).

The danger has already been noted that a sinking fund, fed from income and not from capital, may be deflationary. It may depress trade and create unemployment, by causing savings to exceed investment.[1] In terms of policy, full employment must take precedence of debt reduction.

I may, therefore, refer, in concluding this discussion, to a proposal made by me to the Colwyn Committee, a proposal which, though it did not find favour in their sight, still seems to me to have economic merits, though it might be difficult to sell politically.[2] This might be called a plan for a gradual capital levy. It contemplates the issue of terminable annuities by the Treasury, in compulsory exchange for a certain proportion of all inherited estates above a certain size. This proportion would be handed over by the inheritors in the form of government securities, other approved securities, suitable real estate, or cash. The annual value of the annuities would equal the annual value of the wealth exchanged for them. The effect of such a plan would be the gradual transformation of public debt, the principal of which would be due to be repaid sooner or later, into terminable annuities which would automatically run off with the lapse of time,[3] and into publicly held real estate. The relevance of this proposal to the preceding discussion is that it might both gradually reduce the debt and, since it was mainly financed through capital transactions, avoid the deflationary danger of a sinking fund fed from income.

[1] See Ch. XVIII, § 9.

[2] See Ch. X, § 8, for a reference to this proposal from the point of view of inheritance taxation, and Ch. XXVIII, § 5.

[3] Terminable annuities were a device much favoured by Gladstone for reducing debt. But they were offered in the market, like other securities, and their annual value, therefore, contained a 'redemption factor' or element of sinking fund, in excess of the annual interest on the initial present (capital) value of the annuities. Terminable annuities, on my plan, would contain no redemption factor.

# CHAPTER XXIV

## RATE OF INTEREST ON PUBLIC DEBTS

§ 1. We can sometimes reduce the interest payments on public debts by conversion. Conversion is not repayment; it is only the exchange of new debts for old. But, if the interest on the new debts is less than on the old, the immediate burden of debt is reduced. Whether the burden is reduced in the long run depends also on the other conditions of conversion. Here I deal only with voluntary conversion, involving no breach, or unilateral revision, of loan contracts.

Voluntary conversion may take place, either when debt actually matures for repayment, or by the voluntary acceptance before the date of maturity of an offer made by the public authority to its creditors. Generally, a reduction of interest charges through conversion is only possible, if the credit of the public authority has improved since the date of creation of the debt to be converted, that is if the rate of interest at which the public authority can borrow has fallen during this period. If, on the other hand, the rate of interest has risen, conversion will increase the interest charges.

§ 2. Conversion has not been an important factor in reducing the burden of public debts in the past. Thus in this country 'during the nineteenth century conversion gave very little relief. . . . The only refunding operation that made a saving commensurate with the effort involved was Goschen's in 1888 and 1889',[1] and this only resulted in a reduction of less than £1,500,000 in the annual interest charge at that time, and a further, but smaller, consequential reduction in 1903. Similarly, the effect of conversion on the interest charge was practically negligible after the First World War until 1932.[2]

---

[1] Stamp, *Wealth and Taxable Capacity*, p. 186.
[2] In the report of the *Colwyn Committee on National Debt and Taxation* (1927), p. 61, it was estimated that there had only been a reduction of

In that year £2,000 millions of War Loan were converted from 5 per cent to 3½ per cent, making an annual saving in the interest charge of £30 millions. In absolute terms this was the biggest feat of its kind in financial history. But relatively the saving in the interest charge was little more than one-tenth. The success of this conversion exceeded many expectations. But the way was well prepared for it by a combination of three factors, bad trade, a Treasury embargo on new capital issues, and heavy purchases of gilt-edged securities by the banks. All these three forces drove down the rate of interest, and the first two drove down employment also. The British Treasury has often been more preoccupied with the prospects of conversion, and of economies generally, than with employment.

A few minor conversions followed this major operation, and exhausted current possibilities. For some years to come, as regards conversion, we had now shot our bolt.

During the Second World War we were busier contracting new debts than converting old ones. But in 1945, when I became Chancellor of the Exchequer, one of my first acts was to cut, nearly by a half, the interest on the short-term debt. This saved some £30 millions a year, a sum roughly equal to the saving through the War Loan conversion of 1932, but representing a still smaller proportion, only between one-fifteenth and one-sixteenth of the annual interest charge.[1]

A reduction in this charge through conversion does not represent a net saving on the budget. It represents a gross saving, from which must be deducted a consequential loss of revenue. For, if the holders of public securities are receiving a smaller income by way of interest, they will pay less income tax and surtax and, perhaps, less indirect taxes. On the other hand, not the conversion itself, but the fall in the rate of interest which makes it possible, raises the yield of taxes assessed on capital values, such as death duties.

§ 3. A conversion offer by a public authority may contain

£1,500,000 a year on an annual total of more than £300 millions. Between 1927 and 1932 reductions through conversion continued to be trifling.

[1] I then proceeded to some further conversions, which provoked controversy. See Ch. XXVIII, §6.

conditions which, though they facilitate its acceptance by private investors and may even bring an immediate reduction in the burden of the debt, yet increase this burden over a term of years. The issue of new public securities at a heavy discount, but to be redeemed at par, is the most obvious example. Such an issue not only increases the present nominal capital of the debt, but increases the sum which will have to be repaid in the future. For such securities will gradually rise to par, as the date of repayment approaches. Such issues, therefore, are popular with investors more than in proportion to their yield in interest, for they carry a prospect of capital appreciation which, in most countries, is free of income tax. But, for this very reason, they increase the ultimate liability of the State and are a thriftless discounting of the future, for which, equally with the present, the statesman is a trustee. They are condemned, as bad finance, by most competent authorities, but they were a frequent feature of British conversions after the First World War. A very gross example was the $3\frac{1}{2}$ per cent Conversion Loan issued in 1921, when Sir Robert Horne was Chancellor of the Exchequer, and not redeemable before 1961. £163 of this loan was given in exchange for £100 of maturing debt. This loan was quoted at the start at 63 and by 1932 had risen above par, thus having realised in eleven years a capital appreciation of more than 50 per cent.[1]

Another form of the same objectionable device is the issue of new public securities at or below par, to be repaid at a substantial premium. Similar objections apply to other special inducements to lenders, such as exemption of interest from income tax.[2] A clean and beneficial conversion will either reduce the interest charge without appreciably increasing the principal sum to be eventually repaid, or will reduce the principal without

[1] 'The Conversion Loan had a mixed reception in the City yesterday. . . . It was argued that to put British credit on a $5\frac{1}{4}$ per cent basis for at least forty years was extravagant finance. But the greater the truth of this criticism, the greater are the advantages of conversion' (*The Times*, City Editor, April 27th, 1921).

[2] Except, perhaps, for securities primarily intended for small investors, such as British Savings Certificates. But the case for this concession applies, of course, to all such securities, not specially to conversions.

appreciably increasing the interest, or will reduce both at once.

The success of a conversion operation can be, and often has been, much assisted, if, in the period leading up to it, the public authority, or public agencies under its control,[1] steadily buy the stock about to be converted. This not only tends to raise the price of the stock, and so improve the look of any given conversion offer, but also ensures the wide acceptance of the offer, through the loyalty of public stockholders to the public credit.

§ 4. The floating debt raises a special problem. By definition it is in a continual state of conversion. But should it be converted into fresh floating debt, or funded into debt at moderate or long term? The decision at any given time turns partly on the relative height of the short and long term rates of interest. If the former is above the latter—as sometimes in the past, though seldom now—there is a clear economy in funding; in the contrary case such an operation will increase the interest charge.

The decision also turns partly on the size of the floating debt. A large floating debt may embarrass a government, subjecting it too much and too continuously to the caprice of lenders. But modern technique, such as the Treasury Deposit Receipts[2] invented in the Second World War, have made this much less likely. On the other hand, too rapid a reduction of the floating debt may, by reducing unduly the volume of short-term securities, cause an undesired restriction of credit. If, however, it is desired to restrict credit indiscriminately, funding part of the floating debt is as good a way as any other.

§ 5. I now turn from conversion to the more general question of the rate of interest on public debts. There are clear social

[1] Including in Britain the National Debt Commissioners, the National Insurance Funds, the Exchange Equalisation Account and the Issue Department of the Bank of England. These and other minor auxiliaries command in total a formidable financial mass of manœuvre, never yet, perhaps, fully used to drive, and hold, down interest rates.

[2] Compulsory short-term loans from the banks to the Treasury. These were not popular with the banks and have now been replaced, as before the war, by Treasury Bills. 'T.D.R.s' could be revived either by agreement or under my Bank of England Act of 1946.

advantages in keeping this rate low. First, and most obviously, a low rate helps the budget by keeping down the debt charge. Britain financed her share in the First World War on a 5 per cent, in the Second on a 3 per cent, basis. But for this welcome change, our budget problem in 1945 would have been quite insoluble, except by most difficult and desperate measures, amid grave risks of uncontrollable inflation and social confusion. And in less dramatic situations there are less dramatic and smaller, but not less definite, gains.

Second, a low rate of interest means a better distribution of income than a high rate; not only a less unequal distribution, but a distribution more favourable to the active and less favourable to the passive and functionless elements in society.

Third, a low rate of interest is better for investment than a high rate and, fourth, a low rate is also better for full employment. These last two advantages of a low rate hang together and fit into the picture, to be completed later,[1] of a stabilising budgetary policy.

Keynes in his *General Theory of Employment, Interest and Money*, published in 1936, coined the famous phrase 'the euthanasia of the rentier' and contemplated as a practical, and most desirable, possibility that 'within one or two generations' at the most the rate of interest might fall to zero and 'the scarcity-value of capital' disappear, as the result of a sustained high level both of investment and consumption in a society enjoying full employment.[2]

It has been objected that a falling rate of interest enriches rentiers by giving them capital gains, and that a rising, rather than a falling, rate is good for distribution, since this depreciates rentiers' securities and discourages them from spending capital, which they do on a large scale when they make capital gains, thus raising their personal expenditure, and hence their

---

[1] See Ch. XXVII.

[2] *General Theory*, pp. 220–1 and 375–7. He adds that 'it will be a great advantage of the order of events which I am advocating, that the euthanasia of the rentier, of the functionless investor, will be nothing sudden, merely a gradual but prolonged continuance of what we have seen recently in Great Britain, and will need no revolution' (p. 376).

standard of living. There is some force in this objection, though
Keynes dismissed it lightly, and it is certainly true that the distribution of *income* and the distribution of *personal expenditure*
(income minus savings plus dissavings) may be moved in
opposite directions by a change, either up or down, in the rate
of interest. But I doubt whether it is worth while to try, as a
deliberate policy, to make distribution of income more unequal
in order to make distribution of personal expenditure less
unequal. Better a policy which would make both these distributions less unequal. This could be done by combining a falling
rate of interest (sometimes becoming constant for a time, but
never rising) with taxation aimed at capital gains, especially if
spent. Either a capital levy, or a tax on capital gains, or on
personal expenditure, as distinct from income,[1] might serve
this purpose.

I conclude, therefore, that the case for a gradually falling rate
of interest is firm.

§ 6. How can the rate be lowered? By words, or by deeds, or
by both. Sometimes the rate can be 'talked down' by those in
favour of 'cheaper money', or 'up' by those against it. Such
talk works by forming new expectations in men's minds about
future price movements. If it is expected that the rate will fall
lower, and stay there, the bulls take charge, prices of securities
rise and the rate *does* fall. Conversely, with the bears in charge,
if the rate is expected to rise.

These efforts at persuasion involve no necessary change in
the quantity of money. But, though talking down the rate may
have some success—it did in 1945–6—there are limits to what
can be done by words alone. More can be done if words are
supported by deeds, if, for example, the government, either
itself or through some governmental agency, buys public securities, so forcing up their price and forcing down the rate of
interest. But this means an increase in the quantity of money,
generally in the form of increased bank deposits.

Some critics have argued that a policy of lower interest rates,
brought about by increases in the quantity of money, is necessarily inflationary. But this is not so. What raises prices is not

[1] See Ch. XXVII, § 4.

an increase in the *quantity* of money, but an increase in money *expenditure*. There is no reason why expenditure should rise simply because people are holding more of their wealth in liquid form, in bank deposits rather than in bonds which they have just sold to the government. After a while, if expectations become adjusted to the lower interest rate, depositors may repurchase their bonds at the higher price, or others may buy them, and the quantity of money will decrease again. Meanwhile there may have been some 'unfunding' of the debt—borrowing short in order to redeem long-term debt—and an increase in the quantity of money sufficient to keep down the short-term rate. But the principle of action by the government is to go on buying long-term securities, until their price, reflecting the lower rate of interest, is established, and then to announce that it will go on buying from anyone who wants to sell at that price. If these tactics succeed, private investors also will begin to buy at this price, the government can 'refund', moving back from shorts into longs, and a reflux of money will enable the basis of credit, expanded for this battle, to be reduced again.

Whether these tactics will succeed or not, depends on all the circumstances of the battle. But they did succeed, for some years following the last war, in the hands of the United States Treasury, which kept down the rate of interest on its bonds to 2½ per cent, announcing that it would maintain this rate by buying back its own bonds without limit.[1]

Another method of lowering the rate of interest on public

[1] The following passage from an American textbook already cited supports my argument that the process here described is not necessarily inflationary. 'Increasing or decreasing an economic unit's cash balance by a given amount does not mean that the expenditure of that unit for goods and services will be increased—particularly since the change in cash balances will be offset by an opposite change in securities holdings. Many of the economic units—banks, insurance companies and some industrial corporations—which would purchase or sell the bulk of the securities are units which are likely to merely substitute securities for money (or *vice versa*) in their portfolios of assets. Their expenditures for goods and services might remain unchanged. The impacts upon production and employment or upon prices in the rest of the economy might be negligible' (Allen and Brownlee, *Economics of Public Finance*, p. 82).

securities would be for the government to exercise more influence over the investments of wealthy individuals and institutions. Such big investors might, for instance, be legally required to hold a prescribed part of their funds in public securities. Such a requirement might take various forms, but it would involve no increase in the quantity of money. Nor would it be, even remotely and improbably, inflationary.

I shall return to this idea, and to some other questions mentioned in this chapter, in more detail in Chapter XXVIII.

# CHAPTER XXV

## INTER-GOVERNMENTAL DEBTS

§ 1. A special class of public debts are those owed by one national government to another. These are external debts for the debtor governments and the communities they represent, but public assets for the creditor governments and communities. Such relationships between governments arose, as a result of the First World War, on a scale and in a variety unparalleled in previous history. In the Second, in what was thought to be the light of experience, there was a different approach.

After the First War inter-governmental debts fell, as regards origin, into two groups. First, debts imposed by the Peace Treaties upon the defeated, in favour of the victorious, States. Second, debts imposed, by arrangements made among themselves, upon the poorer, in favour of the richer, victors. The former might have lost more lives, but the latter had lent more money, 'in the common cause'. In an examination, from a strictly economic point of view, of inter-governmental debts, their origin may be disregarded. Historically some may be debts for services, others for disservices, rendered. But we ask now, not on which side did these men, or their fathers, fight years ago, but are they debtors or creditors today?

§ 2. What is the process, and what are the economic effects, of actual payments?

There are two separate aspects of debt payments, whether on account of interest or principal, from one government to another. There is, first, the aspect of public finance and, second, the aspect of private finance or private trade. As regards public finance, the position is very simple. A debtor government, A, transfers purchasing power to a creditor government, B, receiving in exchange only a receipt. In A's national balance sheet there is, in consequence, an item of expenditure, in B's an equivalent item of revenue. A is accordingly compelled to increase taxation, or to borrow more, or to reduce other expenditure, or to pay out gold reserves, while B is enabled to reduce taxation, or to borrow less, or to increase expenditure, or to increase gold reserves. And, apart from remote reactions, this is all.

But the second aspect is less simple. A must obtain from individuals the purchasing power to be transferred, B must pass on the purchasing power received to other individuals, and the purchasing power, in the course of transfer, must be changed from A's currency into B's. These three processes give rise to a number of transactions within the sphere of private trade. The third process, which may influence the rates of foreign exchange, will be considered separately. But the first two may be taken together.

Their effect must be that over a period of years the debtor community must have an 'export surplus', or, in other words, must part with a quantity of exports unbalanced[1] by imports. The creditor community must likewise accept an import surplus. But the period during which these surpluses will actually emerge may differ from the period during which inter-governmental debt payments are being made. This divergence may be caused by further external borrowing by A, or by its nationals, or by further external lending by B, or by its nationals. Thus the German Government paid reparations under the Dawes Scheme for several years, while the German trade balance showed, not an export, but an import, surplus. This was because large loans were made by American and other foreign investors to German municipalities and private enterprises.

§ 3. I turn to the third process, which operates through the foreign exchanges. The unilateral transfer of purchasing power from A to B, where currencies differ, causes an increased demand for B's currency in terms of A's. This tends to lower the value of A's currency and to raise that of B's. Then, if the transfer is large and there is no effective stabilising mechanism for A's currency, and the effectiveness of any mechanism will

[1] Or 'unrequited', to use a term invented, in this context, by me when Chancellor of the Exchequer.

depend upon the strain to which it is subjected, there is risk of a serious fall in the value of this currency, with disturbing consequences both to debtors and creditors.

The possibility of such a danger was recognised by the authors of the Dawes Scheme, who in 1923 provided for a 'transfer fund' into which the German Government should pay its reparation obligations in marks, but out of which payments should only be made in francs, pounds and other creditor currencies, so long as the stability of the mark was not endangered. In earlier times the thing looked simpler. Ancient Rome, when she demanded tributes of corn from Egypt, 'did not ask whether Egypt had an export surplus or not; she made her have one'.[1] The same simple approach is still possible, if reparations, or other inter-governmental debts, are reckoned, not in money, but in carefully selected kind—not in loose purchasing power, but in tight schedules of specific goods and services, drawn up according to the national interest of the recipients.

§ 4. It is the use of loose money for the payment of these inter-governmental debts which has lent plausibility to the paradox maintained by certain writers that, as between nations, it is not only more blessed, but economically more advantageous, to give than to receive. War indemnities, it has been held, damage the recipients, and it has even been suggested that they may benefit the nations which are forced to pay. This argument conflicts with the common-sense view that to get something for nothing is an economic gain, and to part with something for nothing an economic loss. It also implies that the ownership, by some of its members, of investments abroad is a source of economic loss to a community. And it suggests that a flow of imports, unbalanced by exports, is to be deplored, while a flow of exports, unbalanced by imports, is to be welcomed. But all this stinks of the crudest mercantilist fallacies. And, while misconceiving the private trade aspect of debt transactions, it wholly loses sight of the public finance aspect.

The paradox, indeed, in its general form, is an obvious loser. But, in some special circumstances, it contains an element of

[1] Cannan, *Economic Journal*, September, 1933, p. 377.

truth, especially when payment is made in money, which individual recipients are free to spend as they choose, regardless of the interests of the recipient community as a whole. Thus particular industries in the recipient country may be injured and unemployment caused by the import of competing goods from the paying country. To avoid such troubles—which may not even be serious if the recipient country is successfully following a full employment policy—the recipient country must exercise the right to decide in what concrete form the payments shall be made. Most of the gloomy talk about the harmful effects of receiving reparations dates from the experiences of the early nineteen-twenties, when in Britain and elsewhere there was deflationary depression and heavy unemployment. If we had had full employment then, we should have welcomed German reparations warmly.

§ 5. The actual course of events following 1918 in regard to these inter-governmental debts was one of the most astonishing episodes in economic history. It was an amazing prospect which confronted us, the opening of a strange new chapter in international relations.[1] I gave expression in an earlier book to these general reflections on this subject.[2]

'Facts keep moving on. Huge paper obligations, which seemed a few years ago like unsubstantial economic nightmares, wholly incapable of enforcement, have been rapidly assuming

[1] Thus the United States during the early 1920's had been settling with her European 'war-debtors' one by one. No fewer than thirteen of them, from the Baltic to the Adriatic and from the Black Sea to the Atlantic, had been made to toe the line. Payments had been arranged which between 1926 and 1930 would aggregate more than a billion dollars, rising for the period between 1915 and 1955 to nearly two billion dollars and running on for another thirty years at the same level. On the other hand, Germany's total reparation liability had been officially fixed in 1921 at the fantastic figure of 132 billion gold marks, and, even if she had paid the full Dawes annuities of two and a half billion gold marks from 1928-9 onwards for evermore, she would always be paying less than the annual interest on her official debt, so that her total liability, far from diminishing, would be continually increasing by the addition of unpaid compound interest! But the Young Plan, which in 1929 replaced the Dawes Plan, reduced her liabilities to what then seemed quite tolerable figures.

[2] *Towards the Peace of Nations* (1928), pp. 64–6.

solid shape. Reparations, on a large scale, are being punctually paid by Germany, and passed on by the recipients, with additional payments from their own resources, to the United States. In America, as Professor Moulton tells us,[1] "a cycle of discussion and negotiation has practically been completed. Between 1921 and 1926 a whole series of debt and reparation settlements has been negotiated, and practically all the important outstanding obligations have now been funded and regularised with definite annuity payments provided. Aside from the Russian debt, only a few minor obligations remain unfunded." As a result, a large part of Europe, victors and vanquished alike, has bound itself to pay tribute, direct or indirect, to America for more than sixty years, and has actually begun to pay. Within this framework of obligations, the poorer nations, in most cases, pay tribute to the richer, the nations which lost most lives in the war to those which lost least.

'For the United States the war must appear in retrospect as a beautiful idyll of thrift, a gigantic process of profitable foreign investment, the creation of a sure source of income from Europe, which will continue to flow across the Atlantic till the present century is almost at an end. Unborn Americans will wax fat on the labour of unborn Englishmen and Germans, Frenchmen and Italians. Already American investors are lending to Europe the money with which she is to pay what she owes to American taxpayers, so that America is able to charge interest twice over on the same debts! Mr. Wells in the second volume of *The World of William Clissold* has a passage which depicts this situation. "A golden incarnation of Vishnu, the creditor spirit, rules America, as they see it from these broken European countries, rules America absolutely, sitting upon a Treasury full of gold. Indeed, the American Vishnu sits, in this vision, like a golden weight upon all the world, smiling gold stoppings at the figure of Hope."

'To some this situation will seem morally monstrous; to others it will appear as a solemn and majestic vindication of the sanctity of contract. But, however this may be, there are grave doubts as to its stability.'

[1] In his *World War Debt Settlements* (Allen & Unwin, 1926).

P.P.F.—P

That was in 1928. The phase of actual payments was short. In 1934, in another book,[1] I wrote of these inter-governmental debts that 'the crisis is washing them all away. The "solemn engagements" of the Germans at Versailles in 1919, of Mr. Baldwin at Washington in 1923, of the French and Italians to Mr. Churchill in 1925 and 1926, all these and many others like them, are swirling down the stream, following, after an interval of some fifteen years, the promissory notes of the last of the Romanoffs, which the Bolsheviks, from the first hour of their arrival in power, bluntly refused to honour.

'As regards war debts to foreign governments we are all Bolsheviks now. Little face-saving devices—little token payments at Washington, to ease the final bump and dodge a declaration of default, or little slipshod undertakings at Lausanne to pay something more some time in the vague future —make no important difference. Neat schedules of payments, running on till 1984, or even longer, are now only scraps of paper. But for the crisis, and the increasing burden on un-balanced budgets of these tributes fixed in terms of money, this strange system of one-way traffic between State Treasurers might have endured a little longer.' It ended when it did,. because the Great Depression brought the great excuse to debtors whom it irked to go on paying.

§ 6. In the Second World War, and after it, much was quite different. The United States, instead of lending dollars to her Allies, invented Lend Lease, so that, when the war ended, only quite small debts were outstanding between us. Lend Lease, unhappily, never applied as between all members of the British Commonwealth and Empire, so that, at the end of the war, Britain owed large debts, in the form of sterling balances, to a number of her fellow members and to Egypt, where we had spent heavily on goods and services in the course of defending the Egyptians from invasion and subjection by the Germans and Italians.

Remembering the reparation fiasco after the First War, and not, perhaps, drawing quite the right conclusions from it, we let off the West Germans, Italians and Japanese very lightly.

[1] *Unbalanced Budgets*, pp. 450–1.

The United States, Britain and France accepted, though the Soviet Union did not, the principle, much favoured on this occasion by the Germans, of 'no reparations out of current production'. But the Russians gave us all an economic object lesson in their own reparation dealings with Finland. They drew up, according to the needs of their own planned economy, precise lists of the capital goods and other supplies which they required to be furnished by Finland without payment. And all these *were* furnished within the limits of a prescribed time-table.

For Britain, as will be explained in Chapter XXVIII, the sudden stoppage of Lend Lease, as soon as the enemy surrendered, made necessary the raising of new dollar loans from the United States and Canadian Governments. But the broad picture just after the Second War, as compared with that just after the First, is of an international field relatively unencumbered with inter-governmental debts. And this, except for Britain who owes much and is owed little, is not unsatisfactory.

## PART FIVE

# SOME PROBLEMS OF POLICY

★

## CHAPTER XXVI

## BALANCING THE BUDGET

§ 1. Not very long ago it was generally accepted doctrine that a public authority should balance its budget and that, in order to do this, the most strenuous, even if also the most painful, exercises were justified. But recently another doctrine has gained ground, that the budget should be regarded, not as an account to be balanced, but as a stabilising influence on the economic life of the community. In this chapter I shall discuss the earlier, and in the next chapter the later, of these two doctrines.

The common conception of a 'balanced budget'[1] is that, over a period of time, revenue exceeds, or at least does not fall short of, expenditure. If expenditure exceeds revenue, the budget is said to be 'unbalanced'.[2] That budgets should be balanced is often regarded, not only as an unquestioned precept of finance,

---

[1] The word 'budget', as applied to public finance, was traced by Cannan to an anonymous pamphlet, entitled *The Budget Opened*, attacking the policy of Walpole while Chancellor of the Exchequer and likening him to a clown opening his bag of tricks and deceptions. The phrase stuck and in time turned anodyne. 'Opening the Budget' is now the most official Parliamentary language.

[2] This is common usage. But it would be more logical to call the budget 'balanced', only when expenditure exactly equalled revenue, and 'unbalanced' when, as would practically always be the case, either exceeded the other. We might then distinguish between an 'overbalanced' and an 'underbalanced' budget, according as revenue was greater or less than expenditure.

but as a moral precept as well. It is enunciated by orthodox financial experts with a cold puritan pride. In Britain, for example, this moral sentiment, reinforced by a primitive and widespread fear, artificially stimulated, of the consequences of an unbalanced budget, reached a high pitch in 1931. By means of large economies and more taxation the budget was duly balanced. But in 1933 this sentiment had so far weakened that an influential campaign was set on foot to persuade the Chancellor of the Exchequer, Neville Chamberlain, deliberately to unbalance the budget in order to increase employment. The campaign rallied much support.[1] But he was not persuaded.

In 1952 the Republicans in the United States were returned to power after twenty years in opposition, pledged up to the hilt to balance the budget. But in January, 1954, President Eisenhower told Congress that, in the budget for 1954–5, 'the growth in the public debt cannot be entirely stopped. . . . The Administration recognises that a federal budget should be a stabilising factor in the economy.'[2]

[1] The campaign was opened by a leading article in *The Times* on January 25th, 1933, advocating large tax reductions, the gap to be filled by short-term borrowing. And *The Times* stuck to it. On March 10th a letter appeared signed by no less than thirty-seven teachers of economics, from twelve Universities, arguing that, though 'it is a general maxim of financial prudence that all Government expenditure should be financed by taxation . . . it would be pedantic and injurious to regard this as barring the Government from giving assistance to the well-accredited policy of price restoration in present conditions'. The budget estimates should be divided into expenditure on current and on capital account, the latter should be financed by loan and taxation should be reduced. A leading article on the same day blessed this letter. Then followed a series of articles by Keynes, afterwards republished in the pamphlet, *Means to Prosperity*, urging a large loan expenditure for development, and the unbalancing of the budget now, in order the better to balance it later. He was cautiously supported by Stamp, in an address reported on March 23rd, who held that, when savings exceeded investment, it was legitimate to unbalance the budget temporarily, provided foreign opinion was not thereby scared. A leading article on March 31st recalled the budget of 1922–3, when Sir Robert Horne took a shilling off the income tax, reduced other taxes and suspended the sinking fund, and was rewarded by a reduction in unemployment and a budget surplus the next year.

[2] In March, 1933, Roosevelt, during whose Presidency there were more deficits than surpluses, in his first budget message asked for legislation · ·

§ 2. The budget is to be regarded as balanced if, during a given period, expenditure does not exceed revenue. But three preliminary questions arise. What should be included in 'expenditure'? What should be included in 'revenue'? What length of time should be chosen as the accounting period?

As to expenditure, we should exclude debt repayment. If, during the period chosen, there is any net repayment of debt, the budget may reasonably be said to be balanced.[1] Likewise all borrowing for 'reproductive' purposes, such as loan expenditure for public works, should be excluded.

As to revenue, we should exclude receipts which are of the nature of public capital, such as the proceeds of sales of public property, or sums drawn from reserves accumulated out of previous surpluses. For the diminution of public capital assets is equivalent to an increase in the deadweight public debt. But there is no comparable argument for excluding receipts from taxes assessed on private capital, such as death duties.[2]

Thus we may define a budget as being balanced, if during the accounting period there is no increase in the *net* deadweight public debt. But what should be the length of the accounting period? This was the penetrating question which in the end undermined the whole doctrine of the balanced budget. There is no special virtue in a year, though this is the period usually chosen. 'It is a mouldy fallacy,' says Professor Jacob Viner, 'that, regardless of circumstances, the government must balance its budget in each year. Why not in each month, or week, or hour?'[3] Where administration is weak, or financial

help him balance the budget by cutting ex-soldiers' pensions and civil servants' salaries and numbers. He got it, despite the ex-soldiers' lobby, after the Democratic Leader in the House of Representatives had stated that the vote would be put before the President and kept in mind in the allocation of patronage. (See Dalton, *Unbalanced Budgets*, p. 430.)

[1] The May Committee on National Expenditure in 1931 blundered badly on this point. They estimated a prospective budget deficit of £120 millions, but included in this total the current sinking fund of £50 millions.

[2] Though the distinction between taxes paid out of capital and taxes paid out of income is important when we consider the budget as a stabiliser. See Ch. XXVII, § 3.

[3] In an address on *Inflation as a Possible Remedy for the Depression*, delivered at and published by, the University of Georgia, May, 1933.

control slack, there is something to be said for a shorter period than a year. But there is much more to be said for a longer period. Thus it may be argued that there is some gain in keeping rates of taxation stable over a longer period, so that, if expenditure fluctuates within moderate limits, annual deficits and surpluses may roughly balance over a term of years. Or, more austerely, a variable sinking fund may be used as a buffer to keep rates of taxation stable. So long as the sinking fund does not become negative, the annual budget remains balanced, though with a variable surplus. If, on the other hand, expenditure is stable, and still more if it is higher when trade is bad than when it is good—as with expenditure to maintain the unemployed—variable rates of taxation to balance the budget annually mean rates varying inversely with general prosperity, and hence with taxpayers' ability to pay. Thus Keynes argued in Britain in 1933 that 'our existing budgetary procedure is open to the serious objection that the measures which will balance this budget are calculated to unbalance the next, and *vice versa*'.[1] Some American economists have proposed that the accounting period should coincide with that of the trade cycle, surpluses being used to repay debt in years of boom, and deficits met by borrowing in years of slump. But is there a trade cycle any more? And, if so, is its period everywhere the same? The Soviet Union has never known a trade cycle. Their economic institutions and the relative unimportance of their external trade have shielded them from this capitalist fever. And in other countries there is a great variety of institutional and other conditions.

All this strengthens the case for lengthening the accounting period beyond one year, or, at least, in judging, and encouraging public opinion to judge, a series of annual budgets as a whole, rather than separately. This conclusion goes some way towards answering the question, 'Should the budget be balanced?' Clearly, in the long run, it must be, unless we are prepared to contemplate an increase, unlimited both in time and amount, of the deadweight debt. And such a prospect, at first sight, is clearly intolerable, even if lenders were willing. At

[1] *Means to Prosperity*, p. 1.

first sight a chronic deficit is indefensible. Second sight may qualify these negatives in the next chapter. But we may all agree that, in the short run, measured in terms of a year or two, the budget need not be balanced. This proposition is true in two different senses. First, an annual deficit or two will not, of themselves, cause any great disaster.[1] And, second, public policy may sometimes deliberately and legitimately incur temporary budget deficits in the pursuit of larger aims, notably an increase of production and employment through an expansion of credit.

But budget deficits, even in the short run, must not be excessive. The practical question is, not only how long, but how much, a budget is unbalanced. If deficits are so large as to give the sense of a financial situation out of control, the results may be very damaging. And these results depend, not only on the facts of the situation, but on opinions, whether false or true, about the facts.[2]

There remains, also, of course, the general argument against all budget deficits, that they increase the net deadweight public debt and that this is an economic evil. And this argument must be given its due weight. So, until we can educate them out of it, must the primitive sense of apprehension which many people feel, if they are told that they already owe themselves too much, and that the debt is growing.

§ 3. A backward glance across twenty years is still instructive.

[1] Of Mr. Churchill's five budgets from 1925 to 1929 two at least, and perhaps three, were unbalanced. But there was no catastrophe. From 1929 onwards the great majority of budgets all over the world were unbalanced. But this was only a symptom of deeper disorders. In itself, it was a relatively unimportant incident.

[2] On this question of opinion and of 'confidence', in relation to the British 'financial crisis' of 1931, see Snowden's *Autobiography*, Vol. II. He states (pp. 946–7) that, in the course of his vain and, as I think, misguided efforts to keep Britain on the gold standard, he secured a loan from the Federal Reserve Bank of New York, but only when the latter had been assured that 'the Bank of England approved the programme of economies', which he, as Chancellor of the Exchequer, had submitted to this higher authority. I have given some account of these events, and some judgments on them, in Chapter XII of my *Memoirs, Call Back Yesterday* (Muller, 1953).

The cause of the world-wide epidemic of unbalanced budgets in the Great Depression was simple. It was the steep fall of prices, aggravated by the decline in production and the rise in unemployment, which accompanied this fall. Whether this fall of prices be regarded as a cause or an effect of the slump, it was unquestionably the cause of budget deficits. It diminished public revenue from almost every source. The yield of taxes based on the price of goods, whether customs or excise, fell as these prices fell. When, with declining production, the quantity of taxable goods declined, the yield fell further. The value and volume of business transactions fell and with it the yield of stamp duties based on these transactions. The money income of many taxpayers fell and with it the yield of income tax. If the tax was on a progressive scale, the yield fell more than in proportion to the fall in income. Taxpayers, being poorer, tended to delay tax payments. Finally, the profits of State enterprise fell with the decline in the purchasing power of their customers. As against all this, the fall in the rate of interest, which usually accompanies bad trade and falling prices, cheapened the floating debt and facilitated conversion of other debt as it matured and, by raising the value of gilt-edged securities, raised the yield of taxes based on capital values, such as death duties. But these were very insufficient compensations to the budget.

The fall of prices, on the other hand, had no immediate effect on that large part of public expenditure which consisted of fixed money charges. It had some effect, though much even of this was delayed, upon public expenditure which varied with prices, such as the purchase of stores, or wages and salaries on a cost-of-living sliding scale. But, as against this, the cost to public funds of maintaining the unemployed, however low the level of maintenance, rose as their number grew.

Expenditure, in short, was much more rigid than revenue. Today it is still more so. This works both ways. Just as a fall in prices breeds deficits, a rise in prices breeds surpluses.

§ 4. To stop budget deficits, or at least to keep them within bounds, two possible types of policy suggest themselves. The first is deflationary, the second inflationary or, if a term be preferred which emphasises the fact of past deflation, re-flationary. The first accepts the fall in prices, together with the possibility of further falls, and, on this basis, seeks to reduce expenditure and increase revenue. It aims at balancing the budget by direct means. The second seeks to reverse the fall in prices, and relies less on economies in expenditure than on stimulating trade and thus increasing revenue. It aims at balancing the budget by indirect means and is generally willing to leave it out of balance for a while, rather than risk further deflation. Logically these two policies are quite distinct. In practice, some governments have tried to compromise, or have wobbled to and fro, between them.[1]

The first policy was pursued, under orthodox financial guid-ance, in many countries. It generally led to a further fall of prices in a 'deflationary spiral'. It involved, in its most drastic forms, a wholesale breakage of contracts, both public and pri-vate, by legal process, including the compulsory conversion of public debts and the revision of established expectations, in-cluding cuts in the salaries and wages of public servants, in pensions and in social service benefits. Sometimes also the authoritative reduction of prices by decree. It is doubtful whether it anywhere succeeded in its object. Where it seemed to have succeeded best, in Australia and New Zealand for example, in both of which, during the nineteen-thirties, it was pursued with great energy and boldness, inflationary external factors finally turned the scale, with rising export prices, especially for wool and wheat, and an exchange depreciation of 25 per cent. Since it sought to balance the State budget by unbalancing the budgets of private persons, the deflationary policy caused great immediate privations and aroused deep popular resentments. And thus in Germany it helped to bring Hitler to power.

In this country, and in some others, economies in public current expenditure were accompanied, under the influence of the government, by economies in public capital expenditure

---

[1] The practice during the Great Depression of the governments of twelve European countries, and of Australia, New Zealand and the United States of America, is examined in detail by the authors of *Unbalanced Budgets*.

and in private expenditure, both capital and current. This was a stupid blunder, due to gross mental confusions over the meaning of 'economy' and of 'balancing the budget'. For loan expenditure on public works, as pointed out above, should stand outside the ordinary budget and there is no public economy in checking private expenditure, either capital or current, during a trade depression. On the contrary, the effect of this blunder was to slow down the circulation of money, including bank deposits, and thereby to reduce prices, prolong stagnation, increase unemployment and diminish public revenue. Such conduct was exactly wrong. It worked against the success of the policy which it was designed to aid.

The second policy is 'expansionist', as the first is 'restrictionist'. It was tried by fewer countries and therefore afforded less evidence, either of practical success or failure. It aims at raising prices and generally includes large loan expenditures for public works and sometimes also for current public expenditure. It seeks to speed up the circulation of money, to stimulate trade by increasing purchases and to avoid the more brutal and socially dangerous 'adjustments' of the deflationists.

§ 5. These two contrasted policies for escaping from unbalanced budgets corresponded to two wider policies for escaping from the Great Depression. Given an excess, at many points in the industrial field, of costs of production over selling prices—and this is the essential characteristic of depression—the first policy sought to reduce costs, the second to raise prices. At first sight both seemed equally reasonable. On closer examination each had its own difficulties. But, given the actual institutions and temper of the present age, the second, the expansionist policy, seemed the less difficult. It met with fewer human frictions and other obstacles inherent in our present economic arrangements, and it gave easier play to the more obvious forces making for recovery. But in the last twenty years new thoughts and new experiences have changed our approach to old problems, including that of balancing the budget, as will be shown in the next chapter.

# CHAPTER XXVII

# THE BUDGET BALANCING THE WHOLE

§ 1. The new approach to budgetary policy owes more to Keynes than to any other one man. Thus it is just that we should speak of 'the Keynesian revolution'. Others have already carried forward and improved the ideas he launched, but what he launched *was* one of the intellectual revolutions of our time, both in theoretical and practical economics. We may now free ourselves from the old and narrow conception of balancing the budget, no matter over what period, and move towards the new and wider conception of the budget balancing the whole economy.[1]

We may now think of the budget as a powerful instrument for achieving certain aims, (1) full employment, (2) a high level of investment, (3) non-flation, i.e. avoidance both of inflation and deflation, and (4) a better distribution. The combination of (1) and (2) leads to increased production. These aims, it will be seen, correspond with the economic criteria of social advantage set out in Chapter II of this book. It may prove difficult, in practice, to achieve them all at once. In particular, there may be difficulty in combining full employment with absence of inflation.[2]

In case of conflict, which aim should have priority? Opinions

[1] This transition can be seen in Keynes' own writings. In *Essays in Persuasion* (1931), p. 162, and in *Means to Prosperity* (1933), p. 13, he is still for balancing the budget over a period longer than one year. But in the *General Theory of Employment, Interest and Money* (1936) he has freed himself, and his policies, from any such limitation.

[2] Thus Professor R. C. Tress points out that in 1947–52 France achieved full employment, but the cost of living doubled. In Belgium, Italy and West Germany there was 'fairly widespread unemployment', but the cost of living rose in Belgium only by 20 per cent, in Italy by less than this and in West Germany, in the four years following the monetary reform of 1948, hardly at all. *Trends in Public Finance, Lloyds Bank Review*, July, 1953, pp. 44–5.

will differ. Some, haunted by the fear of inflation, even if, in the language of some economists, only 'suppressed' or 'potential', will sacrifice to its avoidance both full employment and high production. Others, for the sake of full employment and rapid development, will be prepared to pay the price of some inflation, even though this brings some social injustice and economic disturbance. Deflation, they will say, would be much worse, and even inflation is better than stagnation. The best choice, or degree of compromise, must depend on the circumstances of particular cases.

§ 2. Broadly, if there is too much inflation, the cure is a budget surplus; if there is too much deflation, the cure is a budget deficit. If there is to be non-flation, the total value of new savings, public plus private, must be equal to the total value of new investment, public plus private. If savings are less than investment, we have inflation and rising prices. With these savings, consumption plus investment is too high. 'We are trying to do too much.' Therefore we should increase savings and reduce consumption, or reduce investment, or both. On the other hand, if savings are more than investment, we have deflation, falling prices and rising unemployment. With these savings, consumption plus investment is too low. We are not trying to do enough. Therefore we should reduce savings and increase consumption, or increase investment, or both.

If we equate savings and investment we close the so-called inflationary (or deflationary) gap between the demand for, and the supply of, final goods, i.e. consumption goods plus capital goods. Much of our lives and efforts are spent in trying to close many gaps, but, in the economics of the budget, this is the most important gap to close.[1]

[1] The best official statement of this modern doctrine is in Mr. Hugh Gaitskell's budget speech on April 10th, 1951, in the course of which he said 'the budget must ensure . . . that what is spent at home is enough, but not more than enough, to buy . . . the goods and services we can afford to consume at home. What we can afford for public and private consumption is what is left over from our total production after adding what is to be imported, and taking away what is required for exports, home investment and defence.' And again: 'How large a budget surplus do we need this

If, however, the budget is to be an economic stabiliser, it must be large enough to have a stabilising influence. The larger the budget, relatively to the total economic activity of the community, the stronger this influence can be. The great growth in recent years in the size of budgets is here a favourable factor.[1] Part of the budget, on both sides of the account, being in practice fixed, is itself an element of stability; and part, being variable, can be varied in either direction so as to counter elements of instability.

§ 3. It has been argued that, in calculating the changes in taxation or expenditure needed to close the inflationary (or deflationary) gap, capital taxes and capital subsidies should be left out of account.[2] And there is much force in this, though it emphasises how rough and inexact such calculations round the gap must be. If a tax, such as death duties, is mainly paid out of capital, it has little effect on consumption. So too with a subsidy, such as war damage payments, mainly paid into capital. But these are extreme cases. Some other taxes are paid by some taxpayers partly out of, and some other subsidies by some of their recipients partly into, capital.

The question has been raised in the last chapter whether a 'chronic deficit', which would involve a continuous increase in the principal of the public debt, can be justified. In putting this

year to bring the level of the nation's total savings—personal and private, public and corporate—up to what is required to finance the total investment by the Government and industry in buildings and plant and machinery and higher stocks?' If investment is controlled, as in Britain between 1945 and 1951, one may ignore the risk of an excess demand for capital goods and aim at closing the consumption gap only.

[1] This point is judged to be very important now with reference to the U.S.A., even as compared with the 1930's, by C. A. R. Crosland, *Britain's Economic Problem*, p. 141. And if in Britain we go back further and compare, say, the first Gladstone budget of 1853 with the first Gaitskell budget ninety-eight years later, it is clear that, even if Mr. Gladstone had wholeheartedly accepted Mr. Gaitskell's approach, manipulation of his tiny budget of £55 millions could have stabilised nothing. Mr. Gaitskell's was more than £4,000 millions. Gladstone's last and thirteenth budget in 1882 was only £85 millions. Even allowing for changes in the value of money and in the national income, our budgets have grown from dwarfs to giants.

[2] Little, *Fiscal Policy*, pp. 160–1.

question it is assumed that deficits are deliberate, and not the result of administrative inefficiency, refusal of taxpayers to pay their dues, or official miscalculations of revenue or expenditure. It seems unlikely that, in any particular community, the gap to be closed would always, or even over a considerable period of years, be deflationary, i.e. such as to justify a series of deliberate deficits. But if this were to happen, and if the doctrine of the gap be rational, it seems to follow that 'fear of a chronic budget deficit is very largely irrational'.[1] This view is supported by Mr. Little by the argument that 'the increase in the national debt could be reduced or even offset by capital taxation and that the "burden" of interest on the national debt must depend on the proportion it bears to the national income'.

A chronic deficit is an extreme case. A more likely situation is one where, over a period, there are both surpluses and deficits, but the sum of the deficits is substantially greater than the sum of the surpluses. Let it be supposed that these surpluses and deficits have been well calculated to maintain full employment and non-flation. But the public debt will have increased over the period, and it has been argued in Chapters XXII and XXIII above that public debts do harm both by discouraging production and worsening distribution, and that, the greater the debt, the greater the harm. How shall we resolve this conflict of considerations?

§ 4. Perhaps by a combination of capital taxes and cheap money.[2] Capital taxes, to the extent noted above, stand outside the gap and can do little to close it. But they can easily be so graduated as to help us to achieve another of our aims, a less unequal distribution of capital, and hence of income. Their proceeds can be earmarked, if desired, for debt reduction, thus offsetting, in some measure, debt increases due to closing deflationary gaps. The principal types of capital taxes, as we

[1] Little, *loc. cit.*, p. 164. The contrary view, that all regular recurrent expenditure should 'in a well-ordered state' be met from taxes, and not from loans, is said by Professor Pigou to be 'universally accepted'—*Public Finance* (third edition, 1947), p. 35. He dwells on the evil of an ever-growing public debt and a declining public credit.
[2] See Ch. XXIV, § 5.

have already seen, are death duties, capital levies and taxes on capital gains.[1] Cheap money has already been discussed in Chapter XXIV, where it was pointed out that a low rate of interest is better, both for investment and for full employment, than a high rate. Also for a more equal distribution of income. Here it may be added that, even if closing deflationary gaps means adding to the principal of the public debt, it need not mean adding to the interest charge, if rates of interest fall meanwhile. But the argument that 'the "burden" of interest on the national debt must depend on the proportion it bears to the national income' is of limited validity. The burden, as analysed in Chapter XXII, is not directly measured by the interest charge, nor by the ratio of this to total income. It is more complex than either of these.

§ 5. Finally we may ask, how far can a nation, in the conditions of today, achieve continuing full employment and the other aims recalled in this chapter by means of the budgetary policy we have been considering? It is not an easy technique, dependent on wildly uncertain estimates, often in most unstable situations. But, subject to this, the United States of America probably *could* achieve these aims, since its external trade is relatively small. Whether it *will*, remains to be seen. The Soviet Union, in accordance with its own way of economic life, probably does achieve these aims, though still at a much lower average level of economic welfare and political freedom.[2] Its

[1] On the comparative merits of these see some interesting observations by Mr. Roy Jenkins in his essay on *Equality* (*New Fabian Essays*, pp. 76–81, Turnstile Press, 1952).

[2] Reviewing *Soviet Economic Growth, Conditions and Perspectives*, edited by A. Bergson, a book published in the United States in 1953, in which thirty-one leading American specialists pooled their knowledge', *The Economist* of February 13th, 1954, observes that 'the claims of Soviet propaganda are normally dismissed with a shrug. . . . Even so, after deflating the exaggerated Soviet claims out of recognition, American experts agree that Soviet national income is probably rising by about six and a half to seven per cent per annum and that industrial production is expanding even more rapidly. This is an incomparably faster rate than that prevailing in any western country. It should also be remembered that Soviet growth is uninterrupted by slumps and that the years chosen to complete this average were not years of "boom" reconstruction but normal peace

external trade, like that of the United States, is relatively small. But in the Russian setting budgetary policy is merged in economic planning as a whole. For other countries, much more dependent on external trade, and particularly on that of the dollar area, budgetary policy can, at the best, lead us only part of the way. All of us are much less masters of our fate, in economics as in international politics, than the Two Giants. For Britain, in particular, the Keynesian Revolution, immensely salutary though it has been, is not enough.

We must also balance our external trade and shield our gold and dollar reserves from dangerous drains. Since 1945 the threat to these reserves has been a pistol always pointing at our heart. What resultant of blind, impersonal economic forces, what 'invisible hand', may lay a fatal finger on that trigger? Some say an American recession. But can we fashion no armour against this?

Economists, mobilised first by the United Nations and then by the Council of Europe, have explained that, if the United States, even in recession, would make over, on any plausible pretext, enough dollars to the rest of the world, then outside the United States it would be as though there *was* no American recession. But this is advice, to the Administration and the Congress at Washington, not very likely to be taken.

Failing some such plan as this, Britain and the rest of the world outside the United States must act, largely, as though the United States, for the moment, was no longer there. These outer regions must trade more actively with each other, perhaps through bilateral agreements; must lend more trustfully to each other; must stockpile, well in excess of their immediate needs, their own and one another's products. If the United States by her own economic policies tears a wide gap in world trade and employment, Britain must look to the Common-

years. . . . At that pace Soviet output in 1970 would be four and a half times as great as in 1950. . . . Unless the West lengthens and steadies its stride, the Soviet Union and its third of the world will progressively narrow the gap. One may dislike the regime, its methods, even the composition and use of its final product; it would be foolish to ignore its economic achievements.'

wealth, Latin America, West Europe and the Soviet Empire to join with her to fill that gap. That gap, though often foretold, is not torn yet.

But we are now well outside the bounds of Public Finance.

# CHAPTER XXVIII

## AT THE BRITISH TREASURY 1945-7

§ 1. For twenty-eight months, from July, 1945, to November, 1947, I held the high office of Chancellor of the Exchequer. During this time I introduced four budgets. I had to deal with many other serious problems within, or on the borders of, the field of Public Finance, and I was mixed up in much vigorous controversy in Parliament, in the country and in the City of London. All the time the threat of dollar bankruptcy hung over Britain like a black thundercloud. After the war, as during it, our dependence on the United States for vital supplies was obvious, painful and extreme. This was a constant preoccupation which absorbed a great part of our energies.

None the less, the Government of which I was a member, supported by a large Parliamentary majority, fulfilled its pledges to the electors and carried through its policies. Mistakes, of course, were made and opportunities missed. Often we were too slow, sometimes too timid or too tired. And generally, a clue to many other defects, too talkative. But we made a lot of history. And we made the years after the Second World War shine brighter for most of our fellow countrymen than those lack-lustre years after the First.

At the Treasury I tried, often in most unexpected situations, and with due respect for the march of time, to apply the principles which I had learned, taught and published more than twenty years earlier. And I have thought that some account of these efforts might suitably end this book, and perhaps throw fresh light from new angles on familiar subjects.

§ 2. I became Chancellor of the Exchequer when Mr. Attlee formed his Government after the Labour victory at the General Election. Before that, from 1942 to 1945, I had been President of the Board of Trade in Mr. Churchill's Coalition Government.

The chief problems of which I was conscious, when I went to the Treasury in 1945, were these. First, reconversion, from war to peace purposes, of industry, manpower and expenditure; second, a special aspect of the first, a smooth transition, maintaining full employment and avoiding strikes and lock-outs and any sharp rise in the cost of living; third, our pledge to extend the social services into a new, much wider, system of social security; fourth, the reshaping of taxation so as to reduce the total and to narrow from both ends the gap between the richest and the poorest; fifth, our pledge to nationalise the Bank of England, the coal industry, and other key industries and services; sixth, more immediate and difficult than all the rest, how for the next few years to pay for the imports necessary to prevent mass unemployment and starvation. In July, 1945, our export trade had been dismantled for the sake of the war effort. Most of our merchant shipping had been sunk by the enemy. Our reserves of gold and dollars were very low. Lend Lease, on the continuance of which, even if on a diminishing scale and only for a few years, we had confidently counted, was cut short by a sudden administrative decision at Washington, without discussion and without warning. The temporary solution of this sixth problem was found, first in the American Loan Agreement negotiated by Lord Keynes, and its Canadian counterpart, and later in Marshall Aid. Keynes, who thirty-six years before had taught me economics at Cambridge, was now, for the last nine months of his life, my most trusted adviser at the Treasury.

The American Loan, of $3,750 millions, was indispensable to us at this time. But we were compelled by the Americans, as a condition of the Loan, to agree to restore full convertibility of the pound with the dollar for all current, as distinct from capital, transactions in July, 1947. No other European state was to be required to do this. Keynes fought hard against this condition, both on his instructions from the British Government and on his own clear understanding of the problem. But the Americans insisted. To have refused would have broken us. Therefore we were committed, in return for the dollars which, at this early stage of our own reconversion, were literally vital, to do our best to fulfil a condition, which I and many good judges believed would be impossible. And so, when the time came, it proved to be. But, by that time, our reconversion had made good progress and, though not yet strong enough to face the world unaided, we were much stronger than in the hour of military victory.

§ 3. Meanwhile, on October 23rd, 1945, I introduced my first budget. There was much talk of incentives at this time and it was the almost universal opinion, both among experts and ordinary people, that substantial tax reductions would raise morale and stimulate effort. I, therefore, made large cuts in the income tax—reducing the standard rate from 10s. to 9s. in the £1, raising the exemption levels both for single and married people and introducing two new 'reduced rates' on the first slices of taxable income. On the other hand, to prevent the richer taxpayers getting more than their fair share of relief, and to maintain the progressiveness of the tax system, I revised the surtax scale, so that, as incomes rose, an increasing proportion of the income-tax reliefs were offset by surtax increases.

I also cut the excess profits tax from 100 per cent to 60 per cent and abolished purchase tax, prematurely as it turned out, on all space-heating and cooking appliances and water heaters. But I had given away less than £10 millions a year in indirect taxes as against £315 millions (net) on income tax.

I had, thus early, formed the opinion that it was better, in our existing conditions, to reduce direct rather than indirect taxation. Income tax, particularly on wages and other small incomes, was more keenly felt, more heartily disliked and more disincentive than any of our indirect taxes. This opinion I often publicly stated. It never provoked serious dissent either from my political supporters or opponents. But it represented a complete reversal of the old-fashioned view of Philip Snowden, accepted by an earlier generation in the Labour Party, that indirect taxation should be done away with, and all necessary revenue raised by graduated direct taxes.

Looking back, I think it might have been better if in this budget I had left the standard rate of income tax and the surtax scale unchanged, and raised higher and quicker the exemption levels and the earned income relief.

But my first budget was not unpopular, except with surtax payers.

§ 4. At the first meetings of the Labour Cabinet we had decided to go off with a legislative rush. In the first session of the new Parliament there were not only two budgets, my first and second, but the nationalisation of the Bank of England, of the coal industry, of civil aviation, and of Cable and Wireless, and the first instalment of the new social security legislation.

I told my colleagues that, apart from budgets, I wanted only three Departmental Bills in this first session, the Bank of England Bill, a Bill to control borrowing, and an Exchange Control Bill. I got the first two in our first session and the third in our second.

These three Bills between them created a new statutory framework for all private operations in the field of finance.[1] These were three 'streamlined Socialist statutes', as I called them, short, simple and strong.

The Bank of England Act took over the private shareholdings in the Bank, treating Bank stock as the equivalent of government securities and stabilising the income of the recipients. It provided that the Governor, the Deputy Governor and the Court should be appointed henceforth by the Crown. It also gave power to the Treasury to give directions to the Bank of England, and to the Bank of England to give directions to any other bank. I was told that it was difficult to define a bank. So we enacted that a bank is any institution which the Treasury deems to be a bank. This Act received the Royal Assent in February, 1946.

The Borrowing (Control and Guarantees) Act, which became law in July, 1946, made permanent the Government's wartime power to regulate new capital issues. It also authorised, as an anti-slump precaution, the guarantee by the Treasury of new loans up to £50 millions in any one year. If a slump had come,

[1] See *Midland Bank Review*, February, 1948, ' The Changing Shape of Britain's Monetary System', for a good and objective statement of this policy.

this figure could have been raised, to any level required, by a one-clause amending Bill.

The Exchange Control Act, which became law in March, 1947, made permanent the wartime controls over foreign exchange transactions.

§ 5. On April 9th, 1946, I introduced my second budget. This was to me the most satisfying of the four. I raised the earned income relief from one-tenth to one-eighth. My distant ambition was to see it raised to one-half, which I felt would be a natural stopping point. I made other income-tax reductions and finally repealed the excess profits tax. I gave a warning here that it might be necessary next year to extend the tax on *annual* profits (as distinct from *excess* profits) which then stood at 5 per cent. I said that I regarded the purchase tax as a permanent tax which must 'help to pay the bill for social betterment', but I exempted pots and pans, kitchen fitments, electric kettles and firebricks and other fuel-saving devices, and I reduced the tax on many other objects. I also cut entertainment tax on football, cricket and a wide range of other outdoor sports.

I was particularly anxious to reform the death duties and pondered long as to the political possibility of introducing what I have called in Chapter X, § 8, the simplified Rignano scheme, and in Chapter XXIII, § 7, a gradual Capital Levy, whereby a certain part of an estate passing at death should be compulsorily exchanged for a terminable annuity of equal annual value. But I reached the conclusion that it would be politically very difficult to put this scheme across in view of its novelty, when there was so much else going on. I put it on the list of good deeds to be done, if ever I got into smooth water. But this never happened. Meanwhile I stuck to the existing estate duty, but raised the level of exemption from £100, at which it had stood since 1894, to £2,000. This change cost little revenue, but it had the effect of exempting no less than three-quarters of the annual number of estates previously liable to duty, 150,000 out of 200,000. I regraded the scale of duty on estates of £12,500 and upwards and, as a result of these changes, brought in an additional revenue of £22 millions. This was a very simple example of equalitarian adjustment of taxation,

I gave away £16½ millions in indirect taxation (£15½ millions in purchase tax and £1¼ millions on entertainments) and £77½ millions in income tax.

In this budget I made a beginning in repaying post-war credits, the first three years' credits of all men over sixty-five and women over sixty, and in financing the first family allowances, higher old age and widows' pensions, and free milk for all children in schools. In this budget also I created the National Land Fund of £50 millions to encourage the handing over, in payment of death duties, of attractive unspoilt open country or beautiful and historic buildings which it was much in the public interest to have in safe public keeping.[1]

This budget too was well received by most sections of opinion. We were being carried forward at this time on a high tide of economic success and political popularity. Inflation came and went during the post-war years. There were always some voices monotonously proclaiming its presence, but most expert opinion at this time held that, for the moment at least, it had been subdued.[2]

In a speech at Bournemouth on June 14th, 1946, I said: 'When the war ended there was a great danger of inflation. That is why I have quite deliberately gone slow with tax reductions and with the increase of purchasing power in other ways, because I was not going to be responsible for landing this country in an inflationary spiral. I had to give time for production for civilian purposes to pick up. As the production of goods for the home market is rapidly rising, the fear of inflation is diminishing. It has largely passed away.'[3]

[1] See Ch. I, § 2, note.
[2] Of this budget *The Economist* said 'it was a competent and sober budget, whose main features it would be difficult to criticise. The Chancellor did not yield to the temptation to distribute inflationary largesse. ... He is still preoccupied, and rightly so, with the dangers of inflation.'
[3] On this speech *The Economist* commented: 'Mr. Dalton had some grounds for his claim that the worst danger of inflation is passing. ... Is he now being too complacent? Probably not. ... He is saying that, though inflationary pressures will beat against the ramparts, the main structure will hold. There is little in the recent trends ... to make this an irrational view.'

In my second budget speech I also promised quicker action in carrying out the Distribution of Industry Act in the Development Areas, and shocked some purists by declaring that in this matter the Treasury would in future be 'not a curb, but a spur' to those who were too slow in building new factories to ensure in these areas 'what they never had in the past, a condition of full and efficient and diversified economic activity'. In this context I used another phrase, much quoted later out of context by my political opponents, that I would find 'with a song in my heart' all the money necessary to achieve this aim in the Development Areas. 'I pledge my word,' I said, 'that this job shall not fall down for lack of finance.' And indeed great progress was made in the next few years in bringing down unemployment in these areas towards the happily very low national average.

At the Treasury there were three lines of expenditure of which I was exceptionally fond—none of them costly in relation to our total outlay; all, in my judgment, yielding exceptional social advantage; none, I thought, sure to have quite so firm a friend when I moved on. These were Development Areas, National Forests—'a sound socialist investment in land and young trees', I said—and Universities, which I wished to see retain their freedom from state interference, but 'be enabled to play a fuller part than ever before in our national life, and to double the pre-war total of their students within ten years'. To all these three favourites I gave more public money than they had ever had before—and more, I think, than their spokesmen expected. But I am quite sure that, in the national interest, my favouritism was justified.

In my second budget speech I also announced that, though in 1945-6 and 1946-7 large budget deficits had been inevitable, in 1947–8 we should be 'within striking distance of a balanced budget', owing to the rapid decline of expenditure arising from the war.

§ 6. Much more debated, and in some financial circles much less popular, was my cheap money policy. I began as soon as I took office, and continued through the next two years, a policy of driving down interest rates.[1] I announced my intention, in broad terms, in my first public speech as Chancellor and thereafter I frequently spoke on this subject and defended my policy in detail.

My general reasons for driving down interest rates were those already mentioned in Chapter XXIV, § 5, of this book; to save public expenditure on interest, to improve the distribution of income, to encourage investment and to make sure of full employment. The third of these reasons was not, in this period, of much importance, since new investment, both public and private, was held in check much less by the rate of interest, whether high or low, than by the need to obtain permissions from the central Government, or from the Capital Issues Committee, or from the local authorities. But I had some further reasons. I wished to help the local authorities to keep down the cost of housing programmes, and thus to keep down rents. I wished, most of all, to help the local authorities in the 'blitzed cities', both by special grants and by cheap loans. And I wished to prepare the way for the series of nationalisation Bills which, during this Parliament, we intended to pass. The higher the national credit, the lower the rate of interest, the less the annual compensation charge corresponding to a given capital value.[3]

In October, 1945, I reduced the interest rates on the floating debt, on Treasury Bills from 1 to $\frac{1}{2}$ per cent and on Treasury Deposit Receipts from $1\frac{1}{8}$ to $\frac{5}{8}$ per cent. This, as already stated, nearly halved the annual cost of the short-term debt and saved some £30 millions a year. This first economy due to my cheap

[1] A good narrative of events, though written by a critic of my policy, is in C. M. Kennedy's chapter on *Monetary Policy* in *The British Economy, 1945–50* (Oxford University Press, 1952).

[2] At some length, for example, in both my second and third budget speeches.

[3] Even if lower gilt-edged interest rates raised capital values on which compensation would be based, they would generally raise them less than proportionately. And in the case of the Transport Act the capital sum had already been fixed and then, before the compensation stock was issued, the rate of interest rose from $2\frac{1}{2}$ to 3 per cent!

money policy continued in force for six years, under both Sir Stafford Cripps and Mr. Gaitskell. Under Mr. Butler the short-term rates were allowed, indeed encouraged, to rise, by a higher Bank Rate and other rearrangements.

I moved next against the medium and long-term rates. The latter stood at just over 3 per cent.[1] I aimed to bring them down to 2½ per cent and repeatedly said so. In February, 1946, maturing Metropolitan Water Board stock was converted into 2¾ per cent, 1971–6, at 99. In May I put on tap 2½ per cent Savings Bonds, 1964–7, which, as I said, was 'the cheapest long-term Government issue ever made within our lifetime'. In the same month I reduced the rate on new issues of Defence Bonds from 3 to 2½ per cent. That spring I authorised local authorities to borrow at 2½ per cent from the Public Works Loan Board for all loans over fifteen years. Such low rates for local authorities had never been arranged before.

My next, and most controversial, move was to go for a 2½ per cent undated stock. I announced in October, 1946, an offer, in exchange for 3 per cent Local Loan Stock, of 2½ per cent Treasury stock, 1975 or after, at par. I also put this stock on tap. The conversion went well; the new tap issue not so well. 'Nevertheless', as Mr. Kennedy observes, 'the Chancellor had the satisfaction of achieving his immediate aim—the issue at par of an irredeemable stock bearing 2½ per cent interest.'[2] No predecessor of mine, not even Goschen, had done this.

The new rate held firm till the beginning of February, 1947.[3] Then came the fuel crisis, when for three weeks there was wide-spread stoppage of industry through lack of coal and electric

---

[1] At the end of the First World War the long-term rate had been 5¾ per cent, and the Treasury Bill rate 3½ per cent in July, 1919, and 6½ per cent in April, 1920.

[2] *Loc. cit.*, p. 199. This stock is often called affectionately by my name, just as Old Consols 2½ per cent, 1923 or after, should be called 'Goschens' and War Loan 3½ per cent, 1952 or after, should be called 'Chamberlains'. The flat yield on Daltons has stood persistently just above that on Goschens —in April, 1954, they have just drawn level!--but comfortably below that on Chamberlains.

[3] On February 4th, 1947, the new stock stood at 99$\frac{9}{16}$ (ex div.).

power, and for one week unemployment rose above two millions. This was the first blow to the new high level of the national credit. Gilt-edged prices fell, then made a fair recovery until May, then fell again. In August came the convertibility crisis, a second heavy blow struck from outside the City. By the end of November my new stock was down to 84, yielding just under 3 per cent.

Meanwhile blows, in the same cause, were being struck from within the City. First a whispering and then a talking campaign started against cheap money and its alleged 'dangerous inflationary consequences'. The annual allocutions of the Bank Chairmen, pronounced in January in a salvo; the weekly, or daily, distresses of financial scribes; the unreported, often indignant, chatter of jobbers and brokers, and of some large institutional investors—'You can't live on 2½ per cent' they said—all this was bad for the national credit. These people all vociferously talked, or assiduously wrote, the rate of interest up. In the end they quite drowned my small voice trying to talk it steady at 2½ per cent.

But I insisted, until the end of my term of office, in sticking to 2½ per cent at par as the rate at which local authorities could both make new issues and offer conversions. I told the National Debt Office to continue to stand behind the local authorities, and to underwrite all their loans without commission. It did so, and often made a profit by selling out later. A friend said to me, 'You have added a new socialistic animal to the City Zoo, the public stag.'

The direct savings in interest due to my cheap money policy (October, 1945, to November, 1947) were roughly as follows:

|  | Capital £m. | Annual Saving £m. |
|---|---|---|
| 1. *Government Securities.* | | |
|   Long | 1,313 | 6·5 |
|   Medium (Defence Bonds) | 279 | 1·4 |
|   Short (Floating Debt)   More than | 6,000 | 30·0 |
| | | 38·0 |

|  | Capital £m. | Annual Saving £m. |
|---|---|---|
| 2. *Local Authorities.* | | |
| New Loans | 254·5 | 1·2 |
| Conversions[1] | 34 | 0·7 |
| Further reductions of interest following | | |
| conversion of Local Loan Stock[2] | 105 | 0·65 |
| | | 2·55 |

### 3. *Private Finance.*

No close estimate, but substantial savings were made both on the conversion of debentures and on new issues. Many industrialists admitted that cheap money enabled them to put their house in order by reducing the interest rate on their prior charges.

I have explained, in Chapter XXIV, § 6, that the rate of interest can be lowered either by words, or by deeds, or by both. I had considerable success in talking down the long-term rate during the first part of this period and in inducing large subscriptions to tap loans by the use of what *The Economist* called the 'last chance technique'.[3]

But deeds, in the form of an increase in the floating debt, and in the total of bank deposits, also became necessary.[4] I have argued in Chapter XXIV that such an increase in the quantity of money is *not necessarily* inflationary, but only when it leads to increased money expenditure. On this, I think, most serious economists are agreed. But was it *actually* inflationary in 1945-7? Not, in my judgment, in any important degree. Here

---

[1] Sixteen local authorities benefited.

[2] Between 1,500 and 2,000 local authorities benefited, including most of those in the Development Areas, which had been forced to pay extortionate rates of interest in the bad years of mass unemployment. All rates in excess of 4½ per cent on outstanding loans were reduced to that figure.

[3] Thus in my second budget speech, on April 9th, 1946, I said: 'I intend to discontinue the present series of Defence Bonds at the end of this month. There are three weeks in which these bonds may still be taken up at 3 per cent—three precious, fleeting weeks. As from May 1st there will be a new offer, bearing interest at 2½ per cent.' This hint worked well.

[4] For details see Kennedy (*loc. cit.*, pp. 199-201).

some of the ablest critics of my policy support my judgment.[1] No doubt private expenditure rose, as part of the large capital gains due to the falling rate of interest were spent. But likewise private expenditure fell in 1947 when the rate rose, causing large capital losses. And no one then claimed that this was an important deflationary factor.

Looking back on my cheap money policy I have two thoughts. First, if I (and my successor) had held on through 1947, through the fuel crisis and the convertibility crisis up to the issue in January, 1948, of over £1,000 millions of British Transport stock as compensation to the railway shareholders, and if we had used to the full all the means at our disposal to hold the long-term rate at 2½ per cent, we *might* have succeeded in 'conditioning the market' to this rate. But this would, without doubt, have required, as a preliminary, a large further increase in bank deposits, with an increased risk, difficult to measure, of a new wave of inflation. The forces against me, in the City and elsewhere, were very powerful and determined.[2] I felt I could not count on a good chance of victory. I was not sufficiently well armed. So I retreated.

[1] Thus Sir Hubert Henderson wrote that 'the cheap money policy', though he thought that I had carried it too far, 'has been only a very minor factor in the inflationary complex, so unimportant relatively to other factors as to be scarcely worth considering' (*Economic Journal*, September, 1947, p. 265). Mr. Harrod goes further. 'Keynesian technique has been adopted. In order to keep interest rates down, the authorities have flooded the capital markets with money and short-term paper. . . . I do not regard this flood of liquidity as having any immediate bearing, if any bearing at all, on the problem of inflation' (*Are These Hardships Really Necessary?*, p. 126). And even Mr. Kennedy observes 'that the cheaper money drive exerted some inflationary influence would not, I suppose, be denied; and it may be that this influence was under-estimated at the outset. But it is also only too easy in retrospect to over-estimate it, and to attribute the inflationary stresses of those years in too large a measure to the controversial monetary policy being pursued at the time' (*loc. cit.*, p. 195).

[2] These forces included the Insurance Companies and other large institutional investors. There was also a strong and vocal vested interest in favour of getting the rate up from 2½ to 3 per cent on the great block of Transport Stock. I had had it in mind, even with the long-term rate at 3 per cent, to issue only half the new stock in this form, and the other half in short-term 2 per cent say for five or six years, thus still averaging 2½ per cent.

My second thought follows from this. I have mentioned it at the end of Chapter XXIV. I had no power to direct capital into the gilt-edged market, or to stop big holders from unloading, as it came to my knowledge that some did in 1947, millions of pounds' worth of government securities in a single day. I formed the firm opinion that, in order to control the long-term rate and to sustain the national credit, the British Chancellor of the Exchequer should be armed with this power of direction.[1] Thus power might be taken to prescribe, by Treasury order, and to vary from time to time, a minimum percentage of the funds of large investors[2] to be held in gilt-edged securities. To raise this percentage, or even to hint publicly that it might have to be raised, would at once lower the gilt-edged rate. With this power I could certainly have held the long-term rate at, or even below, $2\frac{1}{2}$ per cent.[3]

§ 7. On April 15th, 1947, I introduced my third budget. For 1944–5, the last full year of war, the budget deficit had been £2,825 millions; for 1945–6, the year when peace broke out, £2,200 millions; for the year just ended only £569 millions, 'a pretty quick recoil', I said, 'towards a balanced budget'. And, indeed, on the basis of existing taxation, and in spite of the rising costs of the social services, I estimated for 1947–8 a surplus of £248 millions.[4]

[1] I propounded this idea in an article, 'Thoughts on Finance' (*New Statesman*, February 21st, 1948).

[2] Those, principally institutional, whose invested funds exceeded, say, a million pounds.

[3] Under my Bank of England Act there is already power to issue such a direction to banks, but it would be unfair and might be ineffective to direct banks only. Such a direction, if used to lower the rate in the gilt-edged market and the public sector, might, of course, raise the rate in the private sector. It would cause a shift of funds from the latter to the former, but no scintilla of inflation. I do not, therefore, share the pessimism of Mrs. Joan Robinson (*Econometrica*, April, 1951) and others, who believe that, because I was forced to retreat from $2\frac{1}{2}$ per cent in 1947, no future Chancellor, for a long time, will be able to regain the lost ground. He will, if armed with this new gun, specially designed to shoot bears.

[4] All deficits and surpluses are here given according to the 'conventional form of accounts' which has long been, and still is, used in British budget statements. These cover all transactions, in official language, 'above the line'. Transactions 'below the line' are shown in separate tables. These last

This surplus was a surprise to many, and good so far as it went. But I decided that it was not enough and I proposed to increase it to £270 millions by a net addition to taxation. 1947 was a dark year. We had had the fuel crisis in February. Our adverse trade balance was widening, both with the outside world as a whole and with the dollar area. Our exports were rising too slowly and we were spending our American and Canadian Loans too fast, and getting too little for our dollars. Dollar prices in the United States had risen by 40 per cent since the conclusion of the Loan Agreement. All this gloom I deployed.

Inflation, having practically disappeared in 1946, had reappeared in 1947. 'The immediate danger', I said, 'is of inflation breaking through the controls that we have set up.' And, therefore, in terms of the budget, 'this is a good year for a good surplus'. I raised some taxes and lowered others. I again gave preference in tax reductions to income tax. I raised the earned income relief from an eighth to a sixth, and the maximum relief from £150 to £250. And I raised the child allowance and the income limit for dependent relatives' allowance. These reliefs would cost £87 millions in a full year. On the other hand, I made increases in Inland Revenue to yield £54 millions more, and in Customs and Excise to yield £86 millions more, in a full year. Under Inland Revenue, I introduced, for the first time, a differential profits tax, at 12½ per cent on distributed as against 5 per cent on undistributed profits; doubled the rates of legacy and succession duties, except on charitable bequests, while giving further exemptions for small bequests and reducing the probate fees on small estates; doubled most stamp duties and introduced a new tax on bonus issues. These issues had been

include (1) payments for which the Treasury has power to borrow and (2) receipts applicable to debt redemption, or applicable by statute to debt interest which would otherwise be paid out of revenue. Side by side with the 'conventional form', since 1948 an 'alternative classification' of the same figures has been published. This comes nearer to distinguishing between a current and a capital Budget. The biggest item in 'below the line' expenditure has been Housing Loans to local authorities. If these authorities borrowed privately, and not from the Public Works Loan Board, this item would disappear, but there would be little real change in the economic situation.

wholly prohibited by my two predecessors, but I now gave the Capital Issues Committee discretion to allow them, subject to a tax of 10 per cent on the excess of the market value (or, if not quoted on the Stock Exchange, of the par value) of the bonus share over the sum, if any, paid for it by the shareholder. This little tax was more vehemently opposed than any of my other fiscal innovations.

Under Customs and Excise, I halved the purchase tax on sports requisites for football, cricket, hockey, boxing and rowing—but not for golf and tennis which were good export lines. Following the previous year's cut in entertainment tax on outdoor sports, 'I am happy', I said, 'that this year's budget should contain a second concession on behalf of the young and the active.' But, to encourage fuel economy, I brought back purchase tax, at a higher rate than before, on all the electric and gas space-heating and cooking appliances which I had exempted in my first budget.

My most sensational proposal was a sharp increase in the tobacco duty. I raised this by about 50 per cent and appealed for a cut in consumption of 25 per cent. Even so, I should have got an increased revenue of £75 millions. In fact, the increase was £118 millions, with a much smaller drop in consumption than I wanted. For, indeed, we were literally smoking the American Loan away.[1] I eased this increased duty through the House of Commons by making a concession to old age pensioners, who, if habitual smokers, were to be enabled by means of special coupons to go on buying a reasonable ration of tobacco at the old prices.

On the expenditure side for the coming year there was a cut of 46 per cent on Defence, or, excluding terminal charges, of 28 per cent, and I was counting on further cuts later. But there was more for education, housing, family allowances and all the social services. The National Insurance Act, the National Health Act and the Industrial Injuries Act had all been placed

[1] 'The whole total of our exports to the United States', I said, 'barely exceeds, in value, our consumption of American tobacco. The thing has become fantastic and must be stopped. We are smoking much more, as a nation, than we can afford '

this year upon the statue book. 'We have mounted,' I declared, 'without halt or hesitation, the great social programme which the electors voted for, when our majority was returned.' And I announced the payment, in the autumn, of the remainder of their post-war credits to men over sixty-five and women over sixty. I had paid out cost-of-living subsidies, since the war ended, sufficient to hold the old cost-of-living index absolutely stable. This had been fully justified, in my view, as an important factor in our wonderfully smooth transition from war to peace, and as an anti-inflationary safeguard. But these subsidies were now costing £425 millions a year, and the new provisional index, which was now to be introduced, would give food a lower weighting and would be less controllable through food subsidies. I was uneasy, I said, about the outlook on this sector of the front.

Finally, I gave notice of my intention to provide an Exchequer Equalisation Grant to Local Authorities, which would give more help to the poorer authorities, less to the richer, and to the richest nothing at all.[1] A grant on these lines was approved while I was at the Treasury and enacted in the Local Government Act of 1948. Looking back on this budget now, I think I should have gone for an even larger surplus, particularly as some of my tax increases—on legacies, successions and stamps— were taxes on capital, good for distribution but not for closing the inflationary gap.[2]

§ 8. In the next few months things got worse. In July we kept our promise to the United States Government. We restored full convertibility of the pound with the dollar for all current, though not for capital, transactions. My earlier forebodings, rather than some of the reassuring advice which I received as the critical date approached, turned out to be correct. The drain on

[1] See Ch. XVII, § 4, note.
[2] But *The Economist* once more patted me on the back. 'Mr. Dalton's third budget is an acceptable, even a good one. . . . The proposals he made were, with one exception' (the tax on bonus shares) 'based on principles of finance that all authorities would approve. He might have dissipated the surplus in reductions of taxation. . . . But he decided, very wisely and properly, not to do so, but rather to fortify it. He is proposing to move in exactly the direction that his deflationist critics have urged upon him.'

our gold and dollar reserves quickly became intolerable. After six weeks of convertibility we called it off, and we proposed to the United States Government that, for the time being, we should not draw the residue of the credit due to us under the Loan Agreement. The United States Government showed great understanding and was most cooperative at this difficult time.[1]

We were now once more confronted with a very wide and menacing gap in our overseas balance of payments. To narrow this we must at once reduce imports and increase exports. And clearly this would intensify afresh the danger of inflation, aggravated already by the discontinuance of our drawings on the American Loan. To counteract this danger we planned large cuts in the capital investment programme, public and private, and I introduced, on November 12th, 1947, my fourth budget. I maintained the subsidies on food, but abolished those on cotton, wool and leather. I said that I was 'working for a solid reduction' in total expenditure, principally in defence and civilian 'war terminals', but 'so distributed between the items as to avoid damage to essential social interests'. But primarily I was out to check inflation by increasing the revenue, by methods 'simple, straightforward and capable of being administered with the least expenditure of manpower'. In this budget, therefore, I ruled out all elaborate schemes, however attractive. 'Any large changes in the tax structure must wait till the spring.'[2]

I left the income tax unchanged; charged interest, for the first time, on large arrears of income tax, surtax and profits tax; doubled the profits tax, both on distributed and undistributed

[1] We had carefully considered whether we should ask the United States Government for any of the waivers, such as they were, in the Loan Agreement or even for a straight postponement of the date. But we had decided against any action of this kind. Congress would either have refused our requests outright, or would have taken so long discussing them, with so much publicity for all our most unfriendly critics, that more harm would have been done than by going straight on. So we decided just to keep our word and face the consequences.

[2] I had, indeed, been working for some time on a project for a Capital Levy, which I had in mind to make the principal feature of my next year's budget. A trace of this is to be seen in Sir Stafford Cripps' Special Contribution.

profits; raised all the rates of purchase tax, while leaving all the articles in each range unchanged and maintaining the free list; increased the taxes on alcohol; and put a new tax—easy, I hoped, to collect—on money wagered with dog totes and with football and other pools. These tax increases, I estimated, should bring in £48 millions in the remainder of that financial year and £208 millions in a full year.

My term of office at the Treasury ended immediately after the introduction of this budget. Of many friendly letters which I then received, I quote one, from Mr. John J. McCloy, then President of the International Bank. He wrote to me from Washington: 'All know that you have striven hard in a period of utmost difficulty to set things right in the English economy; that the budgetary condition of England remains sound is due to you.'

§ 9. My friend and successor Stafford Cripps inherited from me both a record surplus for the season of the year of £253 millions, and a record surplus when the financial year ended on March 31st, 1948, of £636 millions. Expenditure had been £234 millions below the total estimate, including supplementaries. It had, indeed, proved 'a good year for a good surplus'. Nor had the full revenue-gathering force of my autumn budget then shown itself. My latest tax increases had run for less than six months.

Apart from the Special Contribution from investment incomes—a once-for-all levy assessed on income but mainly paid out of capital, thus having little effect on the inflationary gap—from which he hoped for £50 millions in 1948-9, out of a total yield of £105 millions, Sir Stafford Cripps proposed to reduce taxation by £39 millions in 1948-9 and by £56 millions in a full year. His preferences here were the same as mine had been. He concentrated by far the greater part of his tax reduc· tions on the income tax, raising the earned income relief to one-fifth and the maximum relief to £400, and increasing from £75 to £200 the income subject to the reduced rate of 6s. in the £. He also made substantial purchase-tax reductions. He increased taxation on tobacco—but this time only by another 6 per cent—alcohol and betting. He counted on a fall of £233 millions in total expenditure. He forecast a new record surplus of £790 millions.[1]

This was to be another 'good year for a good surplus', stemming, like that of the previous year, from the tax increases in my two budgets of 1947.

Next year, in 1949–50, Sir Stafford Cripps reduced taxation again, by £22 millions that year and £92 millions in a full year. The largest tax increases were from death duties and betting, the largest reductions once more on income tax—initial allowances were raised from 20 to 40 per cent—and on beer. The prospective surplus was now only £469 millions.[2] It was thought by many that, as in 1946, inflation had now practically disappeared, and that investment, after the cuts of 1947–8, should now again be stimulated. This was the reason for the increased initial allowances.

Looking back, several years later, on all these ups and downs, Mr. Little observes that 'the figures for the period (1945–50) disclose no sharp break; in particular there seems little justification, at least as far as fiscal policy is concerned, for dividing it (as has become fashionable) into Dalton-inflationary and Cripps-deflationary periods. The most that can be said is that, *ceteris paribus*, the rapid reduction of the public deficit in 1945 and 1946 should not have been slowed up so much in 1947. But Mr. Dalton's emergency budget in the autumn of that year retrieved the mistake and largely set the pattern for 1948 and subsequent years.'[3] This seems to me a pretty correct judgment.

In financial, as distinct from fiscal, policy my successor held the low short-term rates which I had set in 1945, but eased up, even a little more than I had done, the downward pressure on the long-term rates.

More recent events in British Public Finance fall outside this study.

[1] 'Above the line', and a surplus of £330 millions above and below the line taken together.

[2] Above the line. Above and below the line together, the 'overall surplus' had dropped to £14 millions.

[3] *Fiscal Policy*, in *The British Economy, 1945–50*, p. 172.

# INDEX